W9-BMN-053

3 9077 01106160 6

JAN 1 5 1991

947.085 A366t

Alekseeva, Liudmila, 1927-

The thaw generation

History & Travel Division
Rochester Public Library
115 South Avenue
ster, New York 14604-1896

Rochester Public Library

The
Thaw
Generation

The
Thaw
Generation

Coming of Age
in the Post-Stalin Era

LUDMILLA ALEXEYEVA
and
PAUL GOLDBERG

Little, Brown and Company
BOSTON   TORONTO   LONDON

Copyright © 1990 by Ludmilla Alexeyeva and Paul Goldberg

All rights reserved. No part of this book may be
reproduced in any form or by any electronic or mechanical
means, including information storage and retrieval systems,
without permission in writing from the publisher, except by a
reviewer who may quote brief passages in a review.

First Edition

Library of Congress Cataloging-in-Publication Data

Alekseeva, Liudmila, 1927–
    The thaw generation: coming of age in the post-Stalin era /
    Ludmilla Alexeyeva and Paul Goldberg. — 1st ed.
        p.   cm.
    Includes bibliographical references.
    ISBN 0-316-03146-1
    1. Soviet Union—History—1953– 2. Alekseeva, Liudmila, 1927– .
3. Historians — Soviet Union— Biography.   4. Dissenters — Soviet
Union—Biography.   5. Perestroïka.   6. Glasnost.   I. Goldberg,
Paul, 1959–   . II. Title.
DK267. A52   1990
947.085 — dc20   90-32280
                                                                          CIP

10 9 8 7 6 5 4 3 2 1

HC

Published simultaneously in Canada
by Little, Brown & Company (Canada) Limited

Printed in the United States of America

For Lara and Tolya

Preface

The voice in this book belongs to Ludmilla Alexeyeva, the writing to Paul Goldberg. From the outset, we decided to write a book that would find the English-language equivalent of the spirit and energy of modern Russian narrative.

Harmonious collaborations have a way of producing dull books, and we did not want our book to be dull. To keep our creative energy going, each of us tried to push the other out of the bounds dictated by his culture and language. Thus, while one of us argued that it is not in the tradition of Russian memoirs to discuss the sort of intimate details American readers (and editors) crave, the other championed the interests of the American readers by letting the characters come alive and trying to shorten the sort of lengthy, detailed analysis and annotation that a scholar of Russian history relishes.

Under such a working arrangement, we came to regard each disagreement as a small triumph. When our tempers flared, we knew that we had tapped into energy produced by the tension that occurs at the joining of two languages and two cultures.

The
Thaw
Generation

Introduction

Five decades ago, future Soviet leaders and future Soviet dissidents sat in the same schoolrooms, listening to the same teachers impart the same, standard wisdom. Even the photograph in those classrooms was the same: Comrade Iosif Vissarionovich Stalin holding a little girl and an enormous bouquet. The little, round-faced girl, wearing a sailor suit, looked like one of the flowers; and Comrade Stalin looked, well, fatherly.

I was born in 1927, three years after he came to power. In 1937, when I was ten, people began to vanish from our Moscow apartment building. I saw nothing wrong with the disappearances and asked no questions. I knew no other life.

Landmark events that defined stages in my generation's development can be pinpointed to the day, sometimes even to the minute. The first occurred on June 22, 1941, at exactly 4:00 AM: the start of the German invasion. At school, we had been told that our armed forces were invincible. Now the army was retreating toward Moscow, losing hundreds of thousands of soldiers. The retreat gave us an inkling of doubt about our teachers. Could they have been lying to us?

The end of the war did not put our doubts to rest. And it did nothing to ease the nebulous sense that something was missing. I was not happy, and I didn't know anyone who was. If the revolution of 1917 was made in the name of our happy future, then where was that future? Could there have been some defect in the system, or in our leaders, or in me personally? Why was I having such thoughts, which could not be shared with others?

On March 5, 1953, when the radio broadcast the news of Stalin's death, I broke into tears. Most of us did. We cried because we were helpless; we cried because we had no rational way of predicting what would happen to us now; we cried because we sensed that, for better or for worse, an era had passed.

Since we knew no other life, we were not prepared to picture what came next: a period of liberalization that was subsequently named "the thaw," after a second-rate novella by Ilya Ehrenburg.

On February 25, 1956, when I was nearing thirty, Nikita Khrushchev shocked the delegates to the Twentieth Congress of the Communist party — and the entire nation — with the revelation that the deceased Great Leader was actually a criminal. The congress put an end to our lonely questioning of the Soviet system. Young men and women began to lose their fear of sharing views, knowledge, beliefs, questions. Every night, we gathered in cramped apartments to recite poetry, read "unofficial" prose, and swap stories that, taken together, yielded a realistic picture of what was going on in our country.

That was the time of our awakening.

We had no leaders and no teachers. All we could do was learn from each other. To us, the thaw was the time to search for an alternative system of beliefs. Our new beliefs would be truly ours; having gone through Stalinism once, we could not stand for another "progressive" doctrine being imposed on us from above.

Eager to shed the Stalinist doctrine of collectivism, we realized that each of us had a right to privacy. There is no word for "privacy" in the Russian language, but we stumbled upon the concept the word defines: we ceased to be cogs in the machine of state; we ceased to be faceless members of the "collective"; each of us was unique, and all of us had a right to uniqueness. Without asking permission from the party or the government, we asserted that writers had a right to write what they wanted; that readers had a right to choose what they read; and that each of us had a right to say what he thought.

We did not invent this pursuit of liberty; we reinvented it for ourselves and our country. Thanks to the efforts of our Father and Genius, we were ignorant about the West, where such ideas had been around for centuries. We also knew little about any political philosophy other than the Bolshevik brand of communism.

Every person who started to live by the new ethic did so for his own sake. The government remained persistent in its adherence to collectivism, but as each of us found himself, Soviet society slowly started to split away from the government.

Still, my friends and I were loyal citizens. I knew of no opponents of socialism in my country. Yes, we were shocked by the inhumanity of our society; but that merely made us embrace the socialist slogans of the Czechoslovak reformers who at that time were waging their own battle against Stalinism. Like the Czechs, we embraced the idea of "socialism with a human face." The hope of "Prague Spring" resonated in Moscow.

On the night of August 21, 1968, Soviet troops rolled into Czechoslovakia, strangling the reforms and, simultaneously, helping to install a new Communist orthodoxy at home. The invasion marked the end of the thaw. Now each of us had to choose between three options: the first was to toe the party line and be allowed to advance professionally; the second was to put a career on hold and wait for another thaw; the third was to stay the course of the thaw and accept the consequences: an aborted career and the life of a pariah.

Only a few intellectuals chose the third option, and I am proud to say that I was among them. Rejected by the government and society, we lived in a small, close community. As we went on with our lives, we failed to notice how our battle for individual freedom from the state became the battle for freedom of expression and human rights, not only for ourselves and our friends, but for all our countrymen.

Many of us paid dearly during that struggle by spending years in prisons and labor camps. Others were forced into emigration, as I was. Still, I would argue that our fate was no worse than that of the majority of our contemporaries, who spent the same two decades advancing their careers while agreeing to whatever treachery had to be committed along the way. Nor did we fare any worse than those who simply waited, trying to retain their decency while not taking sides. During the two decades that followed the invasion of Czecho-slovakia, some of my former thaw friends deliberately dulled their minds, others drank themselves to death, and still others abandoned their old ideals.

Those who fought for human rights became known as "dissidents." That word, too, did not exist in the Russian language, until some translator at a shortwave radio station used it to stand for the massive word *inakomyslyashchiy,* literally translated as "otherwise-thinker." That was all it took to coin the term. Subsequently, to make a point of our connections with the West, the Soviet press began to refer to us as the "so-called *dissidenty.*" Eventually, the word crept into the language of "otherwise-thinkers" as well.

The dissidents condemned all party bureaucrats, making no distinction between Brezhnev's contemporaries and our own. At the time, the distinction seemed to be moot: in their attacks on the dissidents, our contemporaries were just as ruthless as their older comrades.

My friends and I did not believe that it was possible to remain true to the ideals of the thaw while rising through the ranks of an organization as cynical and corrupt as the Communist party.

At first, in the late 1960s, public opinion was with the dissidents, but year after year that support weakened. By the mid-1980s, when most dissidents were either in prisons or in exile, we were simply forgotten. Society had rejected us.

In 1985, when Mikhail Gorbachev took power, no one could have predicted that his policies in the Kremlin would reflect the ideas of our younger days. The opposite seemed more likely. He could have succumbed to the stultifying effect of the decades of serving as a functionary in the party apparatus. It was not easy to recognize the new Soviet leader as a "man of the sixties."

But since Gorbachev's ascendancy, a number of his functionaries have come out in support of reforms reminiscent of Prague Spring. The general secretary has also found backing among the intellectuals who fell silent for two decades after the invasion of Czechoslovakia — those who stayed neutral, waiting for their hour to come. But no dissident has joined his team. Too great is the schism between the pariahs and the establishment. Our spiritual differences may be irreconcilable.

In 1985, Gorbachev said that the USSR had no political prisoners and that Andrei Sakharov was a madman. By 1986, he acknowledged that the Soviet economy could not be reformed without a restructuring of the political system, and that the only way to achieve reform is through recognition of human rights and the rule of law. At this writing, he has taken the hammer to virtually all of the pillars of the Soviet system. At times, he borrows our slogans and draws on our ideas. We take no offense at Gorbachev and his associates for not citing us as sources. We are happy that our ideas have acquired a new life.

Besides, now we know that such ideas are commonplace in the West and have been known to be heard in Russia's past. We lit a tiny flame of freedom and kept it burning for the two decades of the Brezhnev period. Now, my contemporaries who have not rotted away in their hideouts have joined in *perestroika*. I wish them success. All of us shared the bitterness of the Stalin era, and that shared experience gives us hope that the current warming will be more than a thaw in the midst of winter.

One

On my desk I keep a photograph of my parents. It was taken in 1926, when they were both nineteen. They came from impoverished families, and they had joined the Komsomol, the Young Communist League. The revolution had given them opportunities their ancestors never knew existed: Father was studying economics; Mother, mathematics. In the finest revolutionary fashion, they wore peasant shirts — like Leo Tolstoy's.

My parents were history's favorites, and they did their best to raise me to think that I was as well. Even the children's rhymes carried the beat of the times:

> I am a little girl
> I sing and play a lot
> I do not know Stalin,
> But I love him anyway.

I remember looking at a kitten once, thinking how fortunate I was to be human. It would have been awful to be a kitten, living by reflexes, having no thoughts. This led me to consider other possibilities: What if I had been born in a capitalist country, where everyone is unhappy? And what if I had been born to other parents?

At the end of this exercise, I felt fortunate. Not only was I born human, but my parents, Mikhail Slavinsky and Valentina Yefimenko, were the best parents in the world. My country, the Union of Soviet Socialist Republics, was the best and most progressive in the world. I was special.

In 1935, soon after I went to first grade, Father brought home a map of the world. It was enormous. Stalin and Hitler must have had ones just like it.

The map covered an entire wall over my bed. I tied red ribbons to Mother's pins and we marked the front lines where "we" were fighting the fascists in Spain. Sleeping under that map, I dreamed of glorious battles over places with distant, romantic names. Madrid, Valencia, Barcelona, Córdoba, Bilbao, Murcia, Málaga, Teruel, Aragon. Spain was the battlefield of world revolution, and I knew that after our victory Spanish children would live as happily as I. When you are eight and you live in the best country in the world, you want others to share your happiness.

Every morning, we opened *Pravda* to battlefield reports by Mikhail Koltsov. Then, with disappointment, Father and I shifted our pins upward, closer to the French border. We were losing, but I kept waiting for the opportunity to move the pins back down the map. In those days I wore a red *ispanka*, a hat just like those worn by the Republicans.

In a children's drama club, I was cast as a Spanish girl named Anita. My line: "It is better to die standing up than to live on your knees!" In the courtyard, when my friends and I played cossacks-and-brigands, a game identical to cowboys-and-Indians, both sides were known to raise clenched right fists and shout the Spanish phrase *¡No pasaran!* — "They shall not pass!"

At school I heard the story of Pavlik Morozov, a Young Pioneer who had discovered that his father, chairman of a village soviet, had conspired with the *kulaki*, the wealthy peasants, to hide grain from state procurement officials. Pavlik informed the authorities. The father and other conspirators were brought to revolutionary justice, but Pavlik was murdered by the vengeful "enemies of the people."

I couldn't put myself in Pavlik's place. I knew that my parents were loyal Soviet citizens, yet I couldn't see myself informing on them had they not been.

✦

I don't know if Comrade Stalin understood this, but the New Socialist Man — the new kind of man who would be free from vestiges of bourgeois individualism — was being raised by a legion of grandmothers. As our mothers spent their time at the universities and Komsomol meetings, the grandmothers gently rocked our cradles, singing the songs they had heard from their mothers back in the days when the Bolsheviks were just being born.

Whether Comrade Stalin liked it or not, traditional values were being instilled alongside the icons of the new era. And sometimes, as in the case of my instinctive rejection of Pavlik Morozov, old values directly contradicted the new icons.

Traditionally dressed peasant grandmothers were among the most prominent features at the workers' barracks at Ostankino, a place on the outskirts of Moscow where I spent my early childhood. Those wooden barracks, hurriedly constructed in the woods and located about a mile from the streetcar tracks, housed young laborers. Most of them were in their twenties. They had left the villages at the start of collectivization, and after finding work and housing in Moscow, they brought over their mothers to take care of the children.

Grandmothers in those days were in their forties. Mine was forty-two when I was born and forty-six when she moved in with us in Moscow. Her name was Anetta Marietta Rozalia Yanovna Sinberg. She was an Estonian peasant who was born in the Crimea. Her ancestors had settled there a century earlier, when the peninsula was annexed by Catherine the Great.

When Grandmother was nineteen, she married a traveling salesman, a Ukrainian. It is still unknown how they agreed to get married. At the time, Grandmother spoke no Russian and no Ukrainian and the traveling salesman, my future grandfather, spoke no Estonian. Of course, her looks offered some clues. She was tall and stately; her brown hair lay in a heavy braid; her walk was calm and fluid.

Grandmother loved the vaunted "Power of the Soviets," but for reasons of her own. In 1913, when she was twenty-nine, Grandfather contracted gangrene and died, leaving her with three children. She had no skills and no hope of seeing her children get any sort of an education.

"If not for the revolution, who would have educated my children?" she used to say. After the revolution, Mother became a mathematician and my aunt Zhenya an engineer.

Since Grandmother spent most of her married life at Jankoi, a town in the cosmopolitan Crimea, she learned to cook magnificent kabobs, baba ganuj, chebureki, and gefilte fish. Anyone who visited our apartment was struck by its cleanliness. Our white walls sparkled even over the stove. That was because twice a year, Grandmother mixed ground chalk, water, glue, and a blue detergent and painted everything. Our clothes, sheets, and tablecloths were clean to a crisp. And anyone who saw me go out to play in a starched, pleated white dress would have thought me a vision from the past. Just my dresses must have required an hour of starching before I looked good enough to be allowed to walk outside.

I loved my grandmother. I loved my parents. I felt good walking outside in a starched, white dress. These were real people and real objects that constituted my world. Compared to them, Pavlik Morozov was a two-dimensional icon and the "collective" was something so abstract that it defied my imagination.

A child brought up subject to the undivided attention of Anetta Marietta Rozalia Yanovna Sinberg could never grow up to become a cog in the machine of state. Nor could thousands upon thousands of other children raised under the close supervision of other grandmothers. No matter how hard we would try to fit into the system, each of us would be different. And, eventually, we would stop trying to fit in and would instead become ourselves.

✦

In 1937, when I was ten, we moved to 4/20 First Nikolo-Shchepovsky Street, in the center of Moscow. It was a five-story apartment building with parquet floors and big kitchens. The original design also called for balconies, but for reasons that no one could fathom, they were never put up on the steel beams that protruded from the building's facade.

The apartment we moved to was formerly occupied by an official with Centrosoyuz, the bureaucracy charged with regulating eco-

nomic ties between urban and rural sectors of the people's economy. Father worked there, too.

The previous resident had been arrested and his apartment carved
up. One room was retained by his wife and a teenaged daughter,
and two were allocated to us. My parents became friends with
the woman, who made no secret of her long-running affair with the
head of health care facilities of the NKVD, the precursor of
the KGB — the Committee for State Security.

I loved living in the apartment. The water was indoors, the
kitchen stove didn't burn wood, and the toilet flushed. And then
there was the view. I spent hours sitting by the window of the room
I shared with my grandmother, watching the barges on the Moskva
River below.

Soon after we moved, Father brought me a copy of Aleksandr
Herzen's *Past and Thoughts*. It was a three-volume book, but Father
gave me only the first volume, Herzen's memoir of growing up in
Moscow of the 1820s. I used the book's first chapters to guide me
through the winding Arbat streets. Since the revolution, the old
mansions had been turned into enormous communal flats. The
drapes were gone; their swags and jabots had been cut up for
clothing. Mesh bags with butter, cheese, and sausage hung off the
high windows. Spaces between windowpanes were being used to
store milk and kefir.

But if you squinted just enough to blur the street before you, you
could imagine the black carriages, the dashing officers, their ladies
in ball gowns. You could even imagine Pushkin or Herzen strolling
past you, disappearing into the doorway of a mansion with elegant
Venetian windows.

✦

One night they came after our neighbor, the wife of the arrested
bureaucrat.

I have dim memories of the sound of heavy footsteps in the
corridor, doors slamming, and the crying of the mother and daughter. I was in half-slumber. But on the following morning, when our
neighbors' room stood vacant, I was still certain that I was living in
the best country in the world. The time wasn't right for seeing the
truth.

A family of five moved into our neighbor's room. Similar changes occurred in our building's twenty-nine other apartments. The year marked the peak of Stalin's repressions against the party.

The newspapers offered some explanation for disappearances. They were full of stories about bad people who didn't want to see our country succeed in its historic mission of liberating the working class from being exploited by the capitalists. Those bad people were working together: the British, the Americans, the German fascists, the Japanese, the bourgeois Poles. They delegated their foul deeds to the hordes of spies, terrorists, and assassins who were operating inside our country.

I don't recall whether I thought that the people who had disappeared from my apartment building were bad, too. I knew no other life, and I accepted the disappearances as something normal. I also sensed that forces in history worked rather like forces of nature. Class struggle seemed to be no different from a squall that whirls past, takes lives, destroys buildings or even entire cities, then vanishes into the ocean. How can you apply moral criteria to a squall?

It would have taken nothing less than the arrest of my parents to make me ask questions. Had I been told that they were bad, that they were German spies, saboteurs, or enemies of the people, I would not have believed it. I must have sensed that everyone was in danger, and that questions brought danger closer. Thus, by asking no questions, I was protecting myself and my parents.

In 1937 the country was celebrating the centennial of the death of the greatest stylist of the Russian language, Aleksandr Sergeyevich Pushkin. For the centennial, the Academy of Sciences published Pushkin's complete works. Father and I invented a game: he would read two lines of *Evgeny Onegin,* Pushkin's "novel in verse," and I would pick up and continue until I was told to stop. I could recite the entire eight chapters.

That year I found that other children didn't want to play or talk with me. It could have been something about me, but just as easily it could have been the spirit of the year. Everyone's parents were being careful. Adults weren't talking to each other, and children took their cues from the adults.

It would have been unfair to expect the children of 4/20 First Nikolo-Shchepovsky to be especially outgoing. Even our games were odd and detached. Games were played with abandon, but when they were over, everyone went his own way. It was like the end of a workday at some faceless ministry.

Most children in my courtyard discovered Alexandre Dumas's *Three Musketeers,* and we spent much of the day imagining ourselves in another country, at another time. We reenacted the duels, the journeys across France, the balls in the Louvre. I was assigned to play Madame de Chevreuse, but I picked up a stick for a rapier and fought my way into being cast as Athos. (I felt spiritual closeness with the noble, brave, and modest Athos. Other musketeers were less impressive: Porthos was vulgar, Aramis snobbish, and d'Artagnan reckless.)

When the games ended, I found myself alone. Why didn't I have friends? I blamed myself. I was too tall. I was too awkward. I was not pretty enough. I was too different. I wanted to be liked.

Once, Mother caught me looking at myself in the mirror. "Don't look; you aren't pretty," she said. I can't blame her for that act of cruelty. She was only trying to make me modest. A little girl who thinks she is prettier than anyone else would not fit into the collective.

My parents bought a piano and made a valorous attempt to teach me to play. I got as far as memorizing the "Italian Song" from Tchaikovsky's *Album for Children,* and for at least an hour a day I placed *War and Peace, Anna Karenina, Ivanhoe,* or *Madame Bovary* on the music stand while I played the "Italian Song" from adagio to prestissimo — whatever tempo was most appropriate for my place in the book. That was all it took to convince Grandmother that I was devotedly practicing my routines.

Whenever we had a chance, Father and I "traveled" along our map, usually using Jules Verne to guide us. Thus I learned about the eucalyptus tree, found in Australia, where the earth is red and where animals carry their young in pouches. Athos, Porthos, Aramis, Pushkin, Herzen, Anna Karenina, Madame Bovary, and the little girl named Anita simmered in the hallucinatory porridge of the mind of a hyperimaginative, pale girl for whom books were reality. Red earth and the kangaroos leaping through the eucalyptus forest were far more interesting (and a lot safer) than the happenings at 4/20 First Nikolo-Shchepovsky Street.

For some reason, I still remember the night Father told me about

Iceland. He talked about the geysers, the harsh volcanic terrain, the ancient sagas passed from generation to generation.

"The capital of Iceland is Reykjavík. I know nothing about it, but it must be a beautiful city. Because its name is beautiful: Reyk-ja-vík."

Fifty years later, in a Pan Am jet approaching that austere city, I caught myself repeating, "Reyk-ja-vík."

◆

My deliberate ignorance was an insufficient safeguard. In the fall of 1937, Father stopped going to work. He stopped shaving. In the mornings, he remained in his pajamas, lying on his side, staring at the back of the couch. During the day, when I came back from school, he was in exactly the same position as he was in the morning. His chauffeur-driven Emka was missing, too.

Stalin had decided that Centrosoyuz, the bureaucracy where Father worked, had been penetrated by imperialist agents and enemies of the people. I. A. Zelensky, head of Centrosoyuz, was arrested and accused of taking part in a conspiracy responsible for the assassination of the Leningrad party chief, Sergei Mironovich Kirov, and the poisoning of the herald of the revolution, Maxim Gorky. The conspirators also had plotted the assassination of Comrade Iosif Vissarionovich Stalin, but, fortunately, they were stopped.

In the course of the investigation, Zelensky confessed that he had been an agent of the czar's secret police and an active agent of German intelligence. Using his position at Centrosoyuz, he added nails and ground glass to the butter purchased from the peasants, and at one point, he confessed, he deliberately destroyed fifty railroad-car-loads of eggs. He said he did so to create shortages of consumer goods.

Working for the Germans also entailed directing a fascist "bund" that included all three hundred Communist-party members in his employ, Zelensky said. The enemy organization held its meetings at the Centrosoyuz banquets at the country compound near Moscow. The banquets, indeed, were numerous. There were the anniversary of the Great October Socialist Revolution, the anniversary of the founding of Centrosoyuz, the Day of Solidarity of Working People, the Day of the Stalin Constitution, New Year's, retirements, birthdays.

Drunken bureaucrats stumbled out of those banquets, singing about the invincible Red Army and defending the motherland in past and future wars. My father was never among them. Just a thimbleful of wine made him loopy, and he knew that at Centrosoyuz an official who couldn't hold his liquor was certain to lose the respect of his peers. To hide his inadequacy, he avoided the banquets.

The investigation revealed that Father had never attended any of the bund meetings and thus was not part of the German conspiracy. So, as Zelensky faced the firing squad and 297 party members of Centrosoyuz were hauled off to the camps or executed in the cellars of the secret-police building, Father was merely fired and expelled from the Communist party for "lax vigilance."

I wonder what he thought during the months he spent staring at the upholstery of the couch. It could have been his comrades at Centrosoyuz, people he knew were neither spies nor saboteurs. He could have been wondering whether the social experiment he was a part of had gone horribly awry.

After a year, Father found a job as a functionary at a Moscow factory. Within two years he was back in the party and working as that factory's manager.

✦

On June 1, 1941, Father's Emka took Grandmother and me to the Kursky railroad station. It was a little chilly and overcast. Suddenly, at Zemlyanoy Val, a few blocks from the railroad station, large drops formed on the windshield. I looked out and saw enormous, white flakes circling serenely toward the ground. It was snow. Snow in June.

"Oy, this doesn't bode well," said the chauffeur. "I hope it doesn't mean war."

On June 22, a little after four o'clock in the morning, the sound of airplane engines awakened me on my cot in a garden in Feodosiya, the Crimean resort where Grandmother and I spent the summer vacation. I couldn't see the markings on the wings of the three airplanes high in the morning haze. I had no reason to look; if the planes were in the skies above me, they had to be ours. I had been taught that the Soviet borders were "under a padlock," that if there were ever a war, it would be won "with little blood and on enemy soil." There was even a song to that effect. I went back to sleep.

By noon, a radio speech by politburo member Vyacheslav Molotov confirmed that the war had begun. "Our cause is just," he said. "We shall win." History, of course, was on the side of the progressive masses.

Later that day, at the Feodosiya market, Grandmother heard that three German bombers had flown over town after dropping their cargo on the Soviet-fleet base in Sevastopol. When Grandmother returned, I admonished her for believing what she heard at the market. By early evening, we received a telegram from my parents in Moscow: "RETURN IMMEDIATELY."

"Grandmother, the vacation has just begun, why leave?" I said. "They will be driven back in a few days anyway."

Grandmother agreed. "WE ARE STAYING," we wired back. Telegrams from my parents came daily, but we stood our ground. On July 2, a Nazi bomb hit a shed at the Feodosiya anchor factory. The whole town turned out to look. The sight of wartime rubble made Grandmother doubt my political wisdom. On July 3, we took a train for Moscow. It was the last train carrying civilians from the Crimea.

Our train moved only during the day. At night, we waited at one of the stations, with lights off. When German planes were overhead, the train stopped, and all of us piled out and ducked a few meters away. The trip took over three days, twice the normal time.

We got back on July 6. Father was no longer at home. By the time we arrived, he had made arrangements to waive his exemption from the draft. At the apartment, the windows were crisscrossed with strips of paper. At night, we pulled down dark shades.

"Lyudochka, I am going off to defend the Power of the Soviets," Father said to me on July 14, as he was putting me on a train that took children to safety in Kazakhstan, in Central Asia. Two days later, he shipped out to the front.

In one of his letters, he wrote about his commander, who had called him "the finest political officer at the Northwestern Front." That was largely because Father gave him his rations of vodka rather than drinking them himself.

He also wrote about the time he killed a German pilot who had parachuted into the woods. It was just the two of them. Father pulled out his sidearm and fired. "I had to kill him; otherwise he would have killed me," he wrote. It sounded like an apology.

Over the next few months, the voice on the radio invariably announced that "our military forces retreated to previously prepared positions." By October 1941, four months after the invasion, the Germans were positioned in Khimki, twenty kilometers from Moscow. I knew where that was.

The Red Army was the pillar of the progressive world. It was invincible. My parents told me so. So did my teachers. So did countless songs, speeches, and movies. Now the panzer detachments were roaring through Khimki, their guns aimed at Moscow. For the first time, I asked myself if it was possible that my parents, my teachers, the movies, the songs, and the speeches were simply wrong. Victory was not assured. Soviet military forces were not invincible. Everything was falling apart.

I had to act. I had to act as an individual. All of us had to. Our leaders were wrong. They needed us. They needed the public. By realizing that, we became citizens.

Still, I was only fourteen, and at that age I could do little more than stand by the radio, imagining the Nazis goose-stepping down the winding Arbat, past the house where Pushkin took his bride, past the Herzen house, past Zoo-magazin, the pet store where I used to spend hours admiring hamsters and parakeets.

I vowed that if Moscow fell, I would make my way back from Kazakhstan and fight the Nazis. In those fantasies, I saw myself killing at least one of them; I wasn't sure how I would kill him or with what. Those were details that had to be worked out later.

On January 27, 1942, I opened a copy of *Komsomolskaya pravda,* the Young Communist League newspaper. On the bottom of the page there was a photograph of the corpse of a young woman in a noose. "PARTISAN TANYA TORTURED TO DEATH BY THE GERMAN FASCISTS IN THE VILLAGE OF PETRISHCHEVO," said the cutline. The photo was taken by the Germans who tortured the girl.

Little was known about her — only that she identified herself as Tanya from Moscow. In early December 1941, she had walked into the village of Petrishchevo, not far from Moscow, and set fire to a stable that housed what the newspaper called "the German horses."

Phone lines were cut, too. By the morning, Tanya was captured by the Nazis.

During the interrogation, she was beaten, forced to drink kerosene, lacerated with a saw blade, undressed, and thrown out into the snow for twenty minutes at a stretch. According to the newspaper, villagers overheard fragments of the interrogation.

> "Did you burn down the stable last night?"
> "Yes, I was the one."
> "Where is Stalin?"
> "Stalin is at his battle position!"

The Germans built the gallows, put boxes underneath, then called the villagers to witness the hanging.

Standing on a box, a "FIREBUG" sign on her chest and a noose over her head, Tanya addressed the villagers: "Don't look glum, Comrades! Be brave, fight, kill the Germans, burn them, poison them! I am not afraid to die, Comrades. It is a great privilege to die for your people!"

To the Germans, she said: "You will hang me now, but I am not alone. There are 200 million of us, and you can't hang us all. My death will be avenged. Soldiers! Surrender now; victory will be ours! You will pay the price for this."

Then back to the villagers: "Farewell, Comrades! Fight, have no fear! Stalin is with us! Stalin will return!"

Reading the story of Tanya-the-partisan, I asked myself: How would I have behaved under torture? Would I be able to sacrifice my life with such poise and honor?

Eventually I concluded that if the Germans had caught me alone, the way they had caught Tanya, they probably would have broken me. Alone, I would not stand up under torture. But if I were in a group, and if we were tortured together, I would stand firm. I would not be broken in front of my comrades. That made me a bad person, I concluded. I would not be a hero unless the experience was narcissistic.

Meanwhile, more facts about Tanya began to emerge. Her real name was Zoya Kosmodemyanskaya. She was a nineteen-year-old Moscow girl who had joined a guerrilla unit operating behind the enemy lines. "Tanya" was a nom de guerre she'd picked up as a child, while reading the story of Tatyana Solomakha, a Red guerrilla tortured and executed by the cossacks during the Civil War.

"You can beat me all you want," Tanya Solomakha is said to have told her torturers. "You can kill me, but the Reds aren't dead. The Reds are alive. They will return."

Before being led away to execution, Tanya Solomakha said to her cellmates: "Farewell, Comrades. May the blood that will splatter these walls not be spilled in vain! The Reds will return soon!"

Zoya modeled her life on Tanya's. I modeled mine on Zoya's.

That summer I worked in the kolkhoz fields. The elastic band on my pants had stretched out, so the pants were held up with a safety pin. With the bending, the pin would come undone, sticking into my side. Then with every move, the pin shifted inside the wound, and with every burst of pain, I imagined myself under torture. I was testing myself.

✦

"The situation is such that I may not be writing to you for a few months," Father wrote from the northwestern front in June 1942.

Then the letters stopped coming. Clearly, Father wasn't in the regular army. He had to be hiding behind the enemy lines. He could have joined a partisan detachment. He could have been captured. The other possibility was too painful to think about, and for a long time I didn't.

In the winter of 1942, I joined Mother in the industrial town of Izhevsk, east of the Volga. Later, Grandmother and Aunt Zhenya and her two children joined us there, too. All of us lived in the same room, and I shared a cot with Mother.

At night, on our cot, I would wake up sensing dampness on my collarbone. It was tears.

"What's the matter, Mother?" I would ask.

"Oh, nothing."

"Are you crying?"

"No, no, of course not."

Since I was raised by my grandmother, Mother had been an enigma to me. I just knew that she rarely talked about herself, and that I loved her. Now, in Izhevsk, I got to know her.

There was a day Mother and I spent in line to get sausage. It was brutally cold, so it took two people to stand in that line. We replaced each other in half-hour stretches. One of us would stand in line and the other would find a place to warm up. In the afternoon, when we got home, I cut myself a thick piece. Mother cut herself a thin one.

"Why did you take so little?"

"I like them thinner."

I kept eating. She didn't.

"Mother, why aren't you eating?"

"Oh, I've had enough."

Once, when Mother was on her way back from the train station carrying her mesh bag with bread, she was attacked by an adolescent, a student at the Izhevsk trade school.

The boy grabbed her bag, trying to jerk it out of her hands. She held on. He kept pulling. She kept hanging on. His choice now was either to knock her unconscious or to run away. He ran away.

"If I were here alone, I would have let him have it," she said to my aunt, my grandmother, and me, and I understood that another tugging contest was going on within her soul: "The boy is hungry; shouldn't I let him have the food?"

✦

When hospital trains came to Izhevsk, schoolchildren volunteered to carry the wounded to streetcars that took them to a makeshift hospital. All too often, it was children carrying children. There were amputees on those stretchers, and there were husky men with winter coats on top of body casts. Some were so heavy that we had to set the stretchers down on the trampled snow, take a rest, then pick them up again.

It took a full night to unload a train, and in the morning all of us had to return to our school benches. In the hospital, we helped change the dressings on the newly arrived wounded. On the first try, I passed out from the smell of rotted flesh and the screams of pain. The second time, I passed out again. But I was a citizen and I had duties.

My country was in danger, and I couldn't just go to school. In seventh grade, at age fourteen, I dropped out and went to work as a clerk at the Izhevsk Komsomol regional committee. I didn't ask Mother's permission to drop out. I simply informed her.

"But what if you don't return to school?"

"I will, I will," I assured her.

She didn't fight my decision. She didn't believe in forcing me into anything, even education.

Technically, my job entailed little more than typing and filing, but there were only three of us at the regional committee, so I was ordered to lead meetings. At the end of the year, I took school exams and was advanced to the eighth grade. I enrolled in a nursing program, hoping to be sent to the front. But I wasn't eighteen, so I was turned down.

In the spring of 1943, Mother and I returned to Moscow to find most of our possessions and nearly all of our library missing. "Don't be angry; I had to survive," said Aleksandra Petrovna, our neighbor. She told us that the books she couldn't sell she burned to keep from freezing in the winter. Among the possessions she didn't sell or use for kindling were my father's gabardine suit and our seven-volume set of Aleksandr Sergeyevich Pushkin.

After returning to Moscow, I left school again. I asked the Komsomol to send me to the front or to a war-related industry. Instead, I was directed to work in construction of the Stalinskaya metro station. Now it's called Semyonovskaya. My job consisted of pushing wagonloads of dirt out of the tunnel. It was exhausting work, but the times demanded nothing less.

Oddly enough, I stopped feeling different. Everyone around me was working just as hard. We were citizens, and for the first time since childhood, I felt that I fit in.

✦

When you are hungry and there is no food, you drink water. Then you try to sleep, hoping that dreams will come. My dreams were full of color: I was in a faraway land, bathed in fresh breezes and sunshine, among young, healthy, beautiful people. There was a rainbow, and everyone wore its colors. They were happy and whole; the bonds between them were as warm as the clime. I was one of them, and that felt good. We sang a song without words, a song without a score. It had a melody unlike any other. I wish I could reproduce it now.

The faces around me weren't even vaguely familiar. The song I picked up with such ease was not real. The sounds and images before me were the embodiment of all that I thought was beautiful, and as I dreamed, I knew that I had escaped hunger. I had escaped the war.

In my waking hours, I had another escape: poetry. In Izhevsk, my aunt introduced me to the poetry of Sergei Esenin. At night, when everyone was asleep and the last coal was gleaming in the stove, she whispered:

> I do not know if my last hour lies afar or near me,
> Once my eyes were gleaming blue, now they are so bleary.
>
> Where are you, my happiness? Sorrow, gloom, confusion.
> In the fields? Or in the pub? Nothing but illusion. . . .

One of the last letters Father sent us from the front contained a poem, cut out of a newspaper:

> Wait for me and I'll return
> Wait with all your strength
> Wait when sadness comes to you
> With the autumn rains;
> Wait when blizzards howl and swirl
> Wait in summer heat
> Wait when others wait no more
> Wait as they forget. . . .

It was written by Konstantin Simonov, a living poet. Most good poets I knew before had been long dead. Now the newspapers were filled with the front-lines romanticism of Iosif Utkin, Boris Slutsky, Semyon Gudzenko, Dmitry Osin, Aleksandr Tvardovsky, and Simonov. It was good poetry. It was about the war as it affected real people, not "classes." It was humane, and, in the best sense of the word, it was patriotic.

◆

I didn't worry for the first year of my father's disappearance. He said he wouldn't be able to write. So he wasn't writing.

After a year, I understood that he was in some desperate situation. I started to catch myself thinking that at a particular instant, as I was reading a book, doing homework, standing in line, or walking down the street, Father was doing all he could to survive, and I, his daughter, could not help him. It was a terrifying thought. Then I would carry it further, into the realm of fantasy. If I were there with him and he was wounded, I would be able to carry him to safety. If someone was shooting at him, I would shield him with my body. If I could have believed in God, I would have prayed for him and made him safe. But I didn't believe in God, so I couldn't make him safe that way.

Long after the war, I learned that in January 1942 Father's Second Army was ordered to break through to besieged Leningrad. Along the way, it was to rendezvous with the Fourth, the Fifty-second, and the Fifty-fourth armies. But the other armies didn't move fast enough, and the Second was left cut off a hundred kilometers into the enemy territory.

Orders from Stalin prohibited the Second Army from pulling back, leaving it in the woods and swamps near Staraya Rusa. In that situation, there was something macabre in my Father's duties as commissar. He was assigned to drive a sound truck to the German positions and, in broken German, to persuade the enemy to surrender.

By April, the snow began to melt, and the army was left to die in the mud. By July, the Second Army was no more. Its commander, Lieutenant General Andrei Vlasov, had surrendered. Later, he turned up in Nazi uniform, fighting the Soviets.

No one ever told us how my father died, whether it was a bomb, a mortar shell, or a bullet that killed him. If it was a bullet, it could have been his own. Stalin ordered his soldiers to fight to the death, and many did. Just as easily, he could have been burned alive. The Nazis set fire to the woods to eliminate the Red Army's pockets of resistance. His body was never identified; so, at first he was listed as missing, and later, as "killed in action." The carnage was so gruesome that to this day local peasants call that place Myasnoy Bor — literally, "the Meat Forest." Mushrooms are plentiful there, but the locals don't pick them. In the past few years, Komsomol members have come to that forest to find skeletons and bury them in mass graves with military honors.

✦

One April day in 1944, I was walking to a poetry reading at the Tchaikovsky Concert Hall, about a twenty-minute walk from our Moscow apartment. It was a beautiful spring afternoon. I had passed the Moscow planetarium, and just before crossing the Garden Ring road and reaching the Tchaikovsky, I saw a column of motorcycles in the outer loop of the road. Trailing the motorcyclists were prisoners of war — thousands of them. A crowd began to form on the sidewalk.

"Warriors! Invincible! You can break them in half with snot!" said someone in the crowd.

"Hang them all. It is a waste of food to keep them," suggested someone else.

"Bastards! I'd strangle them with bare hands."

For about an hour, I stared at the procession. They hobbled along, blood caked on dirty bandages, barefoot, wounded; it could be that some of these men had shot at my father; possibly one of them had tortured "Tanya." They were pitiful now. Pitiful, humiliated, scared, defeated. I had plenty of reasons to hate, yet hate them I couldn't.

The prisoners were followed by water trucks spraying the Garden Ring pavement. That was a touch of comedy. As the crowd around me broke into laughter, I couldn't muster as much as a smile. Now I was angry at myself: I couldn't share the rage of my countrymen. I couldn't call those Nazis "bastards"; I didn't want to hang them or strangle them with my own hands.

"What I call compassion is really the absence of resolve," I said to myself. The war was ending, and, now, once again, I felt that I was different.

◆

During the war and just after it, Moscow was a poetry lover's paradise. The poetry section at the Arbat used-book store was filled with looted treasures of Moscow bibliophiles. I stood there for hours, reading verse by poets I did not know. Many of the books had been published in the 1920s.

The name Anna Akhmatova meant nothing to me when I picked up a book called *The White Flock*.

> We don't know how to say good-bye
> We keep wandering arm in arm.
> Twilight has begun to fall,
> You are pensive and I keep still.

Let's go into a church — we will watch
A funeral, christenings, a marriage service,
Without looking at each other, we will leave . . .
What's wrong with us?

Or let's sit on the trampled snow
Of the graveyard, sighing lightly,
And with your walking stick you'll outline palaces
Where we will be together always.

Akhmatova, whoever she was, understood the awkwardness of my life. It was as if she were there, in the room, when Mother told me I was not pretty. It was as if she understood my attempts to be like someone else, to be like Zoya.

What's wrong with us? What's wrong with me? Why am I not the same as everyone else? Why do I remain different, no matter how hard I try not to be? It was the question I was trying to ask, but the right words were not there for me.

I didn't know whether Akhmatova was alive or where she lived. All I knew was that had I been blessed with talent, my writing would be exactly like hers.

✦

At four in the morning on May 9, 1945, Mother whispered in my ear, "Lyudochka, *voyna konchilas*." The war had ended.

I remember glancing out the window. Lights were on in two or three windows in the eleven-story building across the street. I got dressed, then looked out again. By now all the windows had lit up. I ran out into the street. People were running past me; everyone had a place to go; everyone needed someone to hold — a friend, a lover, a stranger. Scattered images of that gloriously hectic day have lodged in my consciousness deeper than any childhood memory.

Red Square. An officer in battlefield uniform, tears in his eyes, handing ice cream to strangers. "Here, comrade! We won! Won! Congratulations, comrade!"

The US embassy. A dozen men on the balcony, a crowd below. Everyone cheers. The doors swing open. A woman in a navy blue dress and a starched, white apron comes out into the crowd. On a silver tray, she carries long, elegant flute glasses. Champagne. People closest to her carefully take the glasses off the tray. I look up at the balcony. The men up there raise flutes of their own. A toast that needs no words.

Dusk. A winding Moscow street. My shoes are in my hands; my stockings, too. A woman passes by, slowly. She seems old; everyone does when you are eighteen. She is crying. "Don't cry. Not today."

"I cry from happiness. But I cry alone. I had a husband, I had three sons; they won't be back."

Every one of us had won a small victory, and together they added up to the big one. It was up to each of us to fight his own personal battle with the enemy. Before the war, we were trained to dislike ourselves, revere Pavlik Morozov, and be as "Soviet" as everyone else. Yet, a "collective" of faceless people could not have won the war. Zoya was not faceless, and neither was my father. They acted as citizens. They needed no orders, no edicts to push themselves to the limit. And that meant a great deal.

Now the war was over; all that was wrong seemed so right on May 9, 1945.

Two

The Moscow State University had to be reinvented. It had all but shut down during the war. The school had been evacuated to Sverdlovsk; the more prominent professors had been evacuated to Kazan, with the Academy of Sciences. Upper-classmen numbered about fifty per class in each department.

There were only fourteen men among the four hundred first-year students in the Department of History. "If you put them all together, you get ten whole ones," quipped one of the girls. One of our boys wore a glove to hide his artificial hand; another wore a band over his eye. There was also a former tank crewman with a badly burned face. We called them *frontoviki,* people from the front.

Student songs had been forgotten. I could reconstruct only the first line of "Gaudeamus Igitur," a drinking song that had been sung by students in European universities since the thirteenth century. Instead of "Gaudeamus," we sang "Brigantina."

> We are tired of arguing and talking,
> Tired of our love for weary eyes.
> Setting out are gentlemen of fortune,
> Their brigantine is raising sails.
>
> Their captain, weathered as the sea cliffs,
> Went to sea before the break of dawn.

Higher, higher, we will raise our glasses
Filled with young and bitter-tasting wine.

We will drink a toast to the unyielding,
And to those who scorn the frills of home.
Overhead we fly the Jolly Roger
And we sing the song of Captain Flynt.

There was a bloody undercurrent in this Jolly Roger romanticism of landlocked kids. The song was written by Pavel Kogan, a Moscow University student, in obvious emulation of Akhmatova's husband, Nikolai Gumilev, a poet, officer, explorer, and big-game hunter. Gumilev was accused of taking part in a plot to overthrow the Bolsheviks and executed by the secret police in Petrograd in 1920. Kogan was killed in action in 1942.

We made a few traditions of our own. On the first of the month, the day the stipends were given out, students treated themselves to ice cream at Cafe Morozhenoye — Café Ice Cream — on Gorky Street. Sometimes we ordered glasses of red wine — the sweeter, the better — and poured it on the ice cream.

After the first week at the university, I was elected the Komsomol organizer of a study group of fourteen people — hardly a job of major importance. Still, in a matter of weeks, I was told that there was no quorum at my election and that the post would be turned over to a *frontovik*. I didn't rejoice when I was elected and didn't grieve when I was ousted. Nor did I realize that my replacement by a *frontovik* was part of a pattern. The number of *frontoviki* increased as they replaced the girls who failed or dropped out. By the end of the first year, there were about fifty men in our class. By graduation, there were about a hundred men and two hundred women. To get into the department, the girls had to overcome stiff competition. One in fourteen made it. *Frontoviki,* almost without exception, were admitted on the strength of their service records.

The Department of History got a special breed of *frontoviki:* peasant boys who had become Komsomol and party functionaries in the military. The war had given them a taste of power, and now they were determined to stay in the city for the rest of their lives. Most of them visualized the same career ladder: a degree in the history of the USSR or the history of the Communist party, then a position someplace in the party apparatus. They had no interest in history; they had no burning questions. They were incapable of critical thinking. They studied to become bosses.

They couldn't even write a decent love note. "The ribbon in your hair makes you more beautiful," a *frontovik* attempted to write to a friend of mine at a party. When he got to "more beautiful," the sentence misfired. He wrote "*krasivshe,*" which is folksy and, presumably, was appropriate for his sweetheart at the kolkhoz. *Krasiveye* would have been correct Russian. The note was widely circulated.

Still, *frontoviki* got the last laugh. They had learned the meaning of power in an extreme situation: in the face of death. If any of them had any youthful idealism to begin with, they lost it on the battlefields. Many lost compassion, too. To them, Komsomol and the party meant power, and power can be consolidated through application.

To be noticed by the higher-ups, *frontoviki* needed "personal cases" in which students would be accused of disloyalty, lack of vigilance, or some such thing. In one "personal case," a classmate of mine was accused of failing to return a banner after a public rally. The boy was apologetic. He said he just left the banner someplace, but *frontoviki* interpreted his action as an ideological affront. He was expelled from the Komsomol and the university.

✦

The Soviet power structure was going through changes, bringing closer the day when a university diploma would become a requirement for rising to political power.

The mechanism of succession was simple: the revolutionaries, my grandparents' contemporaries, were exterminated by Stalin in the 1930s. They were replaced by the barely educated *vydvizhentsy,* promoted party functionaries, most of them the same age as my parents. Those *vydvizhentsy* held power for thirty-two years, from Stalin's death in 1953 to Konstantin Chernenko's in 1985. Now they have been replaced by my contemporaries, most of whom are professionals with better manners and impressive diplomas.

But in the 1940s and 1950s, none of us could have suspected just where our education would take us. Consider Mikhail Gorbachev and his network of graduates of the Moscow University Department of Law. His roommate, a Czechoslovak named Zdeněk Mlynář, went on to become one of the leaders of the 1968 Prague Spring. Another of his classmates, a Ukrainian named Levko Lukyanenko, used his legal training to draft a brief that argued that the Ukraine had a constitutional right to secede from the Union of Soviet Socialist Republics. That argument earned him a fifteen-year prison term. In 1976, shortly after his release, Lukyanenko joined the Ukrainian Helsinki Watch Group. For that he got another fifteen-year term. Another of Gorbachev's classmates, Lev Yudovich, later defended dissidents at trials. He has since emigrated, and at this writing he teaches US troops in West Germany.

I was anything but a social butterfly, yet, by virtue of being a student at Moscow University, I met Stalin's daughter, Svetlana, her first husband, Grisha Moroz, and her husband-to-be, Felix Shirokov. I also met Volodya Shamberg, the former son-in-law of politburo member Georgy Malenkov, and Aleksei Adzhubei, Khrushchev's son-in-law. (The school was nicknamed Son-in-Law University.) I met an American named Tim Ryan. Tim looked a lot like his father, Eugene Dennis, the US Communist-party leader. Later, through my university friend Marina Rosenzweig, I met two of the Jewish doctors who ultimately would be accused of plotting to poison Comrade Stalin. I was acquainted with Tata Khariton, whose father, Yuli Borisovich Khariton, would later dismiss and denounce his institute's most illustrious employee, Andrei Sakharov. And later in life, through Moscow University connections, I met Yuli Daniel, then a little-known writer, who introduced me to Andrei Sinyavsky, a writer and literature professor.

But at the time we were at school, few of those connections could be called friendships. Going out of the immediate circle of friends — usually limited to two or three — meant multiplying the chances of having your offhand remarks reported to the authorities. The university, as the society around it, had broken up into its smallest elements; it had become atomized. It took a poet to describe that indescribable era:

> We live, not feeling the country beneath,
> Walk ten paces, and our speeches aren't heard
> But if there's courage for a half-a-chat
> Its subject's the mountain man of the Kremlin.

That poem was never put on paper. Osip Mandelshtam recited it to a group of friends in 1933 and was arrested and exiled shortly thereafter. One of those friends had turned him in. Early in 1937, Mandelshtam reemerged in Moscow, after consenting to write an ode to Stalin. After the ode was finished, Mandelshtam was arrested again. He died in a prison camp.

During my first year at the university, I formulated a theory: the party had been penetrated by people who lacked moral principles and wanted nothing more than personal gain. Good Communists, people like my parents, did not crave power.

That explained the snake pit at the university and gave me two options. The first was to stay as far as possible from the party. The second was to join and reform it from within. The first option was both escapist and defeatist; the second offered hope that someday all ruthless careerists would be replaced by decent people and the party would return to true principles of Marxism-Leninism. However, I could not see myself in the same pit with *frontoviki*. I chose option one.

✦

As a Komsomol member, I was obligated to take on a minimum of "public work." I picked a volunteer job that had nothing to do with the university: running a "political-information club" for laborers building the Moscow metro. They were good, genuine people, and backstabbing was the last thing on their minds. I looked forward to showing up in their dormitory for what amounted to a simple chat.

Also as a means of escape, I picked the most apolitical field of study available: archaeology. I would have picked the history of the Russian revolutionary movement, but that would have required too much piety. I decided to study it on my own. After classes, I read everything I could find on the Decembrists, Russia's first revolutionaries, and their friend Aleksandr Sergeyevich Pushkin.

On the morning of December 14, 1825, on Saint Petersburg's Senate Square, a grenadier battalion led by a group of young officers and civil servants attempted a coup against Czar Nicholas I. They had a plan: on the day of the coronation of Nicholas I, one regiment would start the uprising, then other regiments would join in, and the serfs would follow. That way, even if the Senate Square rebellion failed, their martyrdom would awaken the nation to the need for liberty and rule of law. They were captured, and by the summer of 1826, five of them had been hanged and 120 exiled to Siberia.

The Decembrists were in their midtwenties. They were romantics with sabers, brought up on Byron and the ideals of the French Revolution. They were the vanguard of their generation, young men who grew up speaking French, reading Homer in Greek, and reciting Pushkin in Russian.

To them, Pushkin was a curly-haired young man who wrote brilliant poetry and had a way of getting in trouble. Some knew him from their school days at the Lyceum; others had met him at the balls in Saint Petersburg, Moscow, or Odessa. Pushkin, the genius who shaped my inner being, was a rebel.

There wasn't a Decembrist who hadn't read Pushkin's "Ode to Freedom," the poem eighteen-year-old Aleksandr Sergeyevich wrote in 1817. It dealt with a touchy subject: replacing tyranny with the rule of law — law that would apply uniformly to the czars and their subjects. The alternative, Pushkin warned, was violence:

> And that's a lesson to the czars:
> Your punishments and your rewards
> Your prison walls and all your altars
> Are not protection you can trust.
> Be first to bow your heads
> Under the sanctuary of Law
> And then tranquility and freedom
> Will guard the throne forevermore.

The poem was circulated among Pushkin's friends and eventually got into the wrong hands. That led to the czar's order for Pushkin's confinement at the poet's family estate in the hills of Valday.

I felt an instinctive bond with the Decembrists. Just a few years earlier, their country had won the war with Napoléon. There was no place for functionaries on those battlefields. It is citizens who win wars. But when Russia's hussars and grenadiers returned triumphantly from Paris, they once again felt the grip of bureaucrats, fools, and opportunists. After seeing the West, they were ashamed of Russia's backwardness and, especially, the mainstay of the Russian economy, the institution of serfdom. But the war was over and the tyrant was not about to consider their opinions. The regime no longer had any need for citizens, for citizens have a way of being a nuisance. They demand reforms; they demand the rule of law. And sometimes, as on December 14, 1825, they stand up to defy the state.

I could see what brought those young men to Senate Square. It was frustration identical to the frustration I felt while observing *frontoviki* orchestrating "personal cases" against our classmates. Our war was over. Hitler had been defeated. But at peace our rulers needed something more manageable than citizens.

After studying the Decembrists, I moved on to the two major schools of thought that split Russian intellectuals in the 1840s. One school, the Slavophiles, saw Russia's salvation in the past, the harmonious (albeit fictionalized) era that preceded Peter the Great and his attempt to make the backward Russia more like Europe.

My sympathies were with the other school, the Westernizers, who regarded Russia as part of the greater European culture. As a Westernizer, I sympathized with Aleksandr Herzen. By then I had read all three volumes of his *Past and Thoughts,* as well as most of his other works. Herzen, the boy from the Arbat, grew up to be a revolutionary and, eventually, an émigré.

In the suburbs of London, Herzen ran his Free Russian Press, which published Pushkin's forbidden poetry, the memoirs of the Decembrists, and a journal called *Kolokol* ("The Bell"), which covered the continuing battle for abolition of serfdom. It was Herzen who first published Pushkin's "Ode to Freedom." (That poetic call for constitutional government was first published abroad in 1856, then reprinted in Russia in 1906, eighty-nine years after it was written.)

Years later, I realized that Westernizers were by no means Westerners. Westerners are beneficiaries of the Magna Carta, the French Revolution, and Jeffersonian thought. Thanks to battles won centuries ago, they are born to civil liberties and equal protection under the law. They rightfully take these as their due. Being Russian, Westernizers are not born to rights and liberties. To them, rights and liberties are ideals. At least in terms of logistics, preservation of rights and securing those rights are entirely different problems.

◆

A woman born in 1927 had to consider every marriage proposal. Most boys from my school had been drafted in 1945. The war was almost over, the commanders were hardened, the training was lax. So my schoolmates were sent to the front with rudimentary shooting skills. Very few returned. Older boys would have been drafted in 1941. Even fewer of them survived.

Valentin Alexeyev was an attractive, calm, stable man; he spoke correct Russian; he wasn't crippled; he liked to dance; he wasn't opposed to reading. He was six years older than I, his career was under way, and he was mature. When he proposed, I talked myself into accepting.

Our courtship wasn't even a courtship. We met in 1943, when I was sixteen. Valentin was one of the officers who used to visit a cousin of mine who was staying with us, a beautiful Estonian woman who looked like my grandmother. After my cousin left Moscow, Valentin kept making his visits.

When the war began, Valentin had been a third-year engineering student at the Kiev Technological Institute. He was drafted, but instead of being sent to the front, he enrolled at the Zhukovsky Air Force Academy. He spent the war in Sverdlovsk, and though he didn't get shot at, by the time the fighting stopped he could not get out of the military.

Valentin was a good officer. He was the commander of his class. The problem was that he disliked the military. In the ideal world, he would have been a researcher, a physicist, or an engineer who would quietly go about his work.

After the war, he managed to find a way out. The Soviet A-bomb project was recruiting scientists, and since the project was given high priority, he was allowed to leave the military and enroll as a graduate student at Moscow University.

At first he showed no interest in me. I went about reading my poetry, building the metro, and preparing for entrance exams, not suspecting that Valentin was waiting for me to get older, to cross the all-important line between last year of school and first year at the university.

After I started the university in September, he began to show up more regularly. He brought flowers. He invited me to the theater. In a matter of months, he proposed.

Had there been no war and had there been more men to choose from, I would not have accepted. But reality had to be acknowledged. Besides, the spring of 1945 and the end of the war brought with it a celebration of fertility. By the fall, many women began to show pregnancy. After four years of cold, hunger, and death, the start of a new life was inspiring.

I wanted a child. In fact, when I was growing up as the only child, I decided that I wanted at least three.

The disappointment of my first year at the university made me look for an escape. There wasn't enough out there to fill a life. I needed something personal, something that would be my own. Now I had that escape. By the time I married Valentin, I had convinced myself that I was in love.

◆

In October 1946, *Pravda* published a decree in which politburo member Andrei Zhdanov called the poet Anna Akhmatova "a nun or a whore — or rather both a nun and a whore who combines harlotry with prayer." Akhmatova, he said, was an "overwrought upper-class lady who frantically races back and forth between boudoir and chapel."

By then I had learned that Akhmatova grew up in Czarskoye Selo, the site of the royal summer residence and the place where Pushkin had attended the Lyceum. She had been married to Gumilev. She had her chance to emigrate after the 1917 revolution, yet she stayed on. And she paid the price for staying. Between 1923 and 1940, hardly any of her work was published.

Now, on the pages of *Pravda,* the willowy, graceful Akhmatova, the ballerina of verse, was being called a whore by a pig. And a nun, and whatever else rolled off Zhdanov's venomous tongue.

I walked up to my bookshelf, took down three thin volumes, looked through them one more time. *The Rosary. Anno Domini. The White Flock.* I knew every poem in every volume, and I recited them to myself whenever I felt the need to, which was often. If they are dangerous, so are white clouds on the first day of spring. But dangerous they were, and they had to be put away.

I placed the volumes in my desk's bottom drawer, covered them with papers; and if I had known any prayers, I would have said them.

✦

Zhdanov's denunciation of Akhmatova and humorist Mikhail Zoshchenko put an end to all contemporary literature.

The libraries had been purged of books by non-Marxists and "enemies of the people." Books that mentioned non-Marxists or "enemies of the people" without condemning them were pulled off the shelves, too. That book purge began in the 1930s, and a decade later library shelves stood bare. The Russian revolutionary movement past the 1860s could not be studied in any depth. Materials went just past Herzen and ended with pre-Marxist Hegelians. That wiped out all Russian philosophy and political thought from the 1860s to the 1940s. Not a trace was left of any Russian political party; even Bolshevik records started with 1940.

Newspapers, books, and journals were now devoted exclusively to praises of Comrade Stalin, our Communist party, the Soviet motherland, the Great Russian People, and Our Valorous Armed Forces. No book could be "idealess." A love story, a poem, or an adventure told for its own sake was no longer acceptable. Every work had to be of ideological value. Otherwise, it was classified as "bourgeois diversionism."

I was yet to read anything by Marina Tsvetayeva, Sergei Esenin, or Osip Mandelshtam. Foreign authors were banned, too. They fell under another campaign, the one aimed at stamping out "low-bowing to the West," a kind of Russia-first movement.

The "low-bowing" campaign went beyond literature. One day, at the bread stores, the whole country discovered that French bread was now called city bread. A menu became a nonsensical *razblyudovka* — a "scattering of dishes." Candy called the American Nut became the Southern Nut.

In those days my husband liked to lavish praise on the Mozhaysky flying machine, which, we were being told, had been invented long before the Wright brothers' plane. "A wonderful plane," Valentin used to say. "A beautiful plane. Just one little problem. Doesn't fly."

You could find the official claims that it was a Russian, Popov, who invented the radio. The light bulb was invented by Yabloshkov and the steam engine by the Cherepanov brothers. The tank, too, was invented by the Slavs, in the thirteenth century. It was a horse cart covered with sheets of wood. Later, the idea was stolen by the West.

Those claims gave rise to a series of jokes: A Russian, a Frenchman, and a German are asked to write books about elephants. The German writes three thick volumes titled *All About Elephants*. The Frenchman writes a novel, *Elephants and Love*. The Russian writes a pamphlet, *Russia, the Motherland of Elephants*.

Another joke claimed that it was Ivan the Terrible who invented the X-ray machine. ("He said to the boyars, 'I see right through you.' ") And then there was the story of a physicist who successfully defended a dissertation based on work by the "great physicist Odnokamushkin." Odnokamushkin sounded Russian enough, except for being a literal translation of "Einstein." I don't know if this was indeed a joke. Dissertations were known to be failed for citing too many foreigners.

One day, I ran into Belochka Zinkevich, a school friend. "How is your sister?" I asked.

"Not too well. Her husband has been sentenced to ten years in the camps for telling a joke."

Then she told me the joke:

Two Muscovites meet in the year 2000.

"I've been spending a lot of time looking at the gallows on the Red Square."

"Why?"

"Just trying not to forget the shape of the letter 'T.' I've forgotten all the others."

It seemed logical that the Russian alphabet would be the next target of Comrade Stalin's campaign to create the New Socialist Man. I told that joke to my husband. He told it to his most trusted friends. I told it to one or two of my friends. They, too, told it to their friends. Every one of us risked a ten-year sentence.

Jokes notwithstanding, we continued to believe that Marxism was the most progressive teaching and that socialism was the bright future of mankind. I had heard those teachings from my parents, and not being a peer of Karl Marx, I was unable to come up with anything better. I am not a creator of new teachings.

◆

As soon as he found out that I was pregnant, Valentin cheerfully gave up his civilian status. Having a student wife and an infant was expensive, and the stipend of a graduate student in a military academy was higher than his Moscow University stipend. For a man who disliked the military, that was an enormous sacrifice.

I understood that, and I appreciated it. But I had other worries. For a year after our son, Sergei, was born, I was busily alternating between going to class, catching up on lectures, and washing and boiling his swaddling sheets. All the while, I was either hungry or exhausted or both. In 1946, a year after the war's end, my diet consisted of potatoes and macaroni. That diet and the usual strains of motherhood left me so tired that I would fall asleep while nursing. At least for a while I didn't have time to worry about the Russian revolutionary movement, social justice, and bad people who made their way into the Communist party.

Those worries returned a year later. By then they were augmented by my doubts about the man I married.

"You shouldn't marry just anyone," Valentin used to say jokingly to his friends. "The right way is to pick out a girl in first grade, bring her up, help her with her homework, then, when she is old enough, marry her. Otherwise, you'll have trouble."

It was only a half-joke. He had waited for me to grow up. He made the sacrifices, and now he was ready to settle into a lifetime of tranquility and marital bliss.

It's not that I had any specific grievances. He was a good father, a good family man. He even made the time to read the books I recommended to him. For a busy graduate student, that took a major effort. He was also genuinely interested in what I thought of the books I recommended. He never debated. He just absorbed my opinions, made them his own, then proceeded to express them as his own. That would have been fine, if not for his distortions of what I was thinking. Sitting at someone's dinner table, I would hear my own remarks in a cheapened, castrated form.

Whenever I told my friends that I was not happy, their response was the same: "Are you crazy! He doesn't drink. He doesn't smoke. Doesn't chase skirts! He is in the military!"

Three years into our marriage, when Sergei was just over two, I told Valentin I was leaving.

His response was disarming: "And where, may I ask, will you go?" I considered the alternatives. Since leaving was my idea, it would be up to me to leave. Valentin would keep the room. But where would a student with a two-year-old son go? Magnanimously, he was willing to forget my foolish impulse. Nothing was wrong. The family was intact.

I had no way to fight him, except on the rare occasions when we went out. I would put on pumps. High heels made me taller than Valentin, and he hated that. Over the next decade, our marriage could be tracked by simply watching my shoes. When we got along, I wore low heels. When we didn't, I wore high heels. Ultimately, Valentin was promoted to colonel and was issued the tall hat of gray karakul. It was taller than the highest heels I could find.

◆

I tried to discuss my political views with my uncle Borya, but that led nowhere.

"You talk about the principles of socialism," Uncle Borya would say in his deep baritone. "Well, they don't matter. They keep them around for fools like you." Then he'd add for emphasis: "That's right, there are no principles, there is no socialism. There's just a band of brigands. They took power and they are holding on. That's all. Repeat after me: no principles, no socialism, only brigands, a band of them."

Though he was my father's brother, Uncle Borya drank like a fish, or, to use the correct Russian metaphor, like a horse. In either case, he had the ability to drink without getting drunk. He was a grim, towering man who had few friends. Before the war, my parents used to be shocked whenever Uncle Borya came to stay in our apartment with young and not especially refined women. He would leave his wife in Leningrad.

Uncle Borya had the gift of making you feel uneasy. He had a way of sizing you up silently, then cutting you off in midargument with his powerful, rumbling, "*Nu*." It meant: "I understand what you are trying to say. Stop belaboring the point. I have something to answer."

His explanations were always the same: it's the brigands. They are to blame. Uncle Borya never told me what made him form his opinions — or, more precisely, his opinion. He was, of course, a Communist-party member. He joined at about the same time as my parents, when the revolution was young and the future was bright. I don't know if he joined because of youthful idealism or because a naval officer had to be in the party to advance.

He had the rank of captain and had served as chief mechanic on board a submarine. I know he loved his submarine. On it, the world was finite. There were just so many people, all of them dependent on each other for their lives, all of them dependent on his wizardry with the machine that kept all of them alive underwater.

On land, things didn't go as well for Uncle Borya. His first wife was from an aristocratic family, which made him suspect in the eyes of his superiors. His second wife was the sister of the wife of an admiral who was imprisoned shortly after the war. Uncle Borya was also a friend of the admiral's, which could mean only one thing: they had spent many evenings drinking vodka and trading stories about the brigands. That association made Uncle Borya even more suspect.

And then there was the matter of the fourteen hours Uncle Borya spent floating off the coast of Denmark after the Nazis sunk his submarine in 1943. The authorities seemed to wonder whether sometime during those fourteen unsupervised hours he had turned into an enemy agent. He wanted to be assigned to another submarine, but was permanently stationed at a repair facility in Leningrad.

For almost two decades, Uncle Borya made regular trips to Moscow to lobby his friends in the defense ministry to get him reassigned to a submarine. He stopped only after suffering a heart attack in 1967.

As far as he was concerned, I was asking all the wrong questions, but at least I was asking questions. That made me a worthy interlocutor. He wanted to hear my arguments, and he took great pleasure in shooting them down.

"I keep hearing about the flourishing of Socialist agriculture, but all I can see is poverty," I would say. "Peasants aren't getting paid 'according to their work.' Is that socialism?"

"Socialism. Socialist agriculture. 'To each according to his work.' All of that is for fools like you," Uncle Borya muttered. "You're educated, but you are a fool. You want the truth? They are a band of brigands. They took power. That's all."

I asked Uncle Borya about anti-Semitism, too. It was a deviation from the internationalist principles of Marxism-Leninism, I said.

"Internationalist principles," said Uncle Borya. "Marxism-Leninism. That, too, is for fools like you. There is a band. Of brigands. They have power. And they use it."

"He is a wonderful man, but his thinking is primitive," I used to say to Valentin whenever Uncle Borya left.

✦

I can no longer recall my classmate Zhavoronkov's first name, but I can still picture his face, his Russian good looks, his curly hair, his blue eyes. There was a spiritual, poetic look about him; I thought he looked like Sergei Esenin.

Zhavoronkov always wore a glove. His hand had been blown off in the war. That injury didn't discourage young women from casting glances in his direction. But the girls who ran after Zhavoronkov generally ran back the instant he opened his mouth. He was an idiot and an anti-Semite.

Given that, 1949, our fourth year at the university, should have been a fine time for Zhavoronkov. That year the campaign of "low-bowing to the West" had grown into a campaign against "cosmopolitism." The term applied to anyone who did not feel loyalty to Mother Russia, but for the most part, it was aimed at the Jews.

That year Comrade Stalin arranged the murder of Solomon Mikhoels, the brilliant actor who had played King Lear in Moscow's Yiddish Theater. No one is certain about the exact circumstances of Mikhoels's death, but, according to one account, he was severely beaten, shot in the head, then dropped in the path of an oncoming Studebaker.

After the Mikhoels assassination, the Yiddish Theater was arrested. The whole theater.

That year, the university fired Professor Atzarkin, one of my favorite teachers, who had managed to make the history of the party seem exciting. He was a short man with curly hair and energetic eyes. In beautiful, precise Russian, he lectured about Lenin's ideological disagreements with the founder of the Russian Social Democratic party, Georgy Plekhanov, with Menshevik Julius Martov, and with fellow Bolshevik Leon Trotsky. In Professor Atzarkin's lectures, Lenin's opponents were always wrong, but never evil.

At the ethnography department, an unschooled *frontovik* tried to make the case for expelling two of his professors for "cosmopolite" overtones in their lectures. I remember his peasant speech. *Kosmopolitizm* always came out with a whistling sound that made "z" sound softer: *kosmopolitiz'm*. He also mentioned *anti-Semitiz'm, kapitaliz'm, sotsializ'm,* and *imperializ'm.*

But when he tried to quote the Jewish professors' disrespectful remarks about some ancient Slavic chieftain as evidence of lack of respect for the forebears of the Great Russian People, a student in the audience raised a hand. "That's not what my notes say," he said.

This was followed by the sound of other students flipping through the pages of their notebooks.

"My notes don't say that, either," said someone else. The professor was spared and the accuser had to live with the humiliation of being a poor notetaker.

Sensing that pogroms were near, my classmate Zhavoronkov grew increasingly vocal. While Komsomol leaders insisted that they were attacking "cosmopolitism" rather than hardworking people of "Jewish nationality," Zhavoronkov went a step further. "Fucking kikes," he used to say in the hallways. While the Komsomol leaders stated that Zionism and anti-Semitism were two sides of the same coin, and that both were deplorable, Zhavoronkov talked of little other than his urge to "strangle them all."

Zhavoronkov was becoming so much of an embarrassment that in April 1949, at a Komsomol meeting of the fourth-year class of the Department of History, he was officially reprimanded for anti-Semitism and an appropriate notation was made in his personal file.

✦

Two meetings later, in June 1949, our Komsomol organization heard the personal case of Stella Dvorkis, an adjunct student accused of making a deliberately slanderous statement about the existence of anti-Semitism in the USSR.

Stella Dvorkis was confronted by her accuser, Lyuda Shaposhnikova. Shaposhnikova testified that she had asked Dvorkis whether the Moscow University history department was her first choice. Dvorkis said no, her first choice was the Institute of Eastern Languages.

"So why aren't you there?" Shaposhnikova asked.

"I didn't get in," Dvorkis answered.

"Why not?"

"Because I am Jewish."

As befitted a Komsomol member, Shaposhnikova reported that Dvorkis had made the outrageous claim that Jewish people were not treated as full-fledged citizens and that discrimination existed in admission policies at a Soviet institution of higher learning. That would imply state-sponsored anti-Semitism, a claim that played into the hands of "World Zionism." Further inquiry revealed that Dvorkis had friends among members of the recently arrested troupe of the Moscow Yiddish Theater.

After the accusation was read, citizens of "Jewish nationality" studying in our department were brought out to state categorically that they deplored Zionism. In their heart of hearts, they may indeed have deplored Zionism, but for the moment they had a more urgent task: saving their hides. Humiliation was in their eyes, and the grotesque parade of the Weissbergs, Izenbergs, and Rabinowitzes made me think of those German soldiers hobbling through Moscow in 1944. They looked captured and wounded.

Now it was Stella's turn to testify. The petite young woman whom I had not seen before didn't admit her guilt, didn't throw herself on the mercy of her judges. Instead, she made a vigorous and convincing argument in her defense. I can't recall its fine points, but I distinctly recall her quoting from Lenin.

The meeting was in its third hour, and the two hundred or so people in the audience were lulled to sleep by June heat and the monotone of orators.

The motion came next: to expel Stella Dvorkis from the Komsomol and to petition the administration for her expulsion from Moscow State University.

At that moment, my patience ran out. I raised my hand.

"Slavinskaya," said Pyotr Lavrin, secretary of the Komsomol bureau and a *frontovik*. His skull was dented in around his right frontal lobe and his right eye was always closed.

"You call this punishment logical?" I blurted out as I got up from my seat. "You say that anti-Semitism and Zionism are two sides of the same coin! So they are. But two meetings ago we gave Zhavoronkov a reprimand for anti-Semitism; now, two months later, Stella Dvorkis is being expelled from the Komsomol and the university for Zionism. So, if they are really two sides of the same coin, you have to expel Zhavoronkov, too. Either that, or you have to give Dvorkis a reprimand and nothing else! Let's be consistent!"

My classmates woke up screaming.

"Whom are you defending?" shouted my detractors.

"You didn't understand her!" shouted my defenders.

"We'll find out who *you* are!" shouted Pyotr Lavrin. The majority voted in favor of expelling Stella Dvorkis from the Komsomol, which also meant automatic expulsion from the university.

I didn't worry much about Lavrin's threat to excavate my family history. My maiden name, Slavinskaya, established me as a Russian, a Pole, or, possibly, a Jew. In my case, it was all of the above and none of the above. My father's mother was Jewish; his father, a Pole. They were married in a Catholic church. My mother's father was a Ukrainian; her mother, an Estonian. They were married in a Russian Orthodox church.

My Polish grandfather spoke no Yiddish, my Jewish grandmother spoke no Polish, my Ukrainian grandfather spoke no Estonian, and my Estonian grandmother spoke no Ukrainian. All of them spoke Russian. Their bloodlines notwithstanding, my parents were raised in the Russian tradition, speaking no languages other than Russian; as children, they read Pushkin, Gogol, and Tolstoy.

The concept of "nationality" was not legally defined until the 1920s, when all Soviet citizens were issued internal passports. Asked to define their ethnic origins, my parents said they were Russian. That's what they considered themselves, and for that reason that's what they were.

I was not given such a choice. When I reached sixteen, the age of majority, I had to adopt the established "nationality" of my parents, which meant that I did not have a legal right to call myself Polish, Jewish, Ukrainian, Estonian, or a combination of the four.

Fortunately, I consider myself a Russian. And I wouldn't advise anyone to dispute it.

✦

Sometime in the spring of 1949, Mother returned from a store empty-handed and red in the face.

"I've just yelled at a woman in a queue," she said, still dumbfounded by her own actions. "She said, 'Those Jews prosper, while we, the Russians, do all the work.'" That was more than my mild-mannered mother could handle.

"Who is *we?*" Mother asked.

"The Russian people! That's who we are!"

"Don't you ever say 'we'!" Mother shouted. "I am a Russian, and you aren't speaking for me. You are an anti-Semite and I am not like you!"

The pressure had been getting to Mother in the previous few months. Her department head at the Bauman Polytechnic Institute had been ousted for being Jewish. She was offered the job, but declined. She didn't want to become an administrator, especially if that entailed presiding over the firings of her Jewish colleagues. But since she was a Russian, a doctor of philosophy, and a Communist, the institute would not take her no for an answer. A party organizer ordered her to take over as head of the mathematics department. Under the conditions, she could not refuse.

In her new position, Mother was called into the administrative and party offices and told to look for "errors" made by Jewish professors. "I am not aware of any errors," she kept telling the party men. "They do fine work."

After such sessions, she met with her Jewish colleagues. Together, they plotted strategy to keep them in their jobs.

✦

That summer, I left two-year-old Sergei with Valentin's parents and went on an archaeological dig around Bryansk, a town normally about half a day's train ride from Moscow. Since we were transporting expedition gear by freight train, the trip took nearly a week.

It must have been my statement in defense of Stella Dvorkis that convinced my classmate Vladimir Kabo that he could be frank with me. As we sat side by side with our feet dangling out the freight car's open door, Volodya told me that he, too, had unorthodox views.

Virtually everything was wrong with the Soviet system, Kabo said. The country was being ruled by bureaucrats and fools, and if there ever had been any point to the revolution, it was now either betrayed or forgotten. Everything seemed to confirm his views; on every corner, he saw waste and greed. He said something about money being embezzled at some student function and something about the practice of sending students to collective farms wasting the students' time and not helping the peasants.

"Why are you this open with me?" I asked. "You don't know me. What if I report you?"

"I can tell that you won't." Kabo laughed.

I didn't feel like discussing my views with Kabo. There was no compassion in his arguments, just contempt for the party. His demeanor was always superior, as if I were the only person he considered his equal. What's more important, I disagreed with him. Everything about him began to irritate me — his pudgy body, his receding hairline, his superior tone, his habit of correcting everyone's speech.

As far as I was concerned, the Soviet system was sound, Marxism-Leninism was the most progressive ideology in the world, and all of Russia's problems could be attributed to the large number of "careerists" who had joined the party for personal gain.

We spent the following two months excavating the Vshchizh fortress destroyed by the Tatars in the thirteenth century. Seven centuries after the fortress went up in flames, the village on its site was still known as Vshchizh. All of us, seventeen people, lived in the schoolhouse. There was not much food, and no electricity. In July, a bridge collapsed under a horse-drawn cart carrying additional supplies for the expedition. No one was hurt, but much of the food was ruined.

At night, we sat around a campfire and talked, then, spontaneously, recited poetry. There was no need to announce anything; we just started reciting. Many of us knew enough of the Russian classics to pick up any poem at any verse. One evening, I started off

with Lermontov's "Demon" and his solemn promise to forsake evil
for a woman's love.

> I swear by the first day created,
> I swear by the last day and hour,
> I swear by shame and evil hated,
> By truth triumphant in its power.
> I swear by torments of the heart,
> By dreams of exultation fleeting,
> By every rapture of our meeting,
> And by the hour when we must part.
> I swear by all the spirit hordes
> Of kindred rebel deities,
> By angels of the flaming swords,
> By all my watchful enemies;
> I swear by Heaven and by Hell,
> By all things holy in the spheres
> Above, and by your last farewell;
> I swear by you, by your first tears
> For me, your tenderness and sighing,
> And by your waving silken hair.
> By happiness and pain undying,
> And by my love for you, I swear
> I disavow my thoughts of pride,
> I disavow my vengeance blind!

Then one of my friends joined in, took the lead, and glided away
with Lermontov's graceful verse.

> I vow I shall no more misguide
> By craft and wiles the human mind.
> I ask to make my peace with Heaven;
> I wish to love, I wish to pray
> Again, I wish to be forgiven.
> I will again believe in good,
> And, penitential, wash away
> The flames of my rebellious mood,
> And let the human race at peace
> In joy and labor find release.

It was a beautiful night — too beautiful for me to suspect that there was an informant in our midst.

On July 20, my twenty-second birthday, Valentin showed up with a bottle of Solkhino, a red, sweet Georgian wine. It was a 375-gram bottle, hardly enough for two, but I invited everyone, bought potatoes and a large bowl of wild strawberries, then set the table in an abandoned peasant hut. Split eighteen ways, the Solkhino didn't go far; everyone downed his thimbleful, then it was time to sing. We sang "Brigantina" before moving on to a song about an Australian pioneer sitting on a riverbank and using an ax to split the skull of anyone who tried to cross the stream. It was a silly song that could be heard at any student campfire, but that night it should have been left unsung.

✦

As the summer wore on, my dislike for Kabo became more intense. Once, a few weeks before the end of the expedition, he came by to ask our mutual friend Natasha Chlenova and me to walk outside with him. When we walked out, he told us that he had received a food parcel from home and that he would share it with us.

I was outraged. Food parcels should be shared with everyone in the expedition, not just with a couple of friends. So righteous was my rage that I told him what I thought, then returned to the schoolhouse and announced, "Kabo got a food parcel and he's gobbling it up by himself."

Over the next two weeks, Kabo was virtually boycotted by everyone in the expedition. Then, in mid-August, two weeks before the expedition's end, he came down with a fever and returned to Moscow.

On September 1, 1949, the first day of my final year at the university, I was summoned to Pyotr Lavrin's office.

"You know Kabo, correct?"

"Yes."

"You've had some conversations, correct?"

"We have."

"Do you remember what you talked about?"

"What do a guy and a girl talk about?" I said. My feelings about Kabo notwithstanding, I didn't want to discuss him with Lavrin. If

I reduced our conversations to a boy-girl sort of thing, few other questions would follow.

"Did you talk about politics?"

"Not that I can recall."

"You go back home and think; then, if you think of something, come back here and tell me."

The following day, Lavrin called me back to his office. He asked the same questions and I gave the same answers.

A few days later, I started wondering about Kabo. He was nowhere to be seen. I remembered that he had been dating a student named Nella Khaikina, so I asked her.

"Didn't you know? He was arrested," she said.

I had heard of many arrests, but that one was horrifying. It was I who had made that poor man's last days of freedom miserable. "I want to know everything that happened," I said to Nella.

She said that after his return, Kabo was visited by a friend, Sergei Khmelnitsky, and another man. I didn't know Khmelnitsky, but Nella told me that he was also a history student. He was full of political jokes, wrote passable poetry, and, like Kabo, always acted superior. In fact, Khmelnitsky may have been the person who helped Kabo thrash out his unorthodox views. Apparently, Kabo was reluctant to talk in front of the third man, but Khmelnitsky assured him of his reliability. So, off they went with their denunciations.

The following night, Kabo, still with high fever, was placed under arrest.

✦

Once again, Lavrin called me to his office. He had more questions about the expedition.

"What did you do in your spare time?"

"Walked around, picked mushrooms, took in the scenery."

"Did you recite poetry?"

"Yes."

"Whom did you recite?"

"Pushkin, Lermontov."

"Whom else?"

"Nekrasov."

"Whom else?"

"Mayakovsky."

"Whom else?"

"Surkov."

"Whom else?"

"Simonov."

"Did you recite Akhmatova?"

"No." I had recited Akhmatova, but with only one witness, Natasha Chlenova. I knew Natasha was reliable.

"Think back. Did you recite Akhmatova?"

"No, I didn't."

"Yulya Sinelnikova reports that you did, by the fire."

"She is wrong." Yulya Sinelnikova was a second-year student, a nice but not especially intelligent girl easily capable of misidentifying poets and poetry.

"Now, about your birthday. Was there drinking?"

"Yes."

"What did you drink?"

"A 375-gram bottle of Solkhino for eighteen people."

"Then what did you do?"

"We sang."

"What did you sing?"

" 'Brigantina.' "

"What else?"

"I don't remember."

"Did you sing 'Na beregu rodnoy reki'?" It was the bastardization of that song about the Australian pioneer sitting on the riverbank and smashing the skull of anyone trying to cross.

"No, I didn't sing 'Na beregu rodnoy reki.' I sang 'Na beregu odnoy reki.' "

The difference between *odnoy* and *rodnoy* was crucial. *Odnoy* meant, simply, on a riverbank. *Rodnoy* — literally, "native" — put the pioneer on the bank of a river that flowed past the place where he was born. That linguistic quirk also gave a different meaning to the word "pioneer": it made the skull smasher a Soviet Young Pioneer.

"I sang 'odnoy reki.' "

"Are you certain it wasn't 'rodnoy'?"

"I am. It wouldn't make any sense as *rodnoy*. It's a song of an Australian pioneer. He could not have had a 'native' river in Australia. Australian pioneers were exiles. They could have had a 'native' river in England, Scotland, or Ireland, but not in Australia. That would be illogical."

"You mean to say that you weren't singing about the Young Pioneers?"

"I sang about Australian pioneers — British convicts sent to Australia."

"Yulya Sinelnikova says she heard you sing '*rodnoy*.' "

"She may have sung *rodnoy*. I sang '*odnoy*.' "

"Go home and think hard. Then come back to see us."

The "Young Pioneer" accusation was too inane to hold, I thought. But what was this business about Akhmatova? I would never have recited her in public; no one in his right mind would. So why was Sinelnikova saying that I had recited something I hadn't?

There are few challenges greater than penetrating the mind of an informant. I had to get inside her skull, become like her. If I were she, how much Akhmatova would I have read? What could I have mistaken for Akhmatova? By the evening, I had my answer.

Sinelnikova had read the Zhdanov denunciation of Akhmatova. To illustrate his point that Akhmatova was the hybrid of a nun and a whore, Zhdanov had cited a poem:

> . . . I vow to you by the garden of angels,
> By the miraculous icon I vow
> And by the fiery passion of our nights —
> I will never return to you.

Sinelnikova must have remembered that there was an Akhmatova poem in which someone was making some kind of vows and where there was something about the heavens and something about love. I went back to Lavrin and asked him to call a committee meeting. I wanted to ask Sinelnikova a question.

"Yulya, do you mind if I recite a poem to you? Stop me if you recognize it as Akhmatova." Yulya nodded.

> I swear by the first day created,
> I swear by the last day and hour,

I swear by shame and evil hated,
By truth triumphant in its power.
I swear by torments of the heart,
By dreams of exultation fleeting,
By every rapture of our meeting,
And by the hour when we must part.

"That's it," said Yulya.

Lavrin slumped into his chair. Lermontov was still permitted reading.

The case was falling apart, but dropping it was out of the question. The Komsomol organization of the Moscow State University Department of History had to punish me for my defense of Stella Dvorkis, and nothing was going to stand in its way.

✦

Mine was the first "personal case" of the academic year. Komsomol activist Leonid Rendel came up to me just before the meeting.

"You do realize that considering these circumstances we cannot trust you with Komsomol education," he said. I would no longer be allowed to run my political-information club for workers building the Moscow metro. I was unreliable.

Rendel wasn't a *frontovik*. He was just a good soldier in an imaginary struggle. Poor, hyperpolitical Leonid Rendel. Eight years later, he would become a political prisoner, and our paths would eventually cross again.

My case was the last item on the agenda. Sinelnikova said I recited Akhmatova; I said I recited Lermontov; Sinelnikova said I sang '*rodnoy reki*'; I said I sang '*odnoy reki*.'

Kolya Sokolov, a *frontovik*, took the floor.

"Some people here could say, 'Why are you making this girl's life difficult? So she sang a silly song, so she recited a silly poem, so it was frivolous? So what?'

"But I say, comrades, it is our duty to respond with vigilance and decisiveness. It is our duty to punish such behavior. It is our duty to nip it in the bud, to destroy it before it grows. Because today, comrades, she might sing a little song or recite a little poem, and tomorrow — tomorrow, comrades, she could go out and blow up a defense plant."

"Idiot," blurted out my friend Maya Novinskaya.

I was given an official reprimand for "apolitical orientation expressed through the singing of frivolous songs and propagandizing the works of Anna Akhmatova."

At the following meeting, Maya Novinskaya stood accused of "loss of vigilance." Fortunately, she, too, got off with a reprimand.

Three

Frontoviki were not good Communists. I was certain of that. They were using the party for personal gain. And they were not alone.

This presented a question: What should an honest person do in the face of evil? I knew that in the long run my temperament would make me unable to hide or seek refuge in my personal life, as I did through my first four years at the university. But *frontoviki* left me no room. Their grip on the party and the Komsomol was so tight that an honest, well-meaning person could not have made any difference. They were too strong, and working alongside them would have offended my sense of aesthetics. In short, I had allowed them to bully me into apathy.

Before graduation, I started to wonder if I had a moral right to remain apathetic. My father, who had died for the Power of the Soviets, would not have approved of my stepping aside and allowing the country to become a prize for the opportunists. But there were still few options for coping with them. I was about to reject my first approach, hiding in personal life. And I did not even think of another option: forming an underground organization. Later, I learned that a few resistance cells had been formed, usually with disastrous results for their participants. Even if I had known about such cells, I would not have joined one; covert activity went against my nature. The remaining option was to join the party and attempt to reform it from within.

I decided that as soon as I graduated I would petition to join the party. Moreover, I felt morally obligated to convince all the decent people I knew to follow me. They, too, would convince all the decent people they knew to follow them. The honest, selfless Communists would then work together to force out the opportunists. And even if all our efforts failed, we would draw comfort from knowing that it was our duty to try to bring change, and that we had indeed tried.

These schemes may sound naive today; some said they sounded naive even in 1950. But I was twenty-two, troubled by injustice around me, and frustrated by my inability to bring about change, to be a citizen. I had no access to books that could have helped me reason my way out of my dilemma. And I lacked intellectual guidance from older, more experienced people.

Yes, there was Uncle Borya. But his responses were entirely predictable. The party was run by a band of brigands. A very powerful band of very bad brigands. Mother was not open to discussing such matters. She was a mathematician, not a political theorist.

My husband and his friends at the air force academy were skeptical. "If we join the party, it won't change anything," they said to my calls to activism. The "careerists" were too deeply entrenched, they said. My husband's friends were at least five years older than I; they were military engineers who had seen the workings of the system. Unlike me, they knew what they were talking about.

Of course, my belief that the party could be reformed from within was nothing but an illusion that I constructed to break out of the home — to find another reason for being, and with it, a place in public life. After enough talking, I managed to convince Valentin that, being an honest person, he, too, was morally obligated to petition to join the party. He had become a consumer of all of my theories, no matter how farfetched.

✦

I couldn't wait for graduation. By getting out of school, I would finally be free from the *frontoviki*. I chose not to attend the graduation ceremony. There was no point in sharing their moment of triumph.

I picked up my diploma at the registrar's office and accepted my job placement as a history teacher at Moscow Trade School No. 4.

As a Moscow University graduate with excellent grades, I could have qualified for a far better job than teaching the rejects of the school system. This, too, was my punishment for Stella Dvorkis and Anna Akhmatova. Since it was a placement job, I could not quit for three years. That was the law.

September 1, 1950, the first day of school, was my independence day. I would start a new life. I would turn those rejects into solid Soviet citizens. In the process, I, too, would become a productive member of the collective. And as I heightened the political under-standing of the masses, other decent people would follow my example.

◆

Few teachers at Moscow Trade School No. 4 were politically active. They had no interest in teaching, no interest in the subjects they taught, and were known to lose patience and beat their students. Some drank heavily. The place was crying out for an activist to improve it.

My students were boys between the ages of twelve and fifteen. Some were discipline problems, others lacked intelligence, and many had criminal tendencies. Many of them didn't know their fathers, and each year at least one student per class ended up in prison. (Crimes included breaking into a vending machine, an at-tempt to steal a pen from the pocket of a passenger in the metro, and the rape of a forty-year-old woman by seven boys.)

When I teach, I insist on complete silence. Even a whisper in the back row throws me off course. So I made a rule: if anything didn't get covered in class, all of us would meet after hours. That rule kept me at school two extra hours every night.

"Ludmilla Mikhailovna, what do you want of us?" a student said to me once. "We sit quieter here than in any class except Vasily Ivanovich's."

"I want you to be as quiet as you are in his class."

"That's asking too much. He beats us."

After hours, I led a history club and held conferences with par-ents of students who didn't do homework. On a visit to one of my boys, I found a drunk lying in the doorway of a workers' barrack. "Just step over him, Ludmilla Mikhailovna," my student said. The boy led me to the room he shared with his mother. A table heaped with dirty dishes and leftover food stood in the center. The mother and son slept on a pile of rags in the corner.

"Where do you do your homework?"

"Right here," said the boy, sitting down on the floor and putting his notebook on the only chair in the room.

Another of my students lived in a bathroom of a large communal apartment. Through unexplainable workings of the bureaucracy, his mother and stepfather had lost their room, but not their residency permit. The adults slept on boards placed on top of the bathtub. The boy slept at their feet. They had to vacate the room in the mornings, when other residents used it for bathing and washing clothes.

Whenever I stayed at work after dark, my students insisted on walking me to the trolley stop. "There's a Central Committee apartment building on the way, and the boys there drag women into the entryways and rape them," they warned me. "Their parents are higher-ups, so nothing happens to them."

I don't know if the boys were trying to make points with their young teacher or if the danger was real. Still, I savor the memory of my young hoodlums protecting me from the children of the party bosses.

✦

I became an "agitator" — a volunteer precinct worker. My job was to bring out the voters at an old house that was once owned by a wealthy merchant. Now at least fifty people lived there. When I stopped by, all of them filed into the kitchen.

Since there was just one candidate, we didn't spend much time talking about the elections. Instead, we talked about anything that interested them. Someone wanted me to explain what the Korean War was about; someone else asked about the plan for the redevelopment of Moscow. Then there was a question about Italian cinema. I delivered a short lecture on Italian neorealism and took everyone to see *The Bicycle Thief.*

Vittorio De Sica's indictment of the capitalist system didn't come through to that group. Scenes of poverty and humiliation made them think of their own lives. "They have capitalism, and the people have nothing. We have socialism, and we have nothing," one of them said. "The war has made us all into paupers."

I liked those people, and they liked me. "We've been fortunate with the agitator," the women said to each other in my presence. And since talking for a living gave me chronic laryngitis, men were admonished for lighting up in my presence. "Can't you see Ludmilla Mikhailovna isn't well?"

"Don't you worry, Ludmilla Mikhailovna," I was assured before every election. "We'll be the first ones at the precinct. We'll come out like one family."

No agitator was allowed to leave the precinct until everyone in his district had voted. Many stayed around past midnight. I left before noon.

✦

And then there was the biography of Comrade Stalin. The book's publication was followed with a directive for history teachers to organize student clubs to study the book. Technically, it was an extracurricular activity. But it was mandatory for both teachers and students.

It was a dry, ideological document. Each phrase was like a formula, solidly packed and unchangeable. I pictured myself reading it, page after page, to a classroom of sleeping adolescents. It was a job that called for a more creative approach, something similar to Professor Atzarkin's class at the university. ("Well, Zinoviev comes to Lenin and Trotsky and says . . .")

At the library, I could find no books about Comrade Stalin's childhood and youth. So I tried to imagine a strong-willed, dark-eyed boy growing up in prerevolutionary Georgia, in the town of Gori. I read everything I could find on Georgia and on Gori. I tried to imagine his father, a hardworking shoemaker. What were the influences on this boy? The church, of course. He goes into the seminary, finds that the truth lies elsewhere, and goes into the revolutionary movement.

The wooden language of Stalin's biography was now replaced with images of the boy, the place, and the time. That was something my students could grasp. The first class went well, so I kept on, relying on the "Atzarkin Method" to liven up the biography. After a few months, a Moscow Komsomol official showed up in my classroom. He sat in the back. When I was done, he waited for the boys to walk out, got up, extended his right hand, and, with the hand extended, walked to the front of the classroom.

He wanted to congratulate me. *Moskovsky komsomolets,* the city Komsomol paper, ran a feature about me. Then several of my stories were published in the paper. I wrote about my experiences as a teacher and about other teachers in my "collective." I was invited to "share my experience" with other Moscow teachers.

Meanwhile, other teachers claimed that the book was too advanced for teenagers and, at great peril to their careers, petitioned for ending the program. The Komsomol, however, was using my example to show that the Stalin biography clubs were feasible after all.

I was an unwitting scab.

◆

In the fall of 1950, I signed up as a volunteer lecturer at the Moscow Regional Komsomol Committee lecture bureau. In a matter of months, the head of the bureau quit to finish his dissertation and, seeing fire in my eyes, suggested me as his replacement. I was given a list of lectures suitable for the political education of the masses, and my job was to match a volunteer with every lecture.

For my own lectures, I picked the topic no one wanted: the story of Zoya Kosmodemyanskaya. By that time, Zoya had been given the posthumous title of Hero of the Soviet Union and had become an icon of the caliber of Pavlik Morozov. Her story had become stale with repetition. On top of that, there were competing, unofficial versions of the events in Petrishchevo. According to one such version, the "German" stable Zoya tried to burn housed the collective farm's horses, which the Nazis had requisitioned. Seeking revenge, the peasants surrendered Zoya to Nazi justice.

Also, by that time I began to doubt the newspaper account of the last minutes of Zoya's life. It seemed unlikely that the Nazis would have stood by as she hailed Stalin and forecast the fall of the Third Reich. Still, I felt uneasy about a popular riddle:

Q. What dangles on a rope and begins with a *Z*?
A. Zoya Kosmodemyanskaya.

In my lectures, I faced crowds of laborers, miners, and agricultural workers, and I thought out loud: What is the nature of heroism? What is it that makes a hero do what he does? How do you explain the situations where a person's honor becomes more important than life itself? There are many kinds of heroism. There is the heroism of a soldier. When you come out of a trench, charging, your comrades run next to you. You are not alone. You share the danger, and you can't turn back because you have your orders.

No one told Zoya to leave Moscow for the woods near Petrishchevo. She could have been biding her time in Siberia. No one pushed her out into that cold December night.

She was doomed from the moment of her capture by the Nazis. She was completely within their power. They could torture her in any way they chose, and then they could execute her. There were no comrades to lend her strength. Yet she remained defiant to the end.

And what did Zoya accomplish? She may have singed a couple of horses. Even if it had been more than a couple, was that worth dying for? I thought it was, because a soldier cannot spend his time calculating what is worth dying for and what isn't. Victory is the sum total of many unthinking decisions.

Some of my listeners may not have thought this through on their own. I offered my thoughts for them to follow. They sat in silence. All of us were part of the same generation. We had survived the war, and to us the nature of heroism was not an abstraction. Every one of us personally knew at least one hero, lauded or unrecognized, dead or alive.

In December 1951, I was asked to give my talk at a ceremony commemorating the tenth anniversary of Zoya's death. It was held at the Zoya Kosmodemyanskaya Young Pioneer Palace in Vereya, the town closest to Petrishchevo. The keynote speaker was Zoya's mother, Lubov Timofeyevna Kosmodemyanskaya. I was to speak after her.

Zoya's mother wore a nondescript gray suit, her gray hair was gathered in a small bun, and her eyes and posture showed neither pain nor enthusiasm. She looked like the embodiment of the stereotype of a Soviet teacher. I tried to start a conversation, but Lubov Timofeyevna wasn't eager to talk.

As we were being driven to Vereya, I sat by the car window, looking out at the gigantic, snow-covered firs, thinking of how frightened that woman's daughter must have been walking alone through the snowdrifts. Moscow teenagers aren't used to pitch-darkness and solitude. It was frightening even without the Nazis.

What could be going through the mind of a mother who had seen the photographs of her daughter's corpse plastered all over the newspapers? In the final month of the war, the same woman was notified that her son Aleksandr, a tank commander, had "died a hero's death in the fight with German interventionists." In the summer of 1941, Lubov Timofeyevna had two children. In the spring of 1945, she had two hero's stars and two graves to tend.

At the Kosmodemyanskaya Palace, Zoya's mother took the microphone. She said Zoya was always truthful, obedient, decisive, and full of respect for her elders. Lubov Timofeyevna must have repeated that speech at every stop in her travels on the Komsomol lecture circuit.

I kept looking at her. She was mechanized, automatized, dead. She was introduced as "the mother of Zoya Kosmodemyanskaya," but she didn't sound like anyone's mother. Her intonations had hardened, like so much cement. It could be that when she told her story the first time, she was genuine. There may have been some emotion left on the tenth repetition. But a decade later, being the mother of two dead heroes had become her complacent identity. I wasn't judging her, but I was frightened by the thought that perhaps I, too, had begun to sound like a record.

When I'd first started giving my lectures, they came from the soul. But how much repetition can a soul endure? I was still able to keep my listeners awake. I could even feel their empathy. My lectures were not clipped from *Pravda;* they were based on the questions that had shaped my thinking in adolescence.

While I prepared my lectures, new questions followed in the footsteps of the old. They came naturally, like maturity — like step two after step one, in a logical progression. I began to compare the courage of a warrior with the courage of a citizen. A war hero is a creature of the moment; he does what the situation calls for, and his wartime bravery doesn't always translate into peacetime courage. I had seen men who had won a chestful of medals bow before some lowly bureaucrat. I had seen the *frontoviki* at the university. They may have been good soldiers, but they were inferior citizens.

The next question: Was I any better a citizen than those *frontoviki*? Did my escape into poetry and personal life constitute a surrender to the careerists? It did. I had seen evil at the university and had declined to engage it in battle. But I knew instinctively that such thoughts could not be aired in public.

It would be an oversimplification to say that it was fear of repression that made me censor myself. It was more reminiscent of awareness of the social norm, the self-preservation instinct, herd instinct, and natural awareness of what is taboo. I feared falling out of the collective.

In 1951, when I was twenty-four, my petition was approved and I joined the Communist party. I'd done a fair amount of agitation and propaganda at home, so my husband joined too. That was my personal triumph, and I kept on with my exemplary teaching, agitation, and lecturing.

✦

After reading the newspapers on January 13, 1953, I decided to change the subject of my lesson.

"Boys," I said, "when you look at the newspapers, you will see that there are a number of Jewish names among the doctors accused of plotting to murder Comrade Stalin." It didn't take much to see that a newspaper spread like that could lead to mass hysteria, perhaps even pogroms.

If that were to happen, the lack of critical thinking would have certainly led the students of Moscow Trade School No. 4 to join the rampaging mob.

"If those doctors are guilty, they will be punished; if they aren't, they will be vindicated. Their guilt would be theirs and theirs alone. It will not be a reflection on the Jewish people as a whole. The Jewish people have played an important role in our revolution; they have given the world Karl Marx —"

"Didn't they also crucify Christ?" interrupted one of the boys.

"It was an internal affair. He was a Jew, and they were Jews —"

"Jesus Christ was a Jew?"

"Yes."

"Ludmilla Mikhailovna, are you sure?"

"Yes. Even if you believe in the Immaculate Conception, his mother was Jewish. They lived in Nazareth, a small Jewish town."

"Ludmilla Mikhailovna, are you saying that the Virgin Mary was a Jewess? If I tell my grandmother, she'll kill me!"

"She was."

"Ludmilla Mikhailovna, are you really sure?"

"I am really sure."

"God damn, Grandmother will just kill me!"

✦

I had been an activist for two years, but the system I wanted to reform through participation showed no signs of change. I had been teaching, lecturing, and "agitating" twelve hours a day, but the people I was trying to help were as miserable as ever.

What difference did it make that the house where I served as the agitator was the first in the precinct to vote? What could I do for those people except pity them? And what could I do for my students? Even in my immediate surroundings amid the school's party organization, the atmosphere remained as rotten as it was before my arrival.

I realized that I was the only person who could benefit from my activism. I could build a career, get a better apartment, a bigger salary. But that wasn't what I was after: I wanted the good people to force the bad people out of power. However, there was no stampede of honest people following me into the party.

I can't recall any turning point, any spectacular revelation. I had simply matured, and after two years of fatigue, I allowed myself a few moments of introspection. Being a student keeps you in an infantile state. Now I was the one doing the teaching. The parameters of my thinking had expanded beyond the simplicity of "the victory of good people over the careerists."

I started to wonder about the party's motivation in the building of "the New Society." I had no doubts about the necessity of the revolution. Czarist Russia was an impoverished, unjustly governed country. I had heard that from my grandparents. I also knew it from Russian history and literature from Pushkin to Tolstoy.

I could accept that bloodshed was a necessary ingredient of a revolution and the subsequent struggle between classes. But our society was not becoming more just. Life was not getting better. Could it be that we had been going in the wrong direction? There had to be a problem somewhere, perhaps a wrong turn. I realized that the only way to find that misstep would be to start at the source: I had to read Lenin from cover to cover.

I had read Lenin before, at the university, but the works were either excerpted or picked to back whatever point was being made or whatever policy was being justified. Now I wanted to assess Lenin as a human being, get an idea of his political tactics, and understand his designs for the party he created. Lenin's works had been published in a twenty-nine-volume set, and by reading them all from start to finish, I could follow the development of his thought and the evolution of his positions. All I had to do was find enough reading time.

I could not have suspected that people who would mean so much later in my life — Anatoly Marchenko, Yuri Orlov, and Pyotr Grigorenko — also traced the beginning of their dissent to the instant they turned to page 1 of volume 1 of the collected Lenin.

I made an attempt at maturity in my personal life as well. I examined every marriage I knew of and compared them with my own. That exercise demonstrated that I knew of no marriage I wanted for myself. At least Valentin and I weren't rude and didn't drink or cheat on each other. Except for the fact that I didn't love him, Valentin was an exemplary husband. Love seemed to be something rare and exotic. People around me simply lived together, pulled the strap of their plow, and occasionally snarled at each other.

Having written off love as a dream of adolescent girls, I decided that it was time to make a truce with Valentin, buy a few more pairs of low-heeled shoes, and have another child. Sergei was almost five. It would be nice if he had a brother or sister.

I made the most comprehensive plan of my life: I would enroll in a graduate school to study Lenin and have another child by the start of my first academic year.

✦

On March 5, 1953, before dawn, I was awakened by the sounds of the allegretto from Beethoven's Seventh Symphony. Stalin was dead.

It wasn't my love for Stalin that made me cry. It was fear. I thought of the faceless functionaries who stood with him on the Mausoleum during parades, people I couldn't distinguish from one another. Now one of them would become the Great Leader. God help us all.

On March 7, Mira Samoylovna Malkina and I went to say farewell to Comrade Stalin, whose body lay in state in the Hall of Columns at the House of the Trade Unions. I went because throughout childhood I had heard about the crowds that had turned out for Lenin's funeral. But that was in 1924, three years before I was born. Now an event of equal significance had taken place. I had to be out there, in the streets. I wanted to see it, to be able to tell my children and grandchildren about it.

Now, a few words about Mira Samoylovna. She was a physician. She was Jewish. Her daughter, Marina Rosenzweig, was my best friend at the university. At their house, I met Eliazar Markovich and Ginda Khaimovna Gelshtein, two respected physicians whom Mira Samoylovna had known since medical school. I also met the Gelshteins' daughters, Vika and Maya, and heard so many stories that I could probably write their family history.

The elder Gelshteins were now at the NKVD prison, charged with plotting to kill Soviet leaders on behalf of German intelligence and world Zionism. Mira Samoylovna knew that her friends were fine physicians, not murderers. She recognized the paranoid monstrosity of the charges brought against them. So why did she want to look at the corpse of the tyrant who had put her friends in prison? I don't know, and I am not the one to judge her. My behavior was no better. I was four-months pregnant with my second child, and I should have recognized the danger of being in a crowd that size.

We walked for forty-five minutes. As we came closer to Pushkin Square, the crowd grew bigger. The space around me was getting tighter. Now the crowd was carrying me toward a wrought-iron fence on Tverskoy Boulevard. I felt pressed against the fence. Then I heard Mira Samoylovna's voice: "Help her! She is pregnant!" She was screaming to a mounted militiaman.

The next thing I felt was a militiaman lifting me out of the crowd.

"So why are you here, you fool?" he said, setting me down on the other side of the fence.

✦

One night in April 1953, Eliazar Markovich and Ginda Khaimovna Gelshtein were brought home by the same people who had arrested them. Ginda Khaimovna looked like half of her former self. The rosy cheeks of that well-heeled Jewish matron now hung down in folds. She had the look of a middle-aged person who had suddenly and irreversibly grown old. But her eyes were the same, and that was a sign that not all was lost. She talked about her imprisonment in broad terms. "Such cruelty, such mistreatment!" she said. "There was no way to prove your innocence!" Eliazar Markovich was now an invalid. He had suffered three heart attacks before his arrest. Now he rarely left the apartment.

Later in the spring of 1953, a column of tanks rumbled down Gorky Street to the Kremlin. "There's been a coup" was the rumor of the day. That night, a politburo faction led by Nikita Khrushchev arrested Lavrenty Beria, the chief of Stalin's secret police. In a matter of weeks, the newspapers ran stories accusing Beria of drinking, womanizing, and spying for the British.

One night, my husband didn't return to the dacha we were renting for the summer. Since he was neither a drunkard nor a womanizer, a third explanation was that he had been in an accident. I spent the night chasing away thoughts of having to raise our two children by myself. Valentin returned on the first train of the following morning, at 6:00 AM.

"Let's go. We need to talk," he whispered. It was something he didn't want our nanny to overhear.

The previous day, he had gone to his office at the Zhukovsky Air Force Academy to pick up some papers to take back to the dacha. Then came the announcement of an informational meeting of the core of the party organization. He wasn't at the core of the organization, but it was vacation time and there was hardly anyone around. Valentin was roped into going.

At the meeting, which did not include rank-and-file members, he learned that the just-executed Beria was far more demented than previously announced. Beria had arrested thousands of people on personal grudges and was known to have taken part in torturing prisoners. Apparently, whenever his motorcade passed by a woman he found desirable, he pointed her out to his aides and had her brought in to his offices. After being raped by Beria, the victim was usually sent to the camps. The minister of internal security also had an extensive collection of brassieres.

The way it sounded, Beria had no accomplices. But who would believe in such a thing as a one-man drunken orgy? And who would believe in a one-man crime wave that employed the system of justice and the prison system to destroy a multitude of innocent people? I found myself haunted by the image of our leaders around a dinner table, guzzling wine and vodka and plotting whom to kill next.

"Uncle Borya was right," I said. "They are a band of brigands."

◆

The Komsomol didn't want to see me leave the lecture circuit. Early in 1953, I was offered the job of head of the Department of Agitation and Propaganda of the Moscow Oblast Komsomol Committee. I declined.

The offers kept coming. Now it was another well-paying position: a lecturer in agitation and propaganda at the Znaniye Lecture Association.

"I've already passed exams," I said to my recruiter.

"Where?"

"The Moscow Economics and Statistics Institute."

"You don't have to enroll."

"I've just had a baby."

"Are you through nursing?"

"Yes."

"So what's the problem? With the money you are going to make, you could hire two nannies."

"I really have made up my mind."

"You all live in one room. If you take that job, you'll have a new apartment." That didn't work either.

I would have liked to think that they had to fill a recruitment quota of people who choose honest work over backstabbing and politicking. But I knew that the instant I became a party official, I would lose what little freedom I had. I would give up the opportunity to avoid taking part in particularly idiotic actions. I would have to repeat that "life has become better, comrades, life has become happier"; condemn cosmopolitism, Akhmatova, and low-bowing to the West; and lead whatever crusades the party happened to invent in the future.

By comparison, life in a tiny room seemed preferable.

✦

We were not the only residents of our apartment to bring home a child. In 1953, four babies were born within months of each other, raising the total count of residents in our three-room apartment to fifteen. Our live-in nanny brought the count up to sixteen. Eight of those people, including two of the newborns, were part of an extended family and lived in one room. At least by then all of us had washing machines. The machines didn't spin and didn't dry. They only washed the soiled sheets. At any given time, one machine was operating by the bathtub and two were awaiting their turn in the corridor. The demand for the bathtub was so great that the babies could be bathed only every other day.

The kitchen became the place to dry the swaddling sheets. So many of them hung from clotheslines, you had to crouch all the way to the kitchen stove. The four burners were always on, to speed up the drying time. Even so, the babies' sheets had to be taken down slightly damp.

✦

Changes at the top were starting to be reflected in stories heard on Moscow streets. These were stories of undetermined veracity, but like all urban lore, they were entertaining. One of the first was the story of a secret-police general.

"My cousin works with a woman who is married to an MGB [secret police] general," the story began. "One night the general was found in a cold sweat, screaming, 'Forgive me, Dmitry Ivanovich!' His wife shook him awake and asked him about this Dmitry Ivanovich, but the general said nothing.

"So, soon the general was tossing and screaming every night and was even afraid to go to sleep. After a few weeks of this, he started talking to the invisible Dmitry Ivanovich while awake. After they took him to the insane asylum, the wife asked around about who this Dmitry Ivanovich was, and it turned out he was a man the general had shot with his own revolver in 1937."

About ten thousand political prisoners were released between 1953 and 1956. For the most part, they were old Bolsheviks who had connections in the government. They had been forgotten, written off, and now they were out there, in the streets, like the walking dead. And in their honor Moscow wags invented tales of betrayal and repentance. Thus, thousands of Muscovites claimed that their friend or a distant cousin had witnessed a truly remarkable scene: A released convict, walking through Moscow, ran into the investigator who had put him in prison fifteen years earlier. The investigator froze in his tracks as if he had seen the ghost of Dmitry Ivanovich, then fell to his knees and pleaded: "Forgive me for putting you in prison for nothing. Forgive me, friend, forgive me."

It was a strange time. *Politzeki,* political prisoners, were able to send messages to the Kremlin. One *politzek,* an old Bolshevik named Aleksei Snegov, was able to get letters through to politburo members Khrushchev and Anastas Mikoyan. The letters led to his appearance as a witness at Beria's closed trial.

"You are still alive!" exclaimed Beria.

"An oversight of your machine," retorted Snegov.

Khrushchev wanted to find Snegov after Beria's execution but was told that the old Bolshevik had been sent back to the camp in Kolyma. Khrushchev ordered him released, brought him back into the party, and made him the number-two man in the political department of the bureaucracy running the camps.

Since the story was so widely circulating in Moscow, I concluded that it was akin to the stories of the insomniac general and the pleading investigator. Actually, the Snegov story was true. The distance between real life and an urban story is never great.

In 1956, Khrushchev set up more than ninety commissions to oversee the release of prisoners. Each commission consisted of one representative of the prosecutor's office, one representative of the Central Committee of the party, and one rehabilitated party member. (The secret police were not represented on those panels.)

Politzeki returned speaking the language of the gulag, singing its songs, exhibiting its peculiar habits. After meals, many of them swept off the tablecloths and ate the bread crumbs.

✦

At any given time, at least a dozen people, mostly men, milled around in the smoking room in the basement of the Lenin Library. The walls were painted a particularly acrid shade of yellow. The ceiling had taken on the color of cigarette smoke, as had the ducts by the ceiling. Trash cans in the room weren't big enough to hold all the cigarette butts generated during the day.

Over time, I learned to recognize the faces of some of the men who spent their days in the smoking room. I got to know some by their first names. They were people who didn't work set hours: graduate students, scholars, journalists. Formal introductions were avoided.

On Wednesdays, the days *Literaturnaya gazeta* came out, the crowd grew larger, sometimes splitting into two or three groups, each one in its own corner. On the days *Novy mir,* the daring monthly journal, hit the stands, the crowd grew larger still. Generally, I showed up at one-thirty and stayed for about an hour.

In October 1953, *Znamya,* a monthly literary magazine, ran Ilya Ehrenburg's essay "On the Writer's Work." "Every society goes through the period of its artistic apex," wrote Ehrenburg, who had once been among Stalin's favorite intellectuals. "Such a period is referred to as high noon." Continuing that analogy, Ehrenburg wrote that Soviet society was going through early morning hours. In other words, the night had passed with Stalin's death, and the sun was coming up.

The smoking-room regulars cautiously agreed.

In December 1953, *Novy mir* published an article innocuously titled "On Sincerity in Literature." In it, Vladimir Pomerantsev, a little-known writer, accused the Soviet literary establishment of "varnishing reality" and churning out contrived, formulaic works that portrayed universal prosperity. I agreed with every one of Pomerantsev's points, as did everyone else in the smoking room.

"Lenin, too, warned about bureaucratization of literature," I said. When I wanted to find out about Pomerantsev, I asked the smokers. I learned that he was once an investigator in Siberia, that he was middle-aged, had heart troubles, and lived in Moscow.

Pomerantsev was attacked at writers' meetings and in the press. "He puts sincerity in the first place, ahead of party loyalty!" screamed Aleksei Surkov, a poet and a Pomerantsev nemesis. The smokers agreed, but with the unspoken caveat that honesty would be preferable. For publishing the essay, Aleksandr Tvardovsky lost his editorship of *Novy mir*.

Now and then, other voices were heard in the smoking room: "When you say self-expression, you mean anarchy," or "Any deviation from party discipline serves the counterrevolution," or something of that sort.

"Of course, such a point of view has a right to exist," was our stock answer. Old-line Stalinist views had a "right to exist." Nothing more. They were no longer the truth and the road to the bright future. They had become downgraded to views that could be tolerated alongside something more liberal and humane.

In 1954, the smokers turned their attention to *The Thaw*, a novella by Ilya Ehrenburg. Less than a year after implying that the Stalin era was the dark night of Soviet literature, Ehrenburg fine-tuned his symbolism and published a novel that likened the post-Stalin era to a thaw.

The Thaw was very much a socialist-realism novel. Its plot unfolds at an industrial plant headed by a rigid bureaucrat whose primary concern is his own advancement. The bureaucrat is married to a young teacher, who believes that she can make a difference in the lives of her students. The teacher is an unhappy young woman. One morning, well into her marriage, she wakes up realizing that she doesn't love her husband. So she gives up on love and lives with the bureaucrat because, as she puts it, she has no right to deprive her daughter of a father. Supporting characters include a Jewish doctor who had been shunned by her patients a few months earlier; a cynical artist who specializes in realistic paintings of livestock, poultry, and foodstuffs; and the cynical artist's childhood friend, a genuine artist.

Love and justice triumph in the end: the young teacher leaves her husband and falls into the arms of a levelheaded engineer whom her husband sees as dangerous to his career. The Jewish doctor finds love, the good artist finds recognition, the cynical artist doesn't, and the bureaucrat factory director gets what he deserves. A tempest

blows down the workers' barracks, which alerts the higher authorities to the fact that no money had been allocated to the construction of workers' housing. The plant director is summoned to
Moscow and promptly transferred to a small factory that makes
paper clips. Of course, all of this happens around March of 1953,
just as the snow begins to melt.

A thaw, the Lenin Library smokers concurred, was not quite
spring. The spring is cyclical and irreversible, and it turns to summer as surely as night turns to day. But a thaw is tenuous. A frost
could strike any minute.

Its symbolism notwithstanding, *The Thaw* was a book I read,
then forgot all about. I had no inkling that it would give the name
to an era.

✦

Uncle Borya didn't think much of my idea of reading Lenin from
cover to cover.

"It's all theory," he said. "Reality is much simpler."

But I read on, following Lenin's thought to the revolution and
beyond. My underlining and scribbling in the margins made each
page look like a battlefield.

Lenin didn't write for posterity. He wrote party documents, position papers, and strongly worded denunciations of his opponents.
My major interests were the Bolshevik agrarian policy and the "na-
tionalities problem," the problem of ruling a multinational empire.

When it came to the peasant question, Lenin seemed to be doing
a continuous pirouette. First he wrote that peasants were small-time
capitalists, and, as such, should be united into collectives that would
till the nationalized land. Then, on the eve of the revolution, he
borrowed a clause of the party program advanced by Socialist Revolutionaries, who called for giving all land to the peasants. That
meant abandoning the idea of rapid collectivization. Hence, his
principal slogan: "Peace to the People, Land to the Peasants, Power
to the Soviets!"

Meanwhile, at party congresses, Lenin made no secret of his
decision to replace the original Bolshevik agrarian program with a
clause from the Socialist Revolutionaries' program to trick the peasants into supporting the Bolsheviks. The peasants were the majority; power could not be held without their support. Lenin changed

course without abandoning his belief that socialism can exist only if the peasants are forced out of their individual enterprise. To his cohorts he said that as soon as it became politically feasible he would proceed with some form of collectivization.

As a Marxist, Lenin operated under the slogan "Proletarians of the World Unite." To him, the proletariat had no ethnic characteristics, no national identity. After the proletarians united, world revolution would follow. After that, national borders would become redundant and disappear. Still, Lenin believed that the old Russian Empire had to remain intact, as the first bastion of world revolution. Secession of any territory amounted to dismantling of that bastion, and thus a setback.

Between 1918 and 1919, Poland, Finland, Lithuania, Latvia, Estonia, the Ukraine, Armenia, Georgia, and Central Asia declared independence, and Lenin saw it as his task to get them back. In 1922, most of these territories joined a "federation" called the Union of Soviet Socialist Republics. Each "republic" was promised control over its internal affairs and reserved the right to secede. By the time I started reading Lenin, only Finland remained independent, and, constitutional guarantees aside, no republic had the option to secede or even run its own affairs.

Lenin's personality came out in his writings. I could sense what he really thought of people, what he thought of mankind. I could sense his drive, his goals, his strategies. Slashing, burning, and gorging weren't his main goals; he was a different kind of brigand.

He was a gambler who thought in terms of "class struggle," "historical formations," and other Marxian abstractions invisible to the naked eye. The world he saw was orderly but barren. It had no place for real people.

I could not detect an iota of concern for soldiers, workers, or peasants. Nor could I detect even a glimmer of doubt. He was convinced that he knew precisely what needed to be done at any given moment, and he was capable of vicious attacks on anyone who disagreed with him on even the most minute of points. Devoid of doubt, not burdened by compassion, he forged ahead into the bright future that only he envisioned.

I couldn't help doubting whether Lenin had charted the "correct" path to communism. The country he created was not a happy place.

At least, there were no happy people around me. Even those who were at the top of the pyramid, even those who had caviar for breakfast, did not look happy. They were part of a pyramid, which made them both our masters and someone else's slaves. Even those who had the power to expel a Stella Dvorkis or derail my career were unhappy. Some of them were probably superficially content, but if you got them drunk, they would tell you that they were pigs and that they knew it. By the time I had read up to 1917, I realized that I had lost all respect for Lenin.

"You are right," I said to Uncle Borya. "They are a band of brigands. They are a new type of brigands. But brigands they are."

✦

"Let's talk a bit," suggested Kolya Demidov as we walked out of the party meeting at the Moscow Economics and Statistics Institute.

It was the spring of 1956, and I had known Demidov for three years. I had seen him in the halls and in the classrooms, but to me he was just a conglomeration of stereotypes: a short, stocky *frontovik,* a heavy drinker, and a below-average student.

"What you've just heard at that meeting must be a revelation to you," he said as we neared a park bench. "For me it's not." What we had heard was the text of the four-hour "secret speech" at the Twentieth Congress in which Nikita Khrushchev accused Stalin of fostering the "Cult of Personality," violating the "party democracy," and unjustly imprisoning great numbers of Communists. The man who had run the country for nearly thirty years was, in essence, a criminal.

I cannot say that I was shocked by the revelations. They simply validated views I had held since 1953. But I was amazed to hear such admissions from the Communist-party leader. After the Beria case, I knew that Stalin was a brigand who had surrounded himself with lesser brigands and proceeded to wreck our country and our lives. That was the general principle. The rest was detail. Khrushchev's speech was read at party meetings nationwide, and, in the end, it trickled down to the Komsomol and the trade unions.

"Do you know what I did in my former life?" Demidov said as we sat down. "I was a prosecutor. Criminal cases."

Demidov wanted to confess. "My job was to put people in prisons. Those people kept coming, and I kept putting them away. I pitied them, so I began to drink.

"There was nothing I could do for them. I had to keep asking for long terms; that's what was in the law, and I was the prosecutor, put in my place by the party. That cruelty. Senseless cruelty."

As the confession poured on, we found ourselves at a café, ordering vodka. I had a shot and stopped. He kept drinking.

He told me he had gone through the war, then got into law school as a *frontovik*. He made it through, barely. As a recent graduate, he was obligated to take his first job. He worked for three years and tried to leave, but the party organization ordered him to stay put. So he spent a few more years demanding long prison terms and drinking heavily.

His only escape was graduate school. In the evenings, he studied history, philosophy, and a foreign language, preparing for entrance exams. He was accepted after two tries, but now he wasn't sure he would be able to write a dissertation. "It's not for my brains," he said.

I responded with a confession of my own. I told him what I thought of the Communist party and its history. We sat in that café, two strangers speaking frankly to each other. Such conversations would have been unthinkable a few weeks earlier.

Now, suddenly, they had become normal, commonplace, and necessary.

✦

Before I could make my escape from the study of Marxism-Leninism, the institute required that I hold four seminars on the history of the party. My students had just been told that Comrade Stalin was less than a great leader, and though they were not much younger than I, they took me for the party personified.

"How could you have lied to us?" they screamed. "How could you have lied to us for so long?"

The official line was to blame Stalin personally, emphasizing that the party was without fault. The "Cult of Stalin's Personality" was a deviation from the Leninist line, which remained correct, and, Stalin's "mistakes" notwithstanding, the Soviet people had built socialism and were continuing to lead mankind down the progressive path charted by Lenin.

It wasn't a very good explanation, so I kept it to myself.

I wanted to tell them that I shared their indignation. I wanted to tell them about the continuity of leadership from Lenin to Stalin. But I had a role to play. So, every morning for four days, I walked into the seminar and faced their anger in silence. I felt like I was being flogged in a public square.

When it was over, I announced to my husband that I would not finish my dissertation and would not accept the professorship in the history of the party offered me by the institute. "If something happens to you and I have to feed our children, I will take up prostitution," I said. "It's cleaner."

Four

Modern Russian is short on words for addressing women. *Tovarishch,* or "comrade," is asexual; *grazhdanka,* "citizen," is impersonal; *devushka* — literally, "virgin" — is an invasion of privacy. A waiter at the Prague restaurant in Moscow called us *devochki,* "girls," and for that reason Lida, Gelya, and I always asked for his table. Lida and I were acquainted at the university, but we didn't become friends until after graduation. Gelya Markizova, also a graduate student, was a university friend of Lida's.

"We are finishing graduate school, and he thinks we are tenth-graders," said Gelya. The Prague was located near the Arbat, a few minutes' walk from the Lenin Library. It was opened during Malenkov's brief reign, and it became our favorite lunch place.

Going to the Prague meant nothing would be accomplished the entire afternoon. We would spend two hours lunching on crab salad, coffee, and chocolate cake, talking about old boyfriends, and flirting with the waiter. It was a pleasure to see other patrons stare at the petite, dark-eyed Gelya. She was the kind of woman whose presence at a restaurant made men and women inadvertently drop their forks.

After lunch, I would spend an hour at the Lenin Library smoking room, then go upstairs and put in an order for an obscure journal called *Byloye* ("The Past"). The journal had been published in the 1920s by the Society of Russian Political Convicts. It disappeared from the shelves in the 1930s, and reappeared after the Twentieth Congress. I leafed through its yellowed pages, following the recollections and arcane disputes of the Russian revolutionaries of the generation that preceded the Bolsheviks.

Starting in the 1870s, thousands of university students from Moscow and Saint Petersburg left for the villages to help the peasants. At first, they tried to educate the people — an undertaking that involved explaining that the reform of 1861 had freed the peasants from serfdom but failed to provide them with land. Thus, it was up to the peasants to demand more substantial changes. But the people weren't learning, and the czar's police had arrested hundreds of students.

Having lost hope of helping the people by peaceful means, many of the former students turned to terrorism. By the end of the decade, some of them had formed a group called Narodnaya Volya, the Will of the People. The goal was to disable the system of government through systematic assassinations of the czars, their governors, and their ministers. That wave of terror would continue until no man in his right mind would ascend the throne, accept a governorship, or take command of a ministry. After that campaign of terror, Russia's only choice would be to enact agrarian reforms and to become a republic.

Judging by their writing, the Will of the People terrorists were remarkably intelligent people, and I could sympathize with some of their arguments. Reading *Byloye* and occasionally glancing up at the mosaic of V. I. Lenin that overlooked the reading room, I pondered the pattern of the struggle between the government and society that spanned Russian history from the Decembrists on.

◆

Once, in the spring of 1956, Lida asked me if I had figured out who Gelya really was. I didn't understand the question.

"You do remember the girl in the sailor suit?" Lida asked.

Everyone remembered the girl in the sailor suit. She was the dark-eyed, beautiful child held by Comrade Stalin in the portrait that hung in schools, kindergartens, Pioneer palaces, orphanages, and children's clinics. A sculpture inspired by the photograph stood at the Stalinskaya metro station, which I helped build. The girl in the sailor suit was the official symbol of happy childhood in the Land of Triumphant Socialism.

"That girl is Gelya," Lida said.

The photo was taken on January 27, 1936, at a reception for the working people of the Buryat-Mongolian Autonomous Soviet Socialist Republic. At the reception, hosted by the leaders of the party and the government in the Kremlin, the Soviet leaders handed out decorations, watches, and phonographs. The guests included Gelya's father, Ardan Angadykovich Markizov, the people's commissar of agriculture of the Buryat-Mongolian ASSR. He was awarded the Order of the Red Banner that day.

Six-year-old Gelya wasn't invited, but she wanted to come anyway and bring flowers to Comrade Stalin and Marshal Kliment Voroshilov, the Red Army commander. When her father gave in, Gelya and her mother, a medical student, went out and bought two gigantic bouquets. Bored by the speeches, Gelya got up and announced that she would take the flowers to Stalin. She was stopped at the podium by the party secretary, Comrade Andrei Andreyev.

"Whom would you like to see?" he asked.

Gelya said she would like to see Stalin.

"*K tebe prishli,*" said Andreyev, turning to Stalin. "It's for you."

Stalin lifted Gelya onto the podium and took both bouquets.

"The girl wants to make a speech," announced Voroshilov.

"This is from the children of the Buryat-Mongolian republic," said Gelya.

The exemplary workers of Buryat-Mongolia erupted in applause. Gelya sat proudly at the podium. Then she overheard the word *podarki,* "presents." "Will I get a *podarok?*" she asked, bringing down the house.

At the end of the evening, Comrade Molotov handed Gelya a small, red box. "Let me," said Stalin, taking the box from her and opening it up.

There was a watch inside. Stalin wanted to know if Gelya liked it. She did.

"This is all you can carry. You can't carry a phonograph," said Stalin.

"I can call my father," said Gelya. Her father had received one phonograph that night, and now he had to come up to claim another.

The following day, the newspapers ran the photograph of Comrade Stalin holding an enormous bouquet and Gelya in her sailor suit. The girl's arms were around Stalin's neck, her eyes on the bouquet that was so enormous that she seemed to be part of it. Gelya spent the day carrying the newspaper around the hotel and repeating to everyone she saw, "Look, this is me."

In December 1937, Gelya's father was arrested and accused of working for the Japanese and plotting to assassinate Stalin. The family was told he was sentenced to "ten years without the right to correspond." Gelya wrote to Stalin that she was the girl in the photograph and that her father was a good Communist who fought in the Civil War and helped organize the Buryat-Mongolian republic. There were other indications of his ideological reliability: Gelya's full given name was Engelsina, a she-Engels; her brother's name, Vladlen, was short for Vladimir Lenin.

Stalin didn't write back. Soon after the letter was mailed, Gelya's mother was arrested. After her release two years later, she took Gelya and her brother to Kazakhstan. One day, Gelya's mother was found dead in the hospital where she worked. She was thirty-two. In 1956, Gelya learned that "ten years without the right to correspond" was the Stalin-era code for immediate execution.

A few years later, Gelya showed me the gold watch and the phonograph. "To Markizova, Gelya, from the Leader of the Party, I. V. Stalin. 27-1-36," read the inscription on both presents. When she showed them to me, Gelya said that someday she would like to tell the whole story. I offered her that opportunity in 1976, when I was compiling an unofficial journal. Gelya refused. The time wasn't right, she said.

In July 1988, speaking to a reporter for *Trud,* the Soviet trade-union newspaper, Gelya said: "I am glad that there will soon be a monument to innocent victims of Stalin's terror. It won't help the dead; it will help the living." The story ran with the photo of Gelya, now a retired grandmother, holding a picture of herself in the arms of Iosif Vissarionovich Stalin.

◆

Sometime in 1956, I ran into Natasha Sadomskaya, a university classmate I knew only by name and appearance. In a matter of minutes, she told me that her marriage to our classmate Moisei Tulchinsky hadn't worked out, that her mother had died, and that she hated teaching but could not get into graduate school. I told her that I hated graduate school, that I would never finish my dissertation, and that as far as I was concerned, they could have their communism without me. Then Natasha invited me to a gathering at her place.

Natasha had a room in which she could throw parties, but had no money to throw them. I had more money, but lived in one room with a husband and two sons. Thus Sadomskaya's room became the gathering place of a *kompaniya,* a group of regular guests who, like us, were looking for opportunities to dance to jazz, drink vodka, and talk until dawn. Nearly all of them belonged to *kompanii* of their own, and nearly all of them reciprocated.

On weekdays, I left the library at six, spent an hour in lines at food stores, another hour by the stove, nearly another hour at the dinner table, then a few minutes washing dishes. At ten, I ran out of the house, entered the metro, and went virtually to any part of Moscow because someone who had been a guest in our *kompaniya* said that an interesting person was expected at a friend's *kompaniya.*

Kompanii emerged in a flash in the mid-1950s, stayed vibrant for a decade, then faded away. Russian history has not seen anything like them before or after. It was all remarkably simple: the *kompaniya* had sprung up as a social institution because it was needed. Our generation had a psychological, spiritual, perhaps even a physiological need to discover our country, our history, and ourselves.

Kompanii evolved their own forms of literature, journalism, music, and humor. They performed the functions of publishing houses, speaker bureaus, salons, billboards, confession booths, concert halls, libraries, museums, counseling groups, sewing circles, knitting clubs, chambers of commerce, bars, clubs, restaurants, coffeehouses, dating bureaus, and seminars in literature, history, philosophy, linguistics, economics, genetics, physics, music, and art.

Just about every evening, I would walk through the dark corridor of some communal flat and open the door of a crowded, smoky room filled with people I knew, people I'd never met, people I must have met but didn't know by name. Old *politzeki* would be shouting something at young philologists, middle-aged physicists would be locked in hot debates with young poets, and some people I had never met would be doing unrecognizable dance steps to someone's scratched Glenn Miller record.

In those days, Moscow's intellectual elite spoke like convicts. We referred to the militia as *musora*, "trash," and the songs heard in our *kompanii* included: "You've destroyed, you vermin, you have ravaged / You have ravaged all my precious youth," "Damn you, Kolyma," "We were running through the tundra from their cursed pursuit," "There once was a thief named Kolya Kucherenko, but the enemies executed him," and "I sit in a cell, the very same cell my grandfather sat in."

No matter which *kompaniya* I was invited to, no matter which corridor I walked down and which door I opened, I sensed that those people were like me. They grew up reading Pushkin and Akhmatova, disliking Pavlik Morozov, tuning out party activists, and considering themselves outsiders. They grew up thinking that they were pitiful beings who did not fit into the "healthy collective."

Now these people were discovering that there were others just like them and that the real deviants were comrades Lenin, Stalin, Beria, and their ilk, who had been herding individuals into "collectives." In a collective, each individual subordinated his will to the will of the group as a whole; in a *kompaniya*, there was nothing but people who liked each other.

We didn't drink much in those days. A couple of half-liter bottles were sufficient to fuel a gathering from dusk till dawn.

"I don't think we'll ever drink ourselves to death," my friend Natasha Sadomskaya said once. "We'll talk ourselves to death."

✦

Valentin never went to *kompanii*. They didn't interest him. He had his work, and listening to people talk and posture seemed to be a waste of his time.

Now, with two sons, Valentin had a more powerful argument for keeping me from leaving.

"Go ahead, leave, but we'll have to divide the children," he said. "You keep Sergei and I'll keep Misha." Such splits were mandated by law, he said.

Despite their five-year age difference, Misha and Sergei were very close. It must have been because they sensed that their parents didn't talk to each other much. The two of them had become their own family. I couldn't believe the law would allow such a split; nor could I believe Valentin would lie about something like that.

"They can't be separated," I insisted.

"Fine, I'll keep both of them."

Valentin didn't like to see me go to *kompanii,* but there was not much he could do to stop me. I had already told him that I planned to leave him forever; it would make no sense to argue about my leaving for an evening.

On the rare occasions when I invited guests to our apartment, Valentin was reserved but polite. The children were fine, too. At 9:30 they disappeared to their alcove and immediately went to sleep. The times demanded that children be able to sleep through loud talk and music.

Naturally, my friends knew all about my impending divorce, and some relished every chance to advise me against it.

"Do you know that nine out of ten women would try to hold on to him with their hands and feet, not to mention teeth!" shouted Lida.

"Can I help it if I am the tenth?"

"That's insane. Get yourself a lover! He won't do anything about it. He will make it look like he hasn't noticed!"

Natasha Sadomskaya simply decided that my talk of leaving was just talk. "You are making me sick with your whining. You are used to living with him. His salary makes you comfortable."

There was a strong subtext here: if I had been indecisive for so long, I would never make up my mind.

◆

A smoking-room regular I knew as "the physicist" told the story of four of his colleagues who had been fired from the Institute of Theoretical and Experimental Physics.

At a party meeting, they had demanded something called "total democratization on a socialist base." The meeting supported the recommendation. This went well beyond the decisions of the Twentieth Congress. After all, Khrushchev's secret speech had leveled accusations at Stalin personally. The speech denounced the "Cult of Personality"; it did not call for "total democratization."

On April 5, *Pravda* said that the party members at the physics institute "sang in Socialist-Revolutionary and Menshevik voices." No one could truly decipher that epithet, except to note that it sounded ominously Zhdanov-like. Party identifications were taken away from everyone in the institute and returned only to those who expressed regrets and denounced the resolutions of the meeting. Four men who refused were expelled from the party and fired.

"That's too bad," said the smoking-room physicist. "One of them, Yuri Orlov, is a very promising physicist."

That name stuck in my mind.

Orlov and the others were living on the financial contributions of their colleagues from several institutes in Moscow, Leningrad, and Novosibirsk. The smoking-room physicist was among the contributors.

Just three years earlier, political outcasts would have been abandoned by their friends and even their families. Few would have had the courage to admit helping an "enemy of the people."

◆

Through the network of *kompanii,* Natasha and I met a group of former *politzeki* who called themselves the Sybarites. Before their arrests, they were Moscow students who had met in 1943 and, after conquering their fear, formed an unusually large group of friends: eight people.

The Sybarites were children of the Soviet elite. Leopold Medvedsky was the son of a general who earned his rank during the war. Yura Gastev's father, a laborer and a talented poet, became a Bolshevik before the revolution, then became the director of the Institute of Labor. (He was pronounced an "enemy of the people" and executed during the purges. Yura's brother, Aleksei, spent ten years in the camps for being the son of an enemy of the people, and their mother served a term in exile for being the wife of an enemy of the people.)

Sasha Volynsky was also the son of a prominent Bolshevik, but his father was fortunate enough to die before the start of Stalin's great terror. Slava Grabar was the son of a famous artist and art historian, Igor Grabar. Yura Tsyzin, Lev Malkin, and Mark Shneider were sons of successful engineers. Tsyzin was a star chemistry student and Malkin was a wunderkind in mathematics. Kolya Williams was the great-grandson of Robert Williams, an American engineer who had designed the bridges on the railroad between Moscow and Saint Petersburg. Kolya's grandfather, Vasily Robertovich Williams, became Russia's foremost agricultural scientist. He headed the Russian exhibit at the Chicago World's Fair of 1893, and after the revolution he joined the Bolsheviks.

Kolya grew up in an enormous house. (The deed bore a distinctive signature: "I. Stalin.") He spoke French to his *bonne* — his governess. At dinners, he sat up straight, using two silver knives and four silver forks. Even when the Williamses served buckwheat, they served it properly.

The boys found each other at the university and soon became inseparable. Generally, they gathered at Slava Grabar's apartment near the university. Thanks to the wealth of their parents' libraries, they had access to books published before the revolution or just after it. Medvedsky and Volynsky were connoisseurs of classical music; Grabar was a scholar of a "reactionary writer and monarchist" named Fyodor Dostoevsky; Williams and Gastev wrote good poetry; Malkin wrote bad poetry; Shneider was famous for womanizing and getting in trouble with the militia. Tsyzin, being too much of a chemist to indulge in worldly matters, just listened.

They had other talents. Medvedsky invented an explosive substance. It was named *vedmedite,* after its inventor. Then he invented the more powerful *raspizdite,* an explosive with a remarkably obscene name that implies destruction. *Vedmedite* was used to blow up mailboxes. *Raspizdite* was placed inside plaster busts of Comrade Stalin. A small amount could reduce a bust to dust. Had that been discovered by the investigators, the Sybarites would have been executed.

These actions weren't political, at least in intent. But on April 7, 1945, at a party, the boys made a serious miscalculation. They gave their group a name, the Brotherhood of Impoverished Sybarites, and drafted a charter that said that the brotherhood would admit only those who would invent a free form of entertainment. Grabar couldn't make the meeting. Volynsky and Shneider were absent, too. They were in the army.

The other five Sybarites were arrested during that summer vacation. Using Morse code at the Lubyanka prison, the confined Sybarites voted to extend "honorary membership" to Grabar, Volynsky, and Shneider. On February 27, 1946, at a closed session, the Moscow City Court found the Brotherhood of Impoverished Sybarites an anti-Soviet organization. The sentences ranged from five to seven years in the camps. "Why Tsyzin?" one of the Sybarites exclaimed during sentencing. "He is just a chemist."

I met the Sybarites in 1959. A decade and a half had passed since they'd drafted their ill-fated charter, but they still remained a mutual-admiration society. Meeting Slava Grabar meant hearing all about (and meeting) Kolya Williams, Yura Gastev, Lyovka Malkin, Leopold Medvedsky, Yura Tsyzin, Sasha Volynsky, and Mark Shneider; meeting Williams meant hearing all about (and meeting) Grabar, Gastev, Malkin, Medvedsky, Tsyzin, Volynsky, and Shneider; meeting Malkin meant hearing all about (and meeting) Gastev, Grabar, Williams, Medvedsky, Tsyzin, Volynsky, and Shneider, and so on.

People who ended up in the camps early in life grew up only physically; their personality was preserved as it was before the arrest. Even later, they matured slowly or not at all. Many remain infantile into their old age.

The Sybarites were in their thirties when we met, but they behaved like boys. Four of the Sybarite *politzeki* exhibited a perverse nostalgia for the camps; sometimes it seemed they could talk about nothing else. The fifth, Tsyzin, was another extreme. He never told anyone, even his son, that he had done time. ("It was humiliating. Why talk about humiliation?" he explained to me once.) Still, Tsyzin and the three "honorary Sybarites" went along with the nutty tone set by Williams, Gastev, Medvedsky, and Malkin.

Williams and Gastev had advanced a theory asserting that the word *blya*, short for "slut," is essential for making the Russian language flow. *Blya* could be divorced from its meaning and inserted in any place of any sentence, as in, "I, *blya*, was raised by a *bonne*," or "I, *blya*, was raised by a *bonne, blya*," or "I, *blya*, was, *blya*, raised by a *bonne, blya,*" and so forth. Sometimes they sounded like drunks at a Moscow beer dive.

The Sybarites could recite any part of the dystopia called "GNIIPI," cowritten by Williams and another Sybarite who has yet to admit his role in the project. GNIIPI stands for the imaginary State Scientific Research Institute of Sexual Perversions.

The dystopia unfolds in the city of GNIIPI, which is the capital of the country of GNIIPI, which is located on the island of GNIIPI. The island of GNIIPI is concave.

> Every midnight, the ringing of the bell resonated over GNIIPI. After that the corpse of a sentry fell off the bell tower. This was followed by the social phenomenon called "rollicking." Rollicking involved GNIIPIites of all ages, guided by the profit motive or the pursuit of amusement, stabbing each other with Finnish knives, splitting each other with axes, hacking each other with hatchets, slashing each other with razors, flailing each other with bludgeons, hitting each other with heavy bags of sand and gravel, cutting each other with frame saws, two-handed saws, and chain saws, deadening each other with the blows of a massive steel spring, pushing each other into manholes reeking with toxic fumes, choking each other with hands and feet, as well as employing other methodologies of deprivation of life and infliction of injuries. Despite the multitude of such methods, each was punished by an article of the GNIIPI Criminal Code. By 5:00 AM the mounds of corpses in the streets reached the roof level. Everything became quiet. Then, packs of growling dogs emerged from the forests that surrounded the capital. The dogs devoured the meat and went off to rest. The city began to live anew; then, the night would descend once again. And once again the streets filled with the victorious cries: "You won't get away, you vermin!" And every night since Creation, GNIIPI burned to the ground.

At many of their gatherings, the Sybarites recited a poem Gastev had composed for December 31, 1953.

> On this eve of the coming year,
> I'll get drunk as a bloody savage.

I am terribly, terribly happy.
Still, too bad that the year's passing.

The old, glorious year — Blast it!
Year of grief for the cursed Georgians.
Let us drink till we drop in convulsions
To the death of the rest of the ogres.

May our drinking be long and happy,
There's plenty of vodka and salad.
We don't fear the Lubyanka or Kremlin
And we spit on what they've disallowed.

And as we celebrate the new year
Let us once again raise our glasses
In a toast: For the next 30 years
May the Leaders drop dead two per annum.

Natasha and I were in love with all eight of the Sybarites, and we soon formed a *kompaniya* similar in spirit to the brotherhood that had cost the Sybarites their freedom.

The toast adopted by our *kompaniya* was similar to the one suggested by Gastev's poem: "*Chtob oni sdokhli* — May they all drop dead."

✦

It was Easter when I met Malkin. We had gathered at Natasha's. He walked in looking like the New Socialist Man. He was tall, clean-cut, upright. His eagle's gaze swept the room, landing on me. Valentin wasn't there and I looked like fair game.

Malkin put his chair next to mine and started his Easter speech. ("I remember the time Pontius Pilate and I sat under the scorching sun of Judea. Then, I recall, they brought in some vagrant . . .") It was very nice, but I was curious about something else. Malkin was the only Sybarite whose prison term had been extended by three years. I wanted to know why.

"Oh, I strangled an investigator," said Malkin, breaking off a piece of bread.

"What?"

"I choked an investigator."

"How badly?"

"To death."

I stared at his hands. The very hands this man has just used to break a piece of bread had once clutched another man's jugular, squeezing. The investigators were not among my heroes; still, any murder is repulsive.

"My God, you were lucky to get three years. They could have shot you."

"Smart girl," said Malkin, patting me on the head. I flinched. Those were the hands of a murderer.

"Did he fight back?"

"Yes, but I was stronger."

Later that evening, as Natasha and I were washing dishes, I told her about Malkin's deed. She was as astounded as I. For the next few hours, we talked about the moral implications of taking another man's life, even if that other man was a cog in the machinery of Beria's secret police. The following day, we told Gastev that we had learned Malkin's terrible secret.

"Which secret?" asked Gastev.

"That he strangled an investigator."

"If that's what he says, it must be so," said Gastev. We concluded that even Gastev didn't know. In the next few days, nearly all of our friends heard the story of the refined Lyovka Malkin strangling an investigator.

Malkin's growing fame started to concern the rest of the Sybarites. They dispatched Gastev to put the story in perspective.

"Girls, there is something I have to explain," Gastev began. "You see, Lyovka Malkin is a wonderful guy."

Natasha and I agreed.

"He is a brilliant mathematician. He is a wunderkind. He wasn't even eighteen when we were arrested, but if only you knew how he conducted himself at interrogations. He is an artist by nature. He is a very special person. The good Lord has smiled upon him," Gastev continued.

"And he is so courageous," said Natasha.

"He is. But you see — how can I put it? — as it often happens with creative people, Lyovka . . ." Gastev took a deep breath.

"Lyovka, like an actor, sometimes pictures himself in a role, and he becomes that role. He doesn't realize that in reality he is not the person he is portraying."

"Of course," I said. "I still can't envision him strangling that investigator."

"You see, Lyudochka, that story . . . that story about the investigator. That story he told you last week . . ."

"What are you saying?"

"That story . . ."

"What are you trying to say?"

"That story is, it's one of his fantasies, but you must understand —"

"Wait, what you are saying is that it didn't happen, that it's a lie!"

"But girls, I am telling you, Lyovka is a very special person!"

I caught a taxi and, tears in my eyes, stormed over to Malkin's room. He opened the door, wearing a shirt over his boxer shorts.

"Oh, Lyudochka, come in, come in. Please excuse my appearance," he said, returning to his ironing board. He had a *kompaniya* to go to and his good pair of pants needed pressing.

"How could you? Yura just told me that it was a lie about the investigator! It was a lie!"

"What's this?"

"He told me that it didn't happen, that you didn't strangle that investigator!"

"Oh, yes, that wasn't really true."

My anger dissipated. "Lyovka, that's not nice. I sat there all evening, thinking about it. You'd pick up a piece of bread, and I'd think, 'With these very hands, the hands with which he picks up bread, with these hands he strangled an investigator.' Then, you patted me on the head, saying, 'Smart girl,' and I kept thinking, 'These hands, these very hands once took a man's life!' Please, please, don't tell that lie to anyone again."

A year later, I ran into my friend Irina. She told me that she was seeing Malkin. We agreed that he was a very nice-looking man, a brilliant mathematician, an actor by nature, and an all-around genius. "And you know, he strangled an investigator," she said.

"Don't believe him, Irka," I said to her. "He once gave me that line, too."

"What?"

"It's a lie."

"Couldn't be."

"It is."

"But . . . but you know how he told it to me? He told me, 'With these very hands — the same hands with which I break bread, the same hands with which I pat you on the head — with these very hands, I strangled an investigator.' "

✦

We were having a party. The reclining sofa now seated four dinner guests. On the other side of the table were two stools with a board on top of them. That improvised bench seated four more people. A chair was placed at each end of the table for the other two guests.

At the center of attention was Lena, an instructor at Moscow University. She was talking about the boycott of the student cafeteria. I had heard that some kind of boycott had taken place several years earlier, in the spring of 1956. Now Lena was telling the story in detail.

If there was ever an institution worthy of a boycott, it was that cafeteria. It had failed to improve after the postwar years. The prices were low, but the food was no better than camp grub. The soups were smelly and brown; the salads were made of rotten potatoes, and worms had been spotted floating in the "fruit soup" desserts. The cafeteria specialty, pirozhki filled with farmer cheese, were nicknamed the alabaster pirozhki because even young, strong teeth could not break through them. A year of that diet could cause gastritis, colitis, or chronic ulcers. All complaints got the same answer from the cafeteria staff: "For the few kopeks you pay here, you have no right to expect anything but this shit."

The faculty had its own cafeteria. It was clean, the food there was decent, but students weren't allowed to eat there.

I am not picky about food, but I never went anywhere near the student cafeteria. The place had the tangy smell of cabbage simmering in an unwashed cauldron. Fortunately, as a Muscovite, I was able to bring sandwiches from home.

Lena said it was the alabaster pirozhki that finally led to the boycott. It seems someone finally did chip a tooth.

The action was organized by an ad hoc committee that consisted of foreign students and several Soviet students. First, the organizers ascertained that the horrible quality of food was in no way related to pricing. Prices were low because the cafeteria received a subsidy that was sufficient to produce more or less decent food. Also, the cafeteria at the university's new campus in the Lenin Hills served better food while receiving the same subsidy and charging the same low prices. The students typed up leaflets announcing the boycott and set up a picket line in front of the cafeteria.

Lena said Soviet students did not take part in the picketing, but they did join the boycott. On the day the boycott started, the cafeteria was empty except for the Chinese students who crossed the picket line. They crossed it together, as a collective. Picketing is an effective method of struggle with the capitalist exploiters, and for that reason it cannot be deployed in a socialist state, they explained.

As soon as word of the picketing spread, the university administrators and city Komsomol and party officials showed up at the picket lines. The demonstration was broken up and the organizers were chewed out. (Soviet students among them were expelled, but some were readmitted later.) But the cafeteria went through an audit, which revealed a number of "irregularities." The place was then closed, renovated, and reopened with a better menu and a new staff.

Had such a protest occurred just three years earlier, the entire student body could have been sent off to the camps. The picketers would have been arrested for putting together an anti-Soviet organization and their classmates would have been arrested for not reporting the organization to the authorities.

◆

Every person in every *kompaniya* had an area of expertise. Natasha Sadomskaya's was ethnography, Soviet ethnic policy, and the Spanish Civil War. At the university, she studied Cuba; at the Institute of Ethnography, she studied Spain. She could tell us what she had found in Spanish- and English-language scholarly journals. At conferences, she met Cubans visiting the USSR, and she knew many Spaniards who had been "evacuated" to our country as children at the end of the Spanish Civil War.

I handled the true evolution of Leninism, a condensed review of the party congresses, Herzen, and the Will of the People terrorists. There were also musicians, and people who had studied philosophy, folk art, Western art, architecture, and cinematography. There were those who had read Nikolai Berdyayev, and those who could resolve debates over particular verses of poems that had never been published.

For many of our writers and poets, publication or acceptance by society was not a goal. Poet Boris Chichibabin, who lived in Kharkov, chose to work as a bookkeeper in a bureaucracy that managed that city's streetcars. He owed nothing to the system, and in return the system did not interfere with his life's work: writing about political prisoners. Philosopher Zhenya Baryshnikov worked as a porter. He had dropped out after a year at Moscow University's philosophy department. "What they taught didn't interest me," Zhenya used to say. Marxism bored him. Now he was free to study prerevolutionary Russian philosophy, a subject not offered at the university.

By contrast, Boris Shragin, Natasha's husband, was fascinated by Marx, the Marxists, and Marxism. Boris, a philosopher at the Institute of Art History of the USSR Academy of Sciences, had read Marx from the first volume to the last, as I had done with Lenin. He had also read "other" Marxists, including Karl Kautski, Rosa Luxemburg, Eduard Bernstein, Herbert Marcuse, and C. Wright Mills. Borya's other interest was existentialism.

The most curious area of knowledge discussed in *kompanii* involved *Novy mir*–watching. *Novy mir*, the monthly journal, had been at the center of our attention since the start of the thaw, when its editor, Aleksandr Tvardovsky, published Pomerantsev's essay "On Sincerity in Literature" and lost his job. His replacement, Konstantin Simonov, was ousted after publishing *Not by Bread Alone*, a controversial novel by Vladimir Dudintsev. Tvardovsky returned to the editorship in 1959, and in a matter of months, the journal became even better.

Tvardovsky was a brilliant poet and an outstanding editor. He had an uncanny ability to find obscure gifted writers. *Novy mir* became a periodical that could turn an unknown talent into a celebrity. And as a member of the Central Committee, Tvardovsky was known to have won battles with the censors. *Novy mir* frequently left its readers in suspense: it was impossible to predict when the journal would come out. The May issue could come in July, but no one complained. The delay meant that Tvardovsky had a battle to fight and that the material was worth fighting for. Hence, it was also worth waiting for.

The light blue cover of *Novy mir* sticking out of a coat pocket could be interpreted as a sign of a liberal intellectual. A stranger spotted reading *Novy mir* on a bus could no longer be regarded as a stranger. It was natural to ask him if the new issue had finally come out. If you talked for a few minutes, you discovered that you had mutual friends.

In our *kompaniya,* the news from *Novy mir* was brought by Maya Zlobina, a literary critic and a free-lance editor who did contract work for the journal, and Lena Kopeleva, the wife of the Sybarite Slava Grabar. Lena's father, Lev Kopelev, was a *Novy mir* free-lance editor who had once received an admittedly controversial novel from a prison camp acquaintance of his. The acquaintance was named Aleksandr Solzhenitsyn; the novel, eventually published by *Novy mir,* was called *One Day in the Life of Ivan Denisovich.*

◆

Generally, our discussions boiled down to two questions: "What is to be done?" and "Who is to blame?" We split into two rival camps: "the lyricists," who were the liberal-arts people, and "the physicists," the natural scientists. The debates would go something like this:

THE PHYSICISTS (TO THE LYRICISTS): All you are doing is chitchatting — all this blather about social justice, democracy, equality, "the people," proletarians-of-the-world-unite. Look what it got us: there's nothing to eat. We are up to our throats in shit, and you are still chitchatting.

THE LYRICISTS (TO THE PHYSICISTS): You've counted up all your atoms, your neutrons and shmeutrons, but what does it mean to us? How's a person to live?

Both sides, the lyricists and the physicists, proudly called themselves "the intelligentsia." This much tortured term emerged in the 1840s to describe an educated elite whose members felt intense guilt about their privileges, shunned government service, and devoted their lives to bettering "the people." Their heightened social consciousness led some *intelligenty* to plot the overthrow of the czar, some to seek salvation in Russia's agrarian communes, others to seek the return to Russian roots, and still others to dream of "Westernizing" the country.

Nearly a century after the word *intelligentsia* emerged, Stalin "redefined" it to include everyone with at least an undergraduate education. Had we accepted this definition, Nikita Khrushchev and the Sybarites would have become part of the same social stratum — a preposterous idea.

The old intelligentsia no longer existed, but we wanted to believe that we would be able to recapture its intellectual and spiritual exaltation. Our goal was to lay claim to the values left by the social stratum that had been persecuted by the czars and destroyed by the revolution. (Even the two central questions we asked at our gatherings had first been asked by the intelligentsia of old: *What Is to Be Done?* was the name of a book by Nikolai Chernyshevsky; *Who Is to Blame?* was a Herzen novel.)

At the same time, we weren't burdened by guilt before the people, since we were just as poor and deprived of rights as our compatriots who hadn't reached our level of education. And we were not interested in sacrificing ourselves for a cause. Blissfully ignorant of the fact that we represented the Soviet human-rights movement in its gestation stage, we were basking in the Khrushchev liberalization, discovering what it means to be human.

Our men grew bushy beards and wore homemade sweaters with Russian pagan symbols, avant-garde designs, and primitivist, asymmetrical nature scenes. Most sweaters were knitted in *kompanii,* so we could observe them as works in progress. Under the sweaters, the men wore *kovboyki,* cowboy-style plaid shirts.

They called each other "old man." Hemingway was popular among the intelligentsia. His picture hung in virtually every home. And many of my friends talked in terse sentences. Like the characters in *The Sun Also Rises.*

✦

Sometime in the mid-1950s, poet Nikolai Glazkov decided to act as his own publisher. Glazkov, a fine poet and a bear of a man who made a living in menial jobs, folded blank sheets of paper and typed his verse on all four sides. Then he took a needle and thread and sewed the pages together at the crease. The result was something like a book.

On the bottom of the first sheet, Glazkov typed *"samsebyaizdat,"* which was both an acronym for "I published myself" and a parody of *"gospolitizdat,"* the name of an official publishing house. Later, *samsebyaizdat* lost the reflexive *sebya* and was shortened to *samizdat,* "self-publishing."

Samizdat sprung up on its own, arising naturally from *kompanii.* It could not have existed without them. My friends and I helped each other fill the enormous void of information, and soon the *izdat,* publishing, part of samizdat became a *kompaniya* ritual: if you liked a manuscript, you borrowed it overnight and copied it on your typewriter. Generally, I made five copies. Three went to friends, the fourth went to the person who let me borrow the poem, and the fifth remained in my possession.

Samizdat was needed because *Novy mir,* for all its good points, published only a small fraction of what we wanted to read. Hardly any information about Stalin's prison camps made it into print. Solzhenitsyn's *One Day in the Life of Ivan Denisovich,* a novel that had left the *Novy mir* readers shell-shocked, provided no new information. It was fiction. Even the Khrushchev speech at the Twentieth Congress had never been published.

The story of Gelya Markizova, the story of the Sybarites, the story of the boycott of the Moscow University cafeteria were simply unpublishable. If we wanted literature, history, philosophy, or journalism, we had to publish it ourselves.

The first samizdat was poetry — the unpublished Akhmatova, Gumilev, Mandelshtam, and Tsvetayeva. Poetry is relatively easy to memorize and easy to copy. Along with poetry came the memoirs of *politzeki.* In a race with death, old Bolsheviks, Mensheviks, anarchists, and Socialist Revolutionaries were scribbling what they could recall from the revolution, the Civil War, the Great Purge, and the camps.

In a *kompaniya,* someone handed me a notebook with handwritten memoirs by Mikhail Yakubovich, a Menshevik leader who had spent the Stalin era in the camps and now lived in an old-age home someplace in Kazakhstan. He was first convicted in March 1931, at the so-called Trial of the Menshevik Center. He served his ten years, but was rearrested and sentenced to another ten. He served that term, too, but was kept in confinement for another two years, until Stalin's death.

Then I read the remembrances of Yevgeny Gnedin, an official in Maxim Litvinov's People's Commissariat on Foreign Affairs. His memoir told the story of working in Nazi Germany just before the Hitler-Stalin pact. Around the time I read Gnedin's work, I also read the typewritten prison memoir of a Communist named Yevgeniya Ginzburg and one by Yevgeniya Olitskaya, a Socialist Revolutionary. According to a Khrushchev statement, ten thousand memoirs by old *politzeki,* political prisoners, had been submitted to publishing houses. None of them were published.

After poetry and memoirs came translations. One of the first was Hemingway's *For Whom the Bell Tolls.* It was a beautiful translation that was finished during the war, but the publication was canceled because censors objected to the scene in which Republicans slaughter the Loyalist prisoners, as well as to Hemingway's portrayal of Soviet advisers as manipulative cynics. I read the manuscript in 1956. It was a feast. The book was officially published two decades later.

Then came Arthur Koestler's *Darkness at Noon* and George Orwell's *Nineteen Eighty-four.* The latter seemed to be translated by a person who didn't speak much English. The idioms were translated literally, and most sentences retained their English structure. Still, the message came through. The book was about us. It was about our Big Brother, our Newspeak, our ministries of Love and Truth, even our Pavlik Morozov.

Pasternak's *Doctor Zhivago* started circulating in 1957. Then came Solzhenitsyn's novels *The Cancer Ward* and *The First Circle.*

It was in a *kompaniya* that I first heard about the fate of "the children with famous names" — the sons and daughters of the executed commissars and generals. These children had been brought up in special camps, and today many of them live in Kazakhstan, where they work as salesclerks and laborers. And it was in a *kompaniya* that I first read an unofficial transcript of the trial of a Leningrad poet named Iosif Brodsky, who was convicted in 1964 on "parasitism" charges and sentenced to five years in internal exile in Siberia.

Also in a *kompaniya,* I saw a typewritten manuscript of Anna Akhmatova's magnificent "Requiem," her poem about standing in line at the Kresty prison in Leningrad, hoping to pass along a food parcel to her son, Lev Gumilev, who was arrested in 1936 for quoting Hegel to friends.

I learned how faces fall,
How terror darts from under eyelids,
How suffering traces lines
Of stiff cuneiform on cheeks,
How locks of ashen-blonde or black
Turn silver suddenly,
Smiles fade on submissive lips
And fear trembles in a dry laugh.
And I pray not for myself alone,
But for all those who stood there with me
In cruel cold, and in the summer's heat,
Beneath that blind, red wall.

Once more the day of remembrance draws near.
I see, I hear, I feel you:

The one they almost had to drag to the end,
And the one who tramps her native land no more,

And the one who, tossing her beautiful head,
Said: "Coming here's like coming home."

I'd like to name them all by name,
But the list has been confiscated and is nowhere to be found.

I have woven a wide mantle for them
From their meager, overheard words.

I will remember them always and everywhere,
I will never forget them no matter what comes.

And if they gag my exhausted mouth
Through which a hundred million scream,

Then may the people remember me
On the eve of my remembrance day.

And if ever in this country
They decide to erect a monument to me,

I consent to that honor
Under these conditions — that it stand

Neither by the sea where I was born:
My last tie with the sea is broken,

Nor in the tsar's garden, near the cherished pine stump,
Where an inconsolable shade looks for me.

But here, where I stood for three hundred hours,
And where an inconsolable shade looks for me,

This because even in blissful death I don't want
To forget the rumbling of the Black Marias,

Forget how that detested door slammed shut
And an old woman howled like a wounded animal.

And may the melting snow stream like tears
From my motionless lids of bronze,

And a prison dove coo in the distance,
And the ships of the Neva sail calmly on.

✦

Enter Bulat Okudzhava, a bard who traveled from *kompaniya* to
kompaniya strumming his guitar and singing about love, war, betrayal, and the fate of our generation. He sang about girls left
without bridegrooms because the boys had been killed in the war.
He sang about the Moscow boy named Lyon'ka Korolyov, whom
everyone in the courtyard called Korol, "the King." The war began,
and the King put on his cap "like a crown" and went off to the
front. Now no one is left to mourn his life because "the King was
too young to find himself a queen."

He sang about the last trolley of the night, which "like a ship"
sails along the boulevards, picking up those who have capsized
during the night. And he sang about the place he called his "moth-

erland," which was neither a country nor a city, but the Moscow street he lived on — the crowded, winding Arbat.

> Like a river you flow — and your name is strange!
> And the asphalt is clear in your riverbed.
> Oh, Arbat, my Arbat, you've become my cause,
> you're the torment of me, and you are my joy.
>
> Your pedestrians are people unremarkable,
> their heels pound on you as they rush along.
> Oh, Arbat, my Arbat, you've become my faith,
> and your pavement is what lies beneath my feet.
>
> I cannot cure myself from your love for me,
> even if I walk on 40,000 streets.
> Oh, Arbat, my Arbat, you've become my motherland.
> There is no way to walk to the end of you.

Okudzhava grew up on the Arbat. His father, a party functionary, was executed in 1937. His brother died of tuberculosis contracted in the camps. Like Lyon'ka Korolyov, Okudzhava went off to war at eighteen. He saw his buddies die, and he came back wounded. In 1946, at Tbilisi University in Georgia, he wrote a "student song," his first.

He didn't write another song for eleven years. Then, in 1957, he wrote a poem about a Moscow character named Van'ka Morozov who goes to the circus and falls in love with the girl doing the high-wire act. ("He didn't think she would betray him / You don't expect a tragedy in love.") Then he picked up a guitar and sang the poem to friends.

He made his living as a free-lance editor at *Novy mir*, writing prose and poetry, and always staying at the center of controversy. Singing was something he did for his friends, who taped his songs and let their friends tape them as well.

Meanwhile, the radio stations were still playing songs that reinforced patriotism and called for heroism on the field of battle. In those songs, men and women were as upright as Zoya Kosmodemyanskaya, everyone was faithful, and no one glanced at a pretty girl walking down the street.

> I saw you off to your heroic deed,
> A thunderstorm raged over our land.
> I was saying farewell, but held back my tears,
> And my eyes were dry.

The other extreme in lyrical poetry was a total lack of meaning.

> Oy, the snowball tree is blooming in the field by the creek,
> I have fallen in love with a young lad.

Okudzhava was remarkably different. I first heard him on tape in a *kompaniya* in 1957 or 1958. Then I bought a tape recorder of my own to play Okudzhava at home. Okudzhava sang through the thaw, he sang through the period now called "stagnation," and he is still singing, thank God.

Other poets, realizing that they, too, had something to say, picked up guitars and sang for their *kompanii*. Three of them, Okudzhava, Vladimir Vysotsky, and Aleksandr Galich have since become folk heroes and celebrities.

◆

And then there were the jokes.

The jokes of the thaw ranged from the political to the scatological to the surrealistic. There were jokes about drunkards, cowboys, crocodiles, mental patients, and comrades Khrushchev and Stalin. There was even a joke about the postwar scarcity of men:

> A drunk is sprawled out in front of a dumpster. A woman walks by.
> "What a waste, what a waste," she says. "They've thrown a man out. And he looks like he could still be slept with."

Each joke had a remarkably short shelf life, each *kompaniya* had a repertoire, and most fit into series devoted to a particular topic.

Mental Patients

From a report by the director of the Belyye Stolby insane asylum:

"In honor of the upcoming anniversary of the Great October Socialist Revolution, the working collective has redoubled its efforts to provide quality recreation to the patients by means of construction of a swimming pool. Some patients have already started to use the diving board.

"The pool will be filled in the near future."

The Wild West
[Inspired by the showing of *The Magnificent Seven*.]
  Three cowboys are riding through the prairie.
  "Hey, Joe, what's two times two?"
  "Four."
  Bang. Joe drops dead.
  "Why did you kill him?"
  "He knew too much."

Radio Armenia
Radio Armenia is asked: "What's the difference between socialism and capitalism?"
  Radio Armenia answers: "Under capitalism, man exploits man. Under socialism, it's the other way around."

Comrade Khrushchev, our bulbous, embarrassing leader, gave us some of the finest comedy material. Like the joke about his visit to an art exhibit:

"What's this turd-on-canvas supposed to symbolize?"
  "That, Nikita Sergeyevich, is *Dawn on the Volga*."
  "And what's this fingerpainting?"
  "This, Nikita Sergeyevich, is *A Symphony of Light*."
  "What's this fat ass with ears?"
  "This, Nikita Sergeyevich, is a mirror."

Most Khrushchev jokes were in the question-and-answer format.

Q. Is it true that Comrade Khrushchev's health is declining?
A. Yes. He is suffering from a hernia caused by lifting the level of agricultural production, hyperventilation caused by trying to catch up with America, and verbal diarrhea caused by God knows what.

Q. What will happen after Cuba builds socialism?
A. It will start importing sugar.

Q. What are the four biggest problems in Soviet agriculture?
A. Winter, spring, summer, and fall.

In his uneven and boorish way, Khrushchev was one of the greatest leaders Russia ever had. He released millions of political prisoners; personally allowed the publication of some very fine literature, including *One Day in the Life of Ivan Denisovich;* initiated an open dialogue about the future of the Soviet economy; increased pensions for retirees; ended the Korean War; improved relations with the United States and Yugoslavia; and even made an attempt to curtail central planning in light industry.

My admiration for Khrushchev came some time after he was ousted in 1964. During his reign, my friends and I were quite indignant about his idiotic "kitchen debate" with Vice President Richard Nixon, his shoe incident at the United Nations, his laughable attempts to "catch up with and overtake America in per-capita production of milk and meat," his illiterate pronouncements on art, his attacks on writers whose work was "inaccessible to the people," and his shameful mistreatment of Boris Pasternak over his decision to publish *Doctor Zhivago* in Italy.

◆

The network of interlocking *kompanii* served as the Moscow University alumni bulletin. Through it, I heard that my classmate Tim Ryan had Russified his name to Timur Timofeyev. Ryan-Timofeyev's career was on the way up. I also heard about Boris Mikhalevsky, a young historian who barely escaped a charge of treason. The story came from his sister, Ada Nikolskaya, who, as a friend of Natasha's, was one of the founding members of our *kompaniya.*

Mikhalevsky graduated a couple of years after me, taught himself mathematics and economics, and became one of the nation's leading experts in econometrics. In the *kompanii* circuit, Mikhalevsky was valued for taking the official Soviet economic statistics and interpreting them to show the country's real economic performance. Once or twice, he cited those numbers to a friend, Kolya Pokrovsky, a Moscow University graduate student who specialized in Russian history.

He had no suspicion that Kolya was a member of an underground cell of Marxist reformers and that the cell was writing and distributing leaflets that, among other things, called for total reorganization of the economic system and demanded an open trial of those involved in Stalin's terror. In those leaflets, Khrushchev was referred to as a "drunkard" and a "corn maniac" who "embarrasses us before the whole world."

In the fall of 1957, Mikhalevsky was called to the headquarters of the KGB. The Marxist reformers — nine of them, including Pokrovsky and their leader, Lev Krasnopevtsev — had been arrested and had testified that Mikhalevsky was the source for the statistics.

"Boris Natanovich, I am afraid we have to initiate a case against you for leaking classified figures," the interrogator said, showing Mikhalevsky the Marxists' leaflet and the order for his arrest.

"I have no access to classified figures," Mikhalevsky replied.

"But our consultations show those figures are not available from unclassified sources."

"I made my calculations on the basis of published numbers," Boris said, offering to go to the Lenin Library, check out a stack of books, and guide the KGB investigator through the calculations. The investigator tore up the arrest warrant.

The nine Marxists didn't fare as well as Mikhalevsky. On February 12, 1958, at a closed-door proceeding, they were found guilty of disseminating anti-Soviet propaganda and were sentenced to prison. Three were sentenced to ten years each, three others got eight, and the remaining three got six.

Among those doing ten years was my classmate Leonid Rendel, the Komsomol activist who once told me that reciting frivolous poetry had made me unfit to propagandize the ideas of communism to construction workers.

✦

Sometime in 1961, Kolya Williams introduced me to Aleksandr Esenin-Volpin, an old friend of his who had just been released from a psychiatric hospital. It was the first time I saw a man with such dry, yellow skin. Later, I came to recognize it as a sign of a recently released convict.

He looked nothing like his famous father, the dreamy, good-looking poet Sergei Esenin. Esenin the elder, who was married to the graceful and legendary dancer Isadora Duncan, traveled the world and drank a great deal. Alek was the product of the poet's affair with Nadezhda Volpina, a literary translator.

Esenin died in a bizarre, romantic fashion. On December 27, 1925, he cut his wrist and wrote a poem in his own blood. "Goodbye, my friend, good-bye," the poem began. The following day, he hanged himself. According to legend, for years following Esenin's death, women came to his grave to slit their wrists.

It was hard to imagine Esenin the younger inspiring such romantic excess. Alek's eyes were wild, his hair unkempt, and his shirttail out. He could be seen walking Moscow streets in his house slippers, and if there was anything more frightening than watching him cross a street, it was crossing a street with him. Alek could keep explaining his ideas for hours at a time, and if anyone was still unsure, he could illustrate them with the help of geometric figures. Those figures confused even the finest mathematicians.

There was a magnificent ring to his name: Aleksandr Sergeyevich Esenin-Volpin. It invoked the memories of his father, and of another, even greater poet. Pushkin was an Aleksandr Sergeyevich, too.

Friends told the story of a 1943 resolution in which the Moscow University Komsomol organization ordered Alek to bathe. He didn't comply. Also that year, Alek decided that since butter contained more calories than bread, he would be better off exchanging all his bread rations for butter. He ended up in a hospital.

In 1949, as a Moscow University graduate student, Alek challenged Pyotr Matveyevich Ogibalov, secretary of the party bureau of the Moscow University Department of Mechanics and Mathematics. Ogibalov was denouncing a group of fifth-year students who had banded together and called themselves a "close fellowship." They steered clear of politics. Still, the party and the Komsomol pronounced them a "secret organization" and demanded expulsions.

"What is it that makes you conclude that the organization was secret?" Alek, who wasn't in the group, asked Ogibalov at the meeting called to discuss the matter.

"The fact that I was unaware of its existence," said Ogibalov.

"Forgive me, but until today I was unaware of your existence, but that has not led me to conclude that you exist secretly," said Alek. Members of the fellowship were expelled, but Alek's impertinence went unpunished.

On our first meeting, Alek told me that there would be a lot less evil in the world if people did not lie. Then he went on to define the word *lie:* It's not a lie when a man onstage says he is Hamlet, the prince of Denmark, when everyone knows that he is not. It's not a lie when someone introduces himself as Aleksandr Sergeyevich Pushkin, because everyone knows that Pushkin is dead. It's not a lie when someone makes a mistake, or misspeaks, or says something that isn't true while knowing that no one can hear him. And, finally, it's not a lie to prove a mathematical problem ad absurdum, by ruling out all unlikely solutions. A lie is told when you say that something is true while knowing that it isn't (or vice versa) and your interlocutor has not given you consent, implied or otherwise, to be told something that isn't true.

Alek's was not a puritan ethic. "Feel free to cheat on your spouse, drink in places where you aren't supposed to, inject narcotics, or whatever else you wish to do," he said. "Do whatever you want to do — as long as you don't have to lie to be able to continue doing it."

I am reasonably sure that on our first meeting Alek told me what he thought of the Soviet Union's constitution. At that time he rarely talked about anything else. The constitution, Alek said, was a good document, as was the Soviet legal code. The idea was to get the state to live by its own laws. Soviet citizens had been conditioned to act as if they had no rights, Alek argued. The state had come to encroach on individual rights because individuals had yet to band together to defend those rights. As a result, Stalin was able to murder millions of law-abiding citizens without so much as a hearing.

But what would happen if citizens acted on the assumption that they have rights? If one person did it, he would become a martyr; if two people did it, they would be labeled an enemy organization; if thousands of people did it, they would be a hostile movement; but if everyone did it, the state would have to become less oppressive. One major point was to force the state into conducting all trials openly, under the conditions of *glasnost,* said Alek. His words registered, as they did many times thereafter. But all of it seemed too logical to be applicable to real life.

The word *glasnost* had been in the Russian language for centuries.

It was in the dictionaries and lawbooks for as long as there had been dictionaries and lawbooks. It was an ordinary, hardworking, non-descript word that was used to refer to a process, any process of justice or governance, being conducted in the open. The word had no political meaning, and until Alek Esenin-Volpin pulled it out of ordinary usage, it generated no heat.

✦

I did not hide my views or my samizdat from my sons. When they were young, that meant risking that one fine day they would come to kindergarten or first grade and say something cute, such as, "Yesterday Mother listened to the Voice of America." But if you whisper about "forbidden subjects" and lock samizdat from your children, they grow up to be strangers. Besides, the forbidden subjects were too much a part of my life. If I had attempted conceal-ment, I would have been talking in a perpetual whisper and carrying a purse full of keys. Life would have become impossible.

The boys asked few questions, presumably because they could get their answers by listening to my friends talk at the dinner table. On their own, they developed a healthy skepticism. Once, in 1960, Misha returned from first grade and told me, "Mother, did you know that we, the Russians, invented the radio and the airplane?"

I hesitated with the answer. It's always difficult to tell a seven-year-old boy that his teacher's job description includes spreading cynical lies.

"And you believe that?" Seryozha came to my rescue. "If you let them, they'll tell you we invented the tank, too. Picture a big Slav getting on a horse cart and swinging a stick at the Tatars. You just let them, they'll tell you Russia is the motherland of elephants."

I had nothing to add to that answer.

At thirteen, Misha asked me why all of our guests were either con-victs or mental patients. I reviewed the list of my friends, from Alek Esenin-Volpin to the Sybarites, and realized that Misha was right.

"I guess that's because there are interesting people among them," I said.

✦

Sometime around 1962, in a *kompaniya,* a guest who happened to be a lawyer overheard me say something about being unable to get a divorce.

"Why not?" she asked.

I explained that I couldn't see separating my two sons.

"You can have custody of both children," she told me. "The father can claim custody only if the mother is a prostitute or an alcoholic. Soviet law is on the side of the woman."

The following day, I went to consult another attorney, who also assured me that under Soviet law I would have custody of both children. That night, I came home and confronted Valentin.

"You lied to me."

He didn't respond to the accusation. "Why aren't you thinking about the children?" he asked me instead. "I am a colonel. I am well paid. I can do a lot for them. If I leave, I will pay child support and nothing more."

I assured him that I realized that the boys would now be my financial responsibility. I had a reasonably well-paying job as an editor of history books at the Nauka Publishing House.

At that, our marriage ended. All I had to do was tell Mother. When I did, she broke into tears. "There are so many children without fathers!" she said. "And you are doing it to your children by choice!"

Unhappy as she was, Mother had to do what was natural. She offered to help by moving in with me and letting Valentin have her apartment until he could buy one of his own. She lived with me for a year and a half.

✦

In 1962, in some *kompaniya,* Natasha met Yuli Daniel, a writer and translator of poetry. There seemed to be plenty of days when Daniel wasn't inspired to translate. There were also long stretches when the journals had no demand for his services. On those days, the tall, thin, slightly stooped Daniel made his rounds, dropping in on old friends, casual acquaintances, and bedridden old *politzeki* hard at work on their prison memoirs. I have a feeling that in the mornings he had no idea where he would end up by nightfall, or, for that matter, the following morning.

It was an honor to be included in Daniel's rounds, and being my best friend, Natasha usually invited me to join them for an hour or two of conversation. "An hour or two" usually meant three or four, and "conversation" usually meant listening to Daniel's stories.

He talked about his father, a Jewish writer and a former *politzek*, his in-laws, also former *politzeki*, and his favorite *Novy mir* editor, Bulat Okudzhava, the poet and singer and son of an executed *politzek*. He also talked about his friend Andrei Sinyavsky, a literary scholar, a *Novy mir* author, and a son of a *politzek*. He talked about Pasternak, the man whom he and Sinyavsky considered their mentor.

Daniel also mentioned his friend Anatoly ("Tosha") Yakobson, a tall, broad-shouldered man who, despite his Jewish heritage, looked, acted, and drank like an ethnic Russian. ("You are a disgrace to your people," a militiaman told him after he had spent a night at a drunk tank.) Yakobson, a history teacher, was a scholar of poet Aleksandr Blok.

Daniel talked about Yakobson's wife, a former *politzek*, and her parents, also former *politzeki*. It seemed most people he associated with were either former *politzeki* or the descendants of former *politzeki*.

Uncharacteristically for a man who had been in the front lines and who still carried a shell fragment that had lodged in his shoulder, Daniel never talked about the war. Nor did he talk about his wife, which made me picture her as a *fifa*. (Let me define my terms: a *fifa* is a social butterfly, which in the context of our *kompanii* meant a frivolous woman who crossed her legs, used lots of makeup, chain-smoked, and lived for the moment.) It seemed appropriate for a man like Daniel to marry a *fifa*, who could be dragged out to parties, then stowed away someplace. It seemed a woman of substance would have found it difficult to live in Daniel's shadow.

After a while, we began to meet the heroes of Daniel's stories. We met Tosha Yakobson and his wife, Maya Ulanovskaya, a contemporary of ours who had been sentenced to twenty-five years in the camps because she had joined a political group at the university. The group, called the Young Leninists, was found to be anti-Soviet, and three of its members were executed.

Then we met Maya's parents, Aleksandr Petrovich and Nadezhda Markovna Ulanovsky. Aleksandr Petrovich looked like a retired actor or a professor emeritus. Nadezhda Markovna looked like an elderly countess. He had spent seven years in the camps; she had spent eight. Maya served four.

Aleksandr Petrovich was an anarchist who had joined the Bolsheviks after the revolution, then traveled the world setting up Communist parties that were part of the Soviet Union's espionage network. Among the spies he oversaw was Richard Sorge, a German radical who warned Stalin about the impending war. (Stalin ignored the warning.)

When he held court, Aleksandr Petrovich liked to tell how he could have changed history by assassinating both Hitler and Stalin. Stalin had been a particularly easy target. Before the revolution, Aleksandr Petrovich served as a courier, running messages to anarchists exiled to the Turukhan Krai, in Siberia. As a courtesy to the Bolsheviks, he also stopped over at the hut of Iosif Dzhugashvili.

"Where is he?" he asked a peasant woman.

"In the woods," she said. Then she described the path Dzhugashvili, the man who would soon become known as Stalin, took during his daily walk.

Stalin was indeed in the woods, secluded, far from the road. "I had a loaded pistol in my pocket," Aleksandr Petrovich lamented. "Why didn't I put a bullet through his head? Nobody would have cared about a little-known political prisoner who vanished in the woods."

The other historical opportunity presented itself around 1923, at the Bürgerbräukeller in Munich.

"Who are these people?" Aleksandr Petrovich asked one of his German Communist contacts.

"A bunch of hoodlums," he answered. "They call themselves National Socialists."

"Now, I had a loaded pistol in my pocket," Aleksandr Petrovich used to say. "I could have gone up to that short one with the mustache and put a bullet through his head."

It sounded as easy as ordering a beer.

✦

One evening, Daniel surprised us by showing up with his wife, Larisa Bogoraz. She was tall, thin, and dressed in a way that showed that her interests in life did not include cosmetics and fine clothing. She barely said hello, then went to Natasha's bookshelf, picked up a samizdat manuscript on palm reading, and sat down in the corner. She had already heard most of Daniel's stories.

She was not the person we had imagined. She seemed tired and detached from what was going on around her. Though she was congenial, she made it clear that she was not concerned about being liked or being invited back. She was immersed in the book; every half-hour or so, she raised her head to exclaim, "Just listen to what he is writing," after which she would read a short passage.

"Would you let me see your hands?" she said after a couple of hours of reading. When a few of us complied, she went on to compare our palms with those sketched in the book. She wasn't reading palms. She was just making sure that there were indeed life lines, health lines, career lines.

What struck me the most was her voice. It was the kind of voice you would expect to belong to a gypsy singer. It was so striking that I don't remember much else of what went on at that party. I kept glancing at Larisa, waiting for her to say something else. I think the gods have a way of ringing bells when we meet people who will change our lives.

Later, I told Daniel that he had a remarkable wife.

"I know," he said.

"Yulik, I thought she would be different," I said.

"How's that?"

"I thought she would be a *fifa*."

"A *fifa*? No, my wife is not a *fifa*."

◆

Less than a year after I met Daniel, a friend told me a secret: "Did you know that Yulik and a friend of his have been published abroad under pseudonyms?"

Daniel used the name Nikolai Arzhak, I was told. His friend called himself Abram Tertz. I had heard both names mentioned on shortwave radio stations and I knew that Arzhak wrote satirical short stories and that Tertz's publications included an essay critical of Lenin and socialist realism.

I did not ask the name of the man who was hiding behind the name Tertz. My source may not have known. Besides, learning that Yulik, a person I admired, would allow foreigners to publish his work was shocking enough. It was one thing to tell the truth at home. It was something else to tell it to outsiders, many of whom were genuine enemies of our country.

That was Soviet xenophobia, the remnants of teachings about

"the progressive forces," "the forces of reaction," "class struggle," and other such things that had been crammed into my mind since childhood. By the mid-1960s, I had learned to recognize those thoughts, and each time they cropped up I did my best to combat them.

As my friend continued her story, I searched for an explanation of Yulik's decision to publish abroad. Immediately, I thought of Herzen. Didn't he go abroad to publish his *Kolokol,* the journal that was the bible of Russia's Westernizers? Herzen published it in the West because he couldn't publish it in Russia. Daniel was doing the same thing.

Then something else began to worry me: if my friend was telling me confidentially that Daniel and his mysterious friend were publishing abroad, couldn't she also be telling someone else? When a secret keeps getting passed around, even from one reliable person to another, then, at some point, it ceases to be a secret.

That seemed to be happening. "I can tell you who Arzhak and Tertz really are," an acquaintance offered on another occasion. It was my first clear chance to learn the identity of the man who called himself Tertz; but not wishing to become party to casual disclosure of life-and-death secrets, I declined the offer.

✦

In the fall of 1964, a curious story started to make the rounds among the intelligentsia. It seemed that a scholar was defending his dissertation and before the panel rendered its decision, a man in the audience asked to be recognized.

"I don't wish to sway the panel's decision, but I am forced to take this forum since I have no other," he said. "The man before you informed on me and another man when we were students at Moscow University. Because of him, we spent five years in the camps."

"Yes, but I haven't informed on anyone since 1953," said the scholar. His dissertation got blackballed.

The story kept making its rounds, which did not particularly add to its credibility. I remained unmoved even when I heard the name of the doctoral candidate, Sergei Khmelnitsky. Names have a way of being forgotten.

His accuser was Yuri Bregel, a research associate at the Moscow Institute for the Study of the Orient. Bregel's name, too, didn't mean anything to me. Years passed before I heard the name of Khmelnitsky's other victim: Volodya Kabo, my classmate who was arrested after the archaeological dig in the fall of 1949.

Bregel had been arrested a month after Kabo. It was Khmelnitsky who told Bregel about Kabo's arrest. And Khmelnitsky was present when Bregel, sensing his own approaching arrest, destroyed his diaries. At the subsequent interrogations, Bregel and Kabo learned that it was Khmelnitsky who had informed on both of them. My friends told me that after being humiliated before his academic colleagues, Khmelnitsky asked Bregel and Kabo to discuss the problem with him.

"Why are you putting my family under fire?" asked the indignant Khmelnitsky.

That wasn't the goal, said Bregel.

"Did you think of our families when you were turning us in?" asked Kabo.

KHMELNITSKY: You've lost five years. Now I've lost my whole life.

KABO: That was your miscalculation. If not for Stalin's death, we would have lost our lives, and you would have kept on going.

KHMELNITSKY: Please, give me your advice, what can I do?

BREGEL: You should have asked for our advice in 1949.

Ostracized by his friends and colleagues, Khmelnitsky departed for Central Asia.

Five

Uncle Borya lived in a one-room apartment that had once been the ballroom of a mansion adjacent to the Winter Palace. The room's panoramic, baroque window overlooked the Peter-and-Paul Fortress on the other side of the Neva River.

The remains of Peter the Great, Russia's first Westernizer, still rest in the bastion church. On December 14, 1825, other Westernizers, the Decembrists, were brought to the prison, a stone's throw from the royal crypt. Five of them were hanged in that bastion. Nicholas I, the monarch responsible for their execution, was brought to rest in the bastion, too. Looming beyond the royal crypt and political prison is the infamous Gray House, Leningrad's KGB headquarters.

A hardened *anti-Sovietchik* like Uncle Borya couldn't have asked for a more poignant vista.

It was September 1965, and I was playing tourist while Uncle Borya was running last-minute errands in preparation for our heading off on a long drive together. I walked through the fortress cells that had once held the who's who of the Russian intelligentsia and the Russian revolutionary movement. From there, I walked to "the blind, red wall" of the Kresty prison, where Akhmatova had seen so much horror. Her monument will stand by that prison wall someday, three hundred paces from the gate, in the midst of an imaginary queue of thousands.

Our vacation began in the hills of Valday, where Pushkin had been sent for being young and iconoclastic. Barred from Saint Petersburg, he spent two years in the family mansion, drinking and writing. As Uncle Borya drove, I recited Pushkin. It wasn't hard to tell which poem went with which site.

Barring Pushkin from Saint Petersburg ranked with calling Akhmatova a half-nun, half-whore. But just as Zhdanov was too inconsequential a figure to silence Akhmatova, the czar was no match for Pushkin.

At the Gorky post office, I found a letter from Natasha Sadomskaya. Yuli Daniel and Andrei Sinyavsky had been arrested, the letter said. So, Sinyavsky and Tertz were one and the same.

What a nation. What a history.

✦

We loaded the car on a barge, then, for about a week, floated down the Volga. I stewed over the news. Discussing it with Uncle Borya would have required too much explaining. I would have had to tell him about my friends, the network of *kompanii* that had united the Moscow intelligentsia, the camaraderie, the lifestyles, the songs, the poetry, the debates, the physicists, the lyricists. Uncle Borya's only interest was the power structure, and he understood it. A band of brigands had taken power, and now they were doing whatever they wanted. He did not understand that change can come from below. He did not see any use in people sitting around the table and talking. He did not see that there was real social value in what at first glance was simple chatter. He was a creature of another era, and generational differences, when they cannot be bridged, have to be respected.

Back in Moscow, Natasha gave me the whole story: Andrei was arrested on September 8, as he walked out of his apartment. Yulik was in Novosibirsk, trying to talk Larisa into returning to him. She had finished her dissertation and taken a job as a Russian-literature professor at the Novosibirsk University. The Daniels' fourteen-year-old son, Sanya, was with Larisa. As far as she was concerned, the separation was final.

In Novosibirsk, Yulik was called in to two interrogations and told by the KGB to return to Moscow. That meant that arrest was imminent. A political prisoner needed a wife to hire an attorney, assist in the defense, monitor the trial, report on the proceedings to friends, pass along food parcels, and visit the convict in the camp. Larisa agreed to return.

Yulik was arrested on September 12, as soon as he stepped off the plane at Moscow's Vnukovo Airport.

Right after the arrests, Natasha and our mutual friend Ada Nikolskaya had come to my apartment and left with my poetry books. It was just a precaution, in case the KGB decided to search the friends of the writers. The year was 1965. Stalin had been dead for twelve years, yet it was still not clear whether you could be arrested for circulating unpublished poetry.

The first question we asked each other was, "Did you know?" The second was, "Who told you?" Natasha knew that Yulik was Arzhak and that Andrei was Tertz. So did Ada Nikolskaya. At least fifty of us had been told. But we couldn't figure out who had tipped off the authorities. To this day, I don't know how the KGB found out.

✦

The Daniel apartment seemed cheerful.

After the arrests, Marya Sinyavskaya, Andrei's wife, moved in with Larisa, bringing with her a poster of Moscow's newly dedicated Ostankino television tower standing atop the globe, with television waves, done in red, emanating in every direction. "Go-VORIT MOSKVA" — "THIS IS MOSCOW SPEAKING" — the caption said. *Govorit Moskva* was also the title of a Daniel novella.

The beat-up couch was now replaced with a not-so-badly-beat-up couch, and an artist had built bookshelves from particle board, then covered them with pictures of branches, flowers, and exotic beasts. All of this provided a more suitable backdrop for Carrie, the Daniels' Irish setter.

When I spotted Larisa, she was entertaining a *kompaniya* with stories about Senior Investigator M. P. Kantov, the KGB investigator assigned to Yulik's case.

"He said to me, 'Your husband is guilty, and he will be punished,'" Larisa said.

"And you know what else he said? I shouldn't bother with hiring a defense attorney. He said (a) it would be outside my financial limitations, and (b) a defense attorney is useless in such a case and will not affect the course of the legal proceedings or the outcome. So I said that at this point my husband has not been found guilty of any crime, and until the trial is concluded, he cannot be considered a criminal."

"What did he answer?"

"Nothing. His jaw dropped."

I could see how Larisa would say something like, "I stand by my husband, and I will not help you hurt him." That's what Marya Sinyavskaya was saying, and that was courageous enough. But lecturing an officer of the KGB on the letter and spirit of the Soviet legal system seemed to follow the teachings of Alek Esenin-Volpin.

Larisa kept talking. "Then he said that unless I behave, I will encounter unpleasantness at my job when they find out." Using her negligible programming skills, Larisa had found a job at the Committee on Standards.

"I said, 'What do you mean, unless I behave?'"

"He said, 'You understand what I mean.'"

"'What kind of "unpleasantness" will I encounter, and what precisely will they find out? That my husband is under investigation? Well, he hasn't been found guilty. And what if he had been? What kind of "unpleasantness" would I encounter, and why?'"

"What did he say to that?" I asked Larisa.

"Nothing. They aren't used to that sort of thing."

Larisa laughed, and so did everyone else. The interrogation tactics that were effective in 1937 and that still worked on the wives of thieves and hoodlums did not work on Larisa Bogoraz. Larisa told the story calmly, with just a slight tint of sarcasm, as if she had spent her entire life sparring with KGB investigators.

◆

Alek Esenin-Volpin was planning a demonstration, and just about all of Moscow knew it. It was discussed at the Lenin Library smoking room. It was discussed at the university. It was discussed in *kompanii*. Alek's involvement was treated as a given by anyone who considered the language of the leaflets announcing the demonstration:

Several months ago the organs of state security arrested two citizens: writers A. Sinyavsky and Yu. Daniel. There are reasons to fear violation of *glasnost* of the legal process. It is commonly known that violation of the law on *glasnost* (Article 3 of the Constitution of the USSR and Article 18 of the Criminal Procedure Code of the Russian Soviet Federative Socialist Republic) constitutes an illegal action. It is inconceivable that the work of a writer could constitute a crime against the state.

In the past, unlawful actions by the authorities have taken the lives of millions of Soviet citizens. This blood-stained past demands vigilance in the present. It is more prudent to give up one day of tranquility than to spend years suffering the consequences of lawlessness that has not been stopped in time.

Soviet citizens have a means for resisting capricious actions of the authorities. That method is the Glasnost Meetings whose participants chant only one slogan: "WE DE-MAND GLAS-NOST FOR THE TRIAL OF (followed by the last names of the accused)!" or where the participants display a corresponding banner. Any shouts or slogans that depart from demands of strict adherence to laws must be regarded as counterproductive or, possibly, provocational and must be halted by the participants of the meeting.

During the meeting, it is essential to observe decorum. At the first demand of the authorities it is essential to inform the authorities about the purpose of the meeting, then to disband.

You are being invited to a Glasnost Meeting which will be held on December 5, at 6 P.M., on Pushkin Square, by the monument to the poet.

Invite two other citizens by means of this appeal.

The only demonstrations I was familiar with were the authorized ones held on Red Square on May Day and November 7. I did not particularly like them. I just don't have much affinity for banners and crowds. Now I was horrified by the prospect of Alek unfurling a banner on a square in the center of Moscow. Nothing like that had ever been done, so there was no way to predict the consequences.

Ada Nikolskaya was even more horrified than I. Her husband, Valera, had met Alek in our *kompaniya* and quickly become his apostle. That meant, he, too, was going to Pushkin Square.

Talking Valera out of the idea seemed hopeless. Talking to Alek didn't seem promising, either. He would simply say something like: "You are very nice girls. It's too bad it's not allowed to marry several girls at once. If I could, I'd marry both of you." There was always a chance that the crazy endeavor would fall apart on its own.

But it showed no signs of falling apart. One evening in Larisa's kitchen, the conversation turned toward deciding whether she should go to the demonstration. The nays had it. Larisa could not afford to get involved in a street scene. Her mission was to monitor the forthcoming trial. The same went for Marya Sinyavskaya.

The Sybarites told us they had a previous engagement. Their friend Vitya Yolles was celebrating the anniversary of his conception. Yolles, who didn't believe in celebrating birthdays, maintained that he was conceived on December 5, the Day of Stalin's Constitution. It was an official holiday, so he could spend the entire day drinking.

On December 1 it was clear that, with or without our approval, the demonstration would take place. Ada was going out of her mind. "Oh my God, they are really going to do it," she kept saying. "There's no way to talk my fool out of it."

Alek's wife, Vika, had similar concerns. "That fruitcake will go and get himself back in the loony bin," she lamented to Natasha and me. "What's to be done?"

On the evening of December 4, Natasha and I decided to act. Talking to Valera still seemed hopeless, so we agreed to begin with Alek.

Alek was in hiding. He wanted to avoid being arrested before the demonstration. We called one possible hideout. He wasn't there. We called another, then another. "I may be able to give him a message," was the answer we got on the fifth or sixth try.

"Please tell him to come to Lyuda's as soon as possible."

At ten o'clock that evening, Alek appeared in my room.

We hit him with all the ammunition we had. Think of what they will do to you. Think of what they will do to Valera. Think of what that would do to Ada. Do you want people to lose their jobs? Want them expelled from their institutes? Want them arrested? Do you want to be declared a fruitcake again? Do you miss the medication? How could you want so many people to give up so much just for a few narcissistic moments?

Alek fought back, reciting his leaflet. *Glasnost* of trials was the essential first step to a more democratic system. Yes, it was possible that all participants of the demonstration would be arrested. It would take many a trial and many a Glasnost Meeting before the Soviet system of justice would begin to function in accordance with Soviet laws. We hit him with more guilt, he fought back through recitation of his legal theories.

"Fine, girls, let's say you've talked me out of it," Alek conceded around midnight. "A demonstration will not accomplish anything. But what can I do about it now? All those people you are so concerned about are going to show up with or without me. And what if I am not there? Would that be morally right? Would that make you feel better?" It was a checkmate.

Alek said good-bye, leaving Natasha and me to consider our options.

✦

At 5:45 PM, Ada and I got off the trolley at Pushkin Square. Since there was still time, we decided to pass by the monument and pick up some sausage at Yeliseyev's grocery store.

The minute we got off the trolley, I saw a face I recognized from the Lenin Library smoking room. I nodded. He nodded back. Then I saw a face vaguely familiar from some *kompaniya*. We exchanged nods. "Hello," said Ada to someone.

It seemed we were surrounded by the brotherhood that met regularly for evenings of Gershwin at the Conservatory, Fellini retrospectives at the House of Film, French-impressionists exhibits at the Pushkin Museum, and, of course, Bulat Okudzhava concerts at the Central House of Workers of the Arts. Now that brotherhood had gathered at the bronze feet of Aleksandr Sergeyevich Pushkin to watch Aleksandr Sergeyevich Esenin-Volpin demand *glasnost* for the trial of their brethren.

About twenty people were milling around the monument. Most of them were much younger than we were. We crossed the road to Yeliseyev's grocery, nodding to acquaintances, but saying nothing to each other. We bought some cheese and some sausage, then met Natasha at the street corner.

It was 5:57. The snow beamed back the gaslight of the majestic Saint Petersburg streetlamps around the statue. Fresh roses lay at the pedestal. The neon sign on top of the building housing the newspaper *Izvestia* was lit up. The name of the paper means "news," and *glasnost,* as defined in Russian dictionaries, means "subject to presentation to and review by the public." News is part of *glasnost.* Hence, Alek had decided to hold a protest in front of a building crowned with a neon sign that was fit to be one of his banners.

The crowd of two hundred nervously clung to the pedestal. We had no problem getting to the front row. Everyone wanted to stay in the second.

Alek paced in front of the crowd. It was his prison-cell stroll; detachment in his eyes, hands behind his back, ten paces forward, ten paces back. A pendulum of *glasnost.*

Valera stood motionless in front of the crowd. So did Yura Titov, another of Alek's followers. I looked at my watch: 5:59. I looked at Alek: ten paces forward, ten paces back. I looked at the watch: 6:00 exactly.

Alek stopped, opened his coat, pulled out a piece of white cloth that had been strapped with a belt to his stomach, then raised the piece of cloth over his head. Valera followed. What happened next, I remember in fragments:

Twenty or so young people run past me, surrounding Alek. The banners are still up over Alek's and Valera's heads.

Another wave runs past, overpowering the first. The banners disappear before I get a chance to read them. There isn't a word from Natasha, not a word from Ada, not a sound in front of me, not a sound behind me, nothing but crisp, tense silence.

A bright flash, then another, and another. The square lights up, then, instantly, fills with the sound of camera shutters. Foreign reporters are photographing Alek, the banners, the demonstrators, the KGB, the spectators. The KGB is photographing Alek, the demonstrators, the banners, the spectators, the foreign reporters.

In the glow of photoflashes, two men drag a third past the pedestal. He is slight; they are burly; he is in a short leather jacket; they are in heavy coats. A black Volga pulls up to the curb on Gorky

Street. The man is thrown into the backseat. Another Volga pulls up. Another man is thrown in.

Three minutes later, the demonstrators are gone. So are the spectators. The square is empty, except for the bronze Aleksandr Sergeyevich, arms crossed on his chest, his head bowed.

◆

We waited at Natasha's.

Valera called first. He was taken to the militia precinct station, kept for about three hours, then let go.

Alek called next: "Everything is fine, girls." He, too, had been kept for about three hours, during which a militia officer asked him to explain his reasons for holding the demonstration. "To assure *glasnost* of the trial," Alek said.

"All our trials are open," the militia officer said, after which Alek was asked to describe the banners.

"Unfurl them," Alek said.

"GLASNOST TO THE TRIAL OF SINYAVSKY AND DANIEL," proclaimed one banner. "HONOR THE SOVIET CONSTITUTION," proclaimed the other.

A few days later, at a beer dive, Kolya Williams overheard the story of the demonstration as it had filtered down to the masses: "Esenin has a son. He organized this demonstration of a thousand people to march on Gorky Street, with him marching in front of everyone with a banner; then he walked in to the KGB, threw a list of demonstrators on the table, and said, 'Here are the names of everyone who marched, but keep your hands off them. I answer for everyone.' He isn't afraid of anyone, *blya*. And his name is Wolf."

◆

It was hard to imagine the number of intermediate steps that went into the production of the book I held in my hands. There was the act of smuggling the manuscript to the West, then the no less dangerous act of smuggling the published books back into the country.

Inside was Yulik Daniel's voice and real people in surrealistic situations. There was the story of a young man who in siring children can guarantee which of them will be boys and which will be girls. If at the moment of ejaculation he visualizes Karl Marx, he produces boys. If he visualizes Clara Zetkin, one of the founders of

Germany's Communist party and women's movement, he produces girls. His secret is unraveled, and he becomes a stud for the families of high government officials.

There was *Repentance,* a novella about a man falsely accused of having betrayed a friend during Stalin's purges. As he is ostracized by his friends, he realizes that he has no way to prove his innocence, and that even if he had a way, it would do no good. No one is willing to listen.

In the end, driven to madness, he screams to his fellow *intelligenty* at the Tchaikovsky Concert Hall: "Comrades! The prisons and camps haven't been closed! That's a lie! A lie you get in the newspapers! It makes no difference whether we are in prison or the prison's within us! We are all inmates! No government can free us! We need surgery! We have to cut the camps out of ourselves, we have to let them out! Do you think it was the *CheKa,* the NKVD, or the KGB that had imprisoned us? No, we did it to ourselves. We are the state. Don't drink wine, don't make love to women — they are all widows of prisoners!

"Wait! Where are you going? Don't try to run! You are running from yourselves, and you won't escape!"

Stalin is within us, but it takes a madman to see him.

And then there was *This Is Moscow Speaking.* On page 1 of the novella, I recognized the voices of Yulik's friends deciding what to do for the rest of a leisurely Sunday in the country. The options included playing volleyball, swimming, or going to see a church in a neighboring village.

Their banter is interrupted by a radio broadcast of a ukase, an edict of the Supreme Soviet of the Union of Soviet Socialist Republics. In connection with the ever-increasing material well-being of the masses and responding to requests of the toiling people, Sunday, August 10, 1960, was being pronounced the Day of Open Murders. On that day, Soviet citizens who had reached the age of sixteen would be allowed to "terminate" other citizens, with the exception of those in the uniformed services, those operating the system of transportation, and those who had not reached the age of majority.

The ukase chills the camaraderie of the *kompaniya.* The obvious questions asked include "Why is this necessary?" "Could this be a provocation?" and finally, "Will I be killed?" They are scared of killing, scared of not killing, scared of being killed, and scared of openly opposing this latest official travesty.

One theory, expressed by a character named Margulis, is that the authorities are trying to deprive human life of all value, and that after that is accomplished, the country will be ready for the return of the rule of terror.

One morning, the narrator, who is reminiscent of Yulik, ponders the idea of killing the very people who issued the edict:

> What about them, the fat-faced ones, the makers of our destiny, our leaders and teachers, the true sons of the nation who accept greetings from the kolkhozniki of the Ryazan Oblast, from the ironworkers of Krivoy Rog, from the emperor of Ethiopia, from the congress of educators, from the President of the United States, from the personnel of public bathrooms?
>
> What about those best friends of Soviet athletes, litterateurs, textile workers, lunatics, and the colorblind? What do we do about them? Forgive them? Forgive them for 1937? Forgive them for the post-war madness, when the country was beating in hysteria, feasting upon itself?
>
> They think that just because they've taken a dump on the grave of the Mustachioed One, they are home free. No, No, they require special treatment. You still remember how it's done.
>
> Pull the pin. Throw. Drop to the ground. A blast. Now, leap forward, spraying from the gut. A burst. Another. Another . . . Here they lie, mangled by the explosion, riddled with bullets.

No, says Daniel's narrator. "It's been done." It's been done in 1937, it's been done in the war, it's been done in the death camps. He doesn't want any part of it, even if that means that the "fat-faced ones" go unpunished.

◆

On October 18, 1965, as Sinyavsky and Daniel were spending their second month in the Lefortovo prison, foreign radio stations broadcast their first reports of the arrest of Andrei Sinyavsky, a prominent Soviet critic and literary scholar. Also arrested was someone identified as "Daniello." Daniello's pen name was reported to be "Arzhanov."

It seemed that the editors of Western newspapers didn't know quite what to make of the December 5 Glasnost Meeting. Two weeks later, presumably after they realized that their reporters had witnessed antigovernment stirrings at the heart of a police state, the story got prominent play. On December 18, the Glasnost Meeting was on page 1 of the *New York Times*. Our existence was noticed and acknowledged.

From then on, by turning on our shortwave radios, we could find out if another international celebrity had joined the list of petitioners for the writers' release. That list included Bertrand Russell, Heinrich Böll, Günter Grass, Lillian Hellman, Saul Bellow, W. H. Auden, Norman Mailer, Robert Lowell, William Styron, Philip Roth, Marguerite Duras, and Philip Toynbee. On December 9, Mark Bonham Carter, Sinyavsky's British publisher, made an unsuccessful attempt to enlist Mikhail Sholokhov, the Nobel laureate, to intervene on behalf of his fellow Soviet writers. (Sholokhov, one of the most unsavory characters ever honored by the Swedish Academy, refused to take the calls or open the door of his hotel room.)

Even the *Izvestia* article on January 16, 1966, couldn't hide the government's surprise at the worldwide outcry over the arrest of the two Moscow intellectuals. "What is it that has awakened the black horde of *anti-Sovietchiki?*" asked the article, titled "The Hypocrites."

How has this horde come to include some members of the foreign intelligentsia, who look awkward in such company? Why have some of those gentlemen assumed a mentorlike pose, making it appear that they are guarding our morals and defending two outcasts on behalf of the Soviet intelligentsia?

The enemies of Communism have found what they wanted: two outcasts motivated by shamelessness and hypocrisy.

Under the guise of their pen names, Abram Tertz and Nikolai Arzhak, for several years they covertly supplied foreign publishers with filthy pasquils on their country, the party and the Soviet system. One of them, A. Sinyavsky, alias A. Tertz, published literary criticism in Soviet journals and wormed his way into the Union of Writers, pretending to subscribe to its guiding principle: "To serve the people by revealing in highly artistic manner the greatness of the ideas of Communism. . . ." The second, N. Arzhak–Yu. Daniel, worked as a translator. But all of that was just a facade for the two. Behind it lurked something else: hatred toward our way of life, and vile ridicule of all that is precious to the Motherland and the people.

The targets of those filthy pasquils included Soviet women, scientific Communism, socialist realism, and the heroic Soviet armed forces, *Izvestia* reported.

Through his hero, [Daniel] suggests the following course of action to his reader:

"Pull the pin. Throw. Drop to the ground. A blast. Now, leap forward, spraying from the gut. A burst. Another. Another . . . Here they lie, mangled by the explosion, riddled with bullets."

Now you see the target of this crazed *anti-Sovietchik:* in essence, he calls for mass terror.

That day, a historian whose manuscript I was editing noticed "The Hypocrites" on my desk.

"I see you've read this," he said. "How dare they publish in the West!"

"What's wrong with that?" I said. "Was it wrong for Herzen to do it a hundred years ago?"

"I am glad you see it that way," he said. His initial righteous rage was a test of my political orientation.

We spent the entire day talking about the writers, the threatening posture of the authorities, and the future of the intelligentsia. I tried to bring up the subject of the book we were editing, but the author wasn't concerned. "It will wait. This is more important."

Mother, too, had some thoughts about the *Izvestia* story. "You do realize that you should no longer associate with those people," she said when she visited me the following day. By then she was living in the apartment left to her by her second husband.

I had not told her about Daniel's arrest, and now the tone of the story made her think of Stalin-era exposés of the "doctors' plot" and the Bukharinite-Zinovievite conspiracy. She sensed danger.

"Of course, Mother," I said.

Later in the day, Williams brought a reaction from his institute. "Brave guys," said a young colleague of his after reading *Izvestia*. "Too bad they will shoot them."

"Do you suppose it's possible?" I asked Williams.

He said nothing.

✦

One after another, people whose chief interest was literature began to drop out of the Daniel-and-Sinyavsky *kompaniya* and entertain new friends with their considered opinions of Tertz and Arzhak as litterateurs.

"Of course, their work is extremely valuable from a politico-historical standpoint, and, of course, it's an honor to be among their friends," such statements usually began. "But as literature, their work is not what I would call a major achievement."

"I refuse to discuss the literary merits of their work while they sit in Lefortovo," was my standard answer to such criticism. "When they are free, we will talk."

One day, a little man in a white knit hat showed up at Larisa's. His name was Vadim Meniker. He was an economist at the Institute of Economics of the USSR Academy of Sciences, a job that gave him access to foreign-newspaper rooms at the Lenin Library. Over the next few months, he kept us abreast of the coverage of the trial in American, British, French, and Italian newspapers.

Another young man, Aleksandr Ginzburg, was brought in by Marya Sinyavskaya. Ginzburg, a *samizdatchik* and a former journalism student, had met Sinyavsky some years earlier. I was yet to learn of his role during the trial. My friend Natasha Sadomskaya moved to the center of the *kompaniya*, along with her husband, Boris Shragin.

By the time of the trial, only a dozen of the fifty or so regulars of the original *kompaniya* stood outside the courthouse.

✦

On the evening of February 9, 1966, Natasha called to say that the trial would begin the following morning.

It turned out to be a ferociously cold one. In a courtyard just off

Barrikadnaya Street, I noticed some familiar faces. A couple of dozen friends of the defendants milled around by the five-story yellow courthouse.

The trial was "open," but only those with official passes were allowed to get in. Some passes were orange, others were blue, but there was no place where an ordinary citizen or friends of the defendants could obtain either. Passes were checked at the entrance to the courthouse, then checked again inside the building, to make certain that the name on the pass matched the name on the spectator's passport.

I joined my friends who stood at the doors looking at those going in. The Union of Writers seemed to get a lot of tickets, and Daniel's friends knew many writers.

"Arkady Vasilyev," a friend announced the arrival of the "public accuser," a writer whose function was to assist the prosecution. "Slime."

"Yevtushenko," someone announced. "Looking straight ahead."

"Agnia Barto. Look at that coat. Let's all write for children."

"Tvardovsky."

Some writers exchanged nods with the friends of the accused. Others walked straight through the doors, embarrassed by having been picked to witness a show trial. Looking around the courtyard, I spotted three dozen KGB operatives and a dozen foreign reporters. Foreigners were easy to spot on a Moscow street, and not just because they were dressed better than the Russians. The distinction was in the faces. The foreigners' faces were not marred by fear, concern, and suspicion.

After all the spectators had entered the courthouse, the reporters edged toward us. It was an awkward overture made by one pack to another, with a third watching. When I sensed a reporter or an operative near me, I quieted down and turned away. I didn't want to be overheard, and I didn't want to be quoted in a Western newspaper.

I remember thinking: We are here because our friends are on trial. It's our problem; it's our grief. For reporters, this is just a political thriller. I don't want my life to be the subject of someone's curiosity.

After getting the cold shoulder, the journalists walked away, but

I continued to glance at them with distrust and curiosity. Shivering, red-nosed, and wearing silly, warm-weather shoes, they huddled together exchanging quips I couldn't understand.

At the break, Larisa and Marya came out to give the news to our group. As they did, the reporters and the goons converged from both sides, but we were far too interested in what had happened at the trial to pay attention to either group of intruders.

I did not know that one of the relatives had smuggled a tape recorder into the courtroom. It recorded one of the oddest spectacles ever staged in the name of jurisprudence. Daniel and Sinyavsky had the honor of becoming the first writers or poets in the USSR to face criminal charges stemming from the content of their works. Even Stalin had never prosecuted writers for writing. Unfortunate accidents, murders, and executions without trials after forced confessions to espionage were just as effective and were easier to arrange.

The Brezhnev clique had the more difficult task of finding a legal rationale to justify its political decision to imprison Daniel and Sinyavsky. By charging the two writers with "anti-Soviet propaganda" under Article 70 of the Criminal Code of the Russian Republic, the prosecution took on the ticklish task of demonstrating that scholarly works and works of fiction constituted propaganda against the Soviet state. Could a responsible jurist argue that Sinyavsky's literary criticism was written with anti-Soviet intent or that fictional characters in Daniel's novellas were made up for the purposes of propaganda and that they actually reflected the point of view of the author?

Such framing of the question paved the way for some odd courtroom exchanges.

PROSECUTOR: Now, Daniel, please demonstrate the ideological direction of *This Is Moscow Speaking*.

DANIEL: I was intrigued by the fact that under a fictional assumption of a "day of open murders" I would be able to explore human psychology and behavior. . . .

JUDGE: Of course, I understand that the author and the character are not one and the same, but in *This Is Moscow Speaking* you write:

Margulis . . . walked in, and immediately asked a stupid question, "Why did they need this ukase?" "They" meant the government. I said nothing and, taking advantage of my lack of opinion on the subject, he began to explain that all this insanity is unavoidable, that all of it is part of the teachings of socialism.

"Why?" I asked.

"What do you mean, why? It's all consistent. They must legalize murder, make it a commonplace occurrence. . . ."

DANIEL: You are correct when you say that the position of the author and the position of his character are not always one and the same. And the principal character in my story objects to that point of view. . . .

JUDGE: That's the one with the "machine gun," "spraying from the gut"?

DANIEL: Yes, one and the same. Here is the point of the story: a man must remain himself no matter what circumstances he finds himself in, no matter what pressure he is under, and no matter who is exerting that pressure. He must be true to himself, and that means not taking part in anything that goes against his conscience. Now, about "spraying from the gut." The prosecution has been parading this passage as a call to massacre the leaders of the party and the government. Indeed, the principal character here refers to the leaders because he remembers Stalin's purges and thinks that those responsible for them must be punished. That's where the prosecution chooses to break off the passage. But that's not the end of the book; that's not even the end of the monologue, in which the character says he's seen enough bloodshed. He's seen it during the war. And the prospect of seeing more bloodshed strikes him as revolting. He says: "I don't want to kill anyone." Let any reader answer this question: does the hero want to kill? Anyone will see that he doesn't."

JUDGE: But you are forgetting the whole point. The hero is able to kill because of an official ukase. That means we have a bad government and a good hero who doesn't want to kill anyone except government leaders.

DANIEL: That's not the implication. The hero says he doesn't want
to kill *anyone*. And he means just that.
JUDGE: But there is a ukase in the story?
DANIEL: Yes.

✦

At the end of the first day, around seven o'clock, back at my apartment, I made a cup of tea and turned on the shortwave radio. As my limbs thawed out under a stack of blankets, I heard about the two writers who refused to plead guilty to charges of slandering Soviet communism in literary manuscripts smuggled to the West for publication.

The news items included the correct names of the defendants and the names of the judge, the prosecutor, and the "public accuser." They said that though the trial was technically open, admission was restricted. There was a list of those invited and a few words about three dozen supporters of the defendants who kept vigil outside the courthouse.

I liked the tone of the broadcast. Unlike the *Izvestia* stories, which without awaiting the trial called the defendants "slanderers," the Western reports presumed innocence.

The next day, the KGB operatives tried to intimidate the reporters. "What are you doing here?" they shouted. "Why are you writing about this?" The reporters ignored them, but for me it was rather like watching Khrushchev's shoe episode at the UN. It was embarrassing.

Tosha Yakobson spotted a man hurrying through the courtyard. "Look, it's that son of a bitch Khmelnitsky!" Yakobson shouted. "He must be the one who turned them in!"

As Yakobson lunged after him, Khmelnitsky made no attempt to escape. The two talked for a few minutes. "He says he isn't the one who did it," said Yakobson. "He says he hasn't betrayed anyone since 1953. If that's a lie, I'll show him."

Later, looking through the transcript of the trial, I saw that Khmelnitsky told the court that he was a childhood friend of Sinyavsky's, that he later became part of the *kompaniya* that included Daniel, and that he had given Daniel the idea for *This Is Moscow Speaking*. Much later, Khmelnitsky went on, he heard someone in a *kompaniya* describe a novella that had just been broadcast by Radio Liberty. It was written by someone named Nikolai Arzhak.

"This is no Arzhak," he recalled saying. "It's Yulik Daniel. I gave him the idea."

After making this public announcement that Daniel and Arzhak were one and the same, Khmelnitsky was ostracized by his friends. "It was rotten of me to name the author of an anti-Soviet work broadcast by an anti-Soviet radio station," he testified at the trial. The testimony was innocuous enough.

Still, I wondered if Daniel had known that the man who gave him the idea for "The Day of Open Murders" had once been an informant for Beria's secret police.

There was no question that Khmelnitsky was also the inspiration for Daniel's *Repentance*. But the novella had been written in 1963, a year before Khmelnitsky was publicly exposed as a Beria informant.

It seemed almost certain that Daniel knew.

✦

On the third day, I was unable to go to the courthouse. I had to attend a scheduled meeting with an author whose book I was editing. In the evening, I got a call from Natasha. There was a problem.

The KGB operatives had tried to provoke a fight with the friends of the defendants, and after some pushing and shoving, everyone, including Natasha, was taken to a police station. Most of those arrested were scholars, scientists, and editors, and most didn't have to be at work more than one or two days a week. But, at least on paper, they had to put in normal workdays at home. Being apprehended outside the courthouse during regular working hours constituted evidence that they had been derelict in their duties. That could constitute grounds for firing.

As Natasha and the others sat in a corridor at the precinct, pondering their sticky situation, a militia officer walked by, whispering: "Turn left, the door is open. Turn left, the door is open. Turn left, the door is open." The crowd of detainees quietly got up and left. The door was indeed open. The entire group got away before the authorities could establish their identities.

That was how we found out that the militia does not always like to take part in KGB operations. Still, Natasha said, most of those rounded up now didn't want to be seen anywhere near the courthouse, at least during working hours.

"Do you realize there won't be anyone there?" Natasha said. "Lara and Marya will come out at the break and there won't be anyone even to give them a sandwich!"

Reluctantly, I concurred that I was morally obligated to go, even if that meant keeping up a solitary vigil in hostile surroundings amid foreigners and goons.

The following morning, I moved slowly. By the metro, I ran into a little man in a white ski cap. It was Vadim Meniker. I ran toward him.

"Are you going to the courthouse?" I asked him urgently.

"Yes."

"You do know we may be the only ones there?"

"I can live with it." He showed no fear. He must have been a Zoya by birth. I was not a Zoya; I'd known that since childhood. I am capable of heroics only when there are others present. But now I was not alone.

Later in the day, others, including the militia-precinct escapees, began to show up outside the courthouse.

✦

We shifted around, clapped our hands, interjected points of law, and debated the minutiae. It was cold. I kept glancing at the reporters. Someone said they didn't seem to know about the *pelmennaya*, a cafeteria that served hot dumplings called *pelmeni*. Instead, the reporters went to Café Ice Cream.

"Let's tell them about the *pelmennaya*," suggested Tosha Yakobson.

The reporters seemed surprised to see us approach them. It must have been difficult for them to realize that our overture was prompted by nothing other than appreciation of the fairness and professionalism of their coverage.

"So, frost-proof *pressa*," said Yakobson in Russian. "Want to see where they sell hot *pelmeni*?"

"Hot what?" asked a reporter.

"*Pelmeni, pelmeni.* Haven't they taught you the word *pelmeni?* They are hot, cheap, and tasty. Let's go before you turn into pillars of ice." The reporters followed us to the *pelmennaya.*

We didn't talk along the way, but the gesture was made and accepted. The alliance that was forged on that day enabled Western reporters to obtain information from the public rather than just from the government. And by virtue of its closeness with the press, the public movement in the USSR became one of the world's best-covered ongoing political stories.

✦

The sentences came down late that evening: seven years for Sinyavsky, five for Daniel. The court said it had treated Daniel with leniency, taking into account that he had been wounded in the Great Patriotic War.

Soon after the trial, I learned that there was more to the already involved story of Daniel and Sinyavsky. Shortly after the war, Sinyavsky was forced to sign a document that made him an informant for Beria's secret police. (At that time, declining such overtures was tantamount to suicide.) Beria's spies were eager to exploit Sinyavsky's friendship with his Moscow University classmate Helen Zamoyska-Pelletier, the daughter of the French military attaché.

Sinyavsky's assignment was to marry Zamoyska-Pelletier. The marriage would have made Helen a Soviet citizen, a Soviet *politzek,* or a Soviet spy. Helen was also being watched by Andrei's childhood friend Sergei Khmelnitsky.

At one point, both men realized that they were being used as informants in the same secret-police operation and that they had the same handler. To keep their reports consistent, Khmelnitsky and Sinyavsky wrote them together. Sometime in the course of the operation, Andrei was assigned to invite Helen to the Sokolniki park in Moscow, sit down at a designated bench, and propose to her. Andrei did take Helen to Sokolniki, but instead of proposing, he told her about his assignment. At the designated bench, he and Helen feigned a spat, which, no doubt was observed by the operatives.

After the spat, Helen ran to Khmelnitsky to tell him that Andrei had proposed to her and that she was insulted. Khmelnitsky was then expected to report the conversation — and the spat — to the officer coordinating the operation.

It was a cheap spy story: Sinyavsky knows that Khmelnitsky is an informant; Khmelnitsky knows that Sinyavsky is an informant; Sinyavsky knows that Khmelnitsky is taking his job seriously and that he may be double-dealing; Sinyavsky plays Khmelnitsky for a fool.

Zamoyska graduated from Moscow University and returned to the West, but the agency didn't want to give up on the plan. In 1952, Sinyavsky was put on a military plane and turned loose in the streets of Vienna.

In a Viennese restaurant, as on the Sokolniki-park bench, Andrei told Zamoyska about the latest secret-police plot against her. Then he and Zamoyska made arrangements for smuggling Andrei's works to the West. The works were passed along by Zamoyska's friends visiting the USSR, and Zamoyska served as a trustee for Andrei's foreign earnings. Daniel, too, smuggled his books through Zamoyska.

The story had another, even more bizarre twist: in 1949, Khmelnitsky had told Andrei that he had reported two students from Moscow University's Department of History. Their names were Yuri Bregel and Vladimir Kabo. After Khmelnitsky's report, both were arrested.

In 1956, Andrei told the entire story to Yulik. The situation presented Andrei and Yulik with a logistical problem. What could they do with Sergei Khmelnitsky? Certainly, he could not remain among their friends. He had to be forced out of the *kompaniya*. But how could that be accomplished without compromising Sinyavsky? After all, his promise to serve as a secret-police informant had no expiration date. As far as the KGB was concerned, Andrei was theirs for life.

Unable to excommunicate Khmelnitsky for his Stalin-era crimes, the two writers had to find another reason.

But Khmelnitsky didn't give them that reason, and throughout the thaw he could be seen at the same tables, drinking vodka, singing *zek* songs, reciting his own poetry, and, sometimes unwittingly, giving Yulik ideas for novellas. He must have thought that he had outlived his past, the way you live through a childhood disease.

In 1964, when Khmelnitsky shouted that he had given Daniel the idea for the novella that had been broadcast over Radio Liberty, Daniel and Sinyavsky got their excuse to ban him from their apartments. The rest of the *kompaniya* learned about Khmelnitsky's past a few months later, when Bregel stood up during the defense of Khmelnitsky's dissertation.

The KGB had been stabbed in the back by its own informant, Andrei Sinyavsky. Sentencing him to two extra years in Mordovia was the agency's way of getting even.

✦

Yulik and Andrei received stiff terms, yet we felt that all of us, the defendants and their friends, had won. The defendants admitted publishing in the West, but did not admit guilt. They did not ask for mercy. Their supporters had demonstrated in the center of Moscow, then kept vigil outside the courthouse. We did not betray them and they did not betray us.

The two writers had become a cause célèbre among civil libertarians around the world. Foreign reporters were interested in giving detailed coverage to every aspect of our defiance. And, thanks to shortwave radio stations, reliable information about our friends was now beamed back to the USSR.

The government attacked; we fought back. It was the beginning of the twenty-year war waged by the Brezhnev government against the intelligentsia.

✦

People knocked on the Daniels' door to offer money, warm clothes, food. At first Larisa and Marya tried to decline, saying that the attorneys had been paid, that Yulik and Andrei had plenty of warm clothes, and that there was no shortage of food on the table.

"In that case, give it to someone who needs it," was the usual reply. Larisa's refrigerator was filling up with smoked sausage, salted fish, and Ukrainian garlic. A pile of flannel shirts, sweaters, fur hats, gloves, mufflers, and felt boots grew in the corner of the room.

Those donations said a lot about the state of mind of the people giving them. As citizens, as survivors of the Stalin era, they had to do something to protect their rights and liberties. For lack of other weapons, they fought Stalinism with felt boots and garlic.

"My God, what will they do in the camps with rapists and murderers?" was the standard fear around Moscow. Stalin-era *politzeki* were particularly worried. Certainly, those camp survivors said, we got longer terms, but we did time with decent people. Political camps back then were filled with the intelligentsia. But by now, most of us believed, Khrushchev had released the last of the *politzeki*.

Yulik's first letter allayed our fears. "Today I was invited for a cup of coffee in the next barrack," he wrote. "The company was truly refined: a Lithuanian priest, an Estonian artist and a Ukrainian writer." So there was still an intelligentsia in the camps. There were political prisoners besides Yulik and Andrei.

Even in the barracks of the Mordovian camp number 11, Daniel was the soul of the *kompaniya*. From his letters, we learned that his new friends included a young man named Anatoly Marchenko. Marchenko was serving a six-year term for an attempt to cross the border into Iran; Svyatoslav Karavansky, a Ukrainian completing a twenty-five-year term for being part of a group that advocated secession from the USSR; and Leonid Rendel, my former university classmate who had been imprisoned in 1958 after joining a group of Marxist revisionists. Now, Daniel wrote, Rendel was sending his regards.

A guard sat in on Larisa's meeting with Daniel in March 1966, so she had to find an indirect way to tell him of the international stir created by his arrest and conviction: "Grandmother Lillian Hellman asked me to say hello. Uncle Bert Russell also sends regards. Your nephew, Günter Grass, talks about you a lot, and so does his younger brother, little Norman Mailer."

The length of the list impressed the guard. "It's nice that you Jewish people have such large families," he said.

On the same trip, Larisa met Karavansky's wife, Nina Strokata, a microbiologist from Odessa. The two unacquainted women had both positioned themselves on the road by the barbed wire of the camp's "work zone." Larisa was trying to catch a glance of Daniel; Nina was trying to spot Karavansky.

Daniel appeared first. He shouted something neither woman could quite understand. He kept shouting until they made out the words: "Introduce yourselves!"

Nina still likes to tell that story: "I said, 'I am Nina Karavanskaya.' She said, 'I am Larisa Daniel.' Then we embraced."

Nina and Larisa returned to Moscow together. When they arrived, a group of friends gathered to meet Nina.

"It's a surprise to find like-thinkers living in the shadow of the Kremlin," Nina said that night.

Strokata took it upon herself to inform her new Moscow friends about the Ukrainian problems, and on her many subsequent visits, she brought along Ukrainian samizdat, translated into Russian especially for us. Through Nina, we learned that the Ukrainians accounted for the largest portion of Soviet political prisoners. They included Western Ukrainian peasants imprisoned for resisting collectivization after their land was annexed to Russia as a result of the Hitler-Stalin nonaggression pact and the subsequent division of Poland. There was also the Ukrainian intelligentsia, imprisoned for opposition to the rewriting of Ukrainian history, the curtailing of Ukrainian-language programs at schools, and the "Russification" of the Ukraine's political and cultural life.

✦

At first, our parcels went only to Daniel and Sinyavsky, but as we learned more names and as gifts and money kept pouring in, we started channeling food and correspondence to every prisoner Yulik and Andrei mentioned in their letters.

Several Moscow women volunteered to write to inmates, telling them about art exhibits and plays, and sending colorful postcards. In a number of cases, correspondence led to romance and matrimony. I started to correspond with Rendel, who promptly mistook my social commitment for romantic interest.

In our circle, aid to prisoners was called "the Red Cross." "Red Cross" volunteer work consisted of running around stores to buy warm clothes, running around stores to buy books and magazines, and running around stores to buy powdered milk, powdered eggs, dehydrated soups, hard sausage, coffee, canned food, and garlic. After all was purchased and packaged, we stood in line at Moscow's main post office to mail it all to the camps.

A prisoner was allowed to receive one four-kilo parcel a year, plus an unlimited number of one-kilo packages and an unlimited number of books and magazines. Money was not permitted, but it was needed to bribe guards and civilian camp employees into purchasing tea, coffee, butter, cheese, or whatever else, then smuggling it into the zone.

So, I learned to conceal ten-ruble bills inside book covers. The procedure involved using steam from a teakettle to unglue the book, inserting the bills between the cardboard cover and the inner lining, and then carefully gluing the book together. To be usable, the books had to have a thick and, preferably, dyed inner lining. In search of such books, I sifted through every bookshelf of every friend I had. "Let me have this for Yulik," I said every time I spotted a volume with the appropriate lining.

No one ever refused.

✦

"I've given one copy to my 'curator' at the KGB and sent one into samizdat," said Alik Ginzburg as he handed me a carbon copy of the manuscript. "Would you hide this one, just in case?"

That was the first time I saw *The White Book,* unofficially compiled documents pertaining to the Daniel-and-Sinyavsky trial.

I was amazed by the thought of Ginzburg openly handing it to the KGB. The implication was that the transcript of the trial, supplemented with appeals to the court, open letters of protest, and clippings from the Soviet and foreign press, did not constitute slander of the USSR.

By saying that he had nothing to hide, Ginzburg was deliberately taking *glasnost* to its logical extreme. He was staying within the law as it was written and was waiting to be arrested.

The manuscript brought together the first Western stories about the arrests, a copy of Esenin-Volpin's leaflet, his legal commentary, the *Izvestia* acknowledgment of the arrests, published letters to the editor, unpublished letters to the editor, official coverage of the trial, letters to the authorities from the wives of the defendants, and appeals by the Pen Club, as well as by Soviet and foreign writers, artists, scholars, scientists, and ordinary citizens.

There was also a letter from sixty Soviet writers who offered to take on the task of "rehabilitating" the defendants in lieu of imprisoning them, and a response by Nobel laureate Mikhail Sholokhov. In the 1920s, when there was still such a thing as revolutionary justice, Sholokhov said, the two would have been shot as traitors. "Humanism should not be confused with spinelessness," said the distinguished man of letters.

Most important, *The White Book* contained the unofficial transcript of the trial.

✦

One Friday in June 1966, after work, I went straight to the railroad station to join Larisa and Sanya, the Daniels' son, on a trip to Mordovia. They needed someone to help them carry bags and backpacks with provisions for a three-day stay.

Since the "Red Cross" was paying for our trip, we took the cheapest tickets available. Sanya went to sleep and Lara and I walked out into the car's lobby, where we spent much of the night comparing our marriages and our decisions to end them. "You know, I think marriage is a no-win game of chance," I said. "I don't know of any marriage that I would want for myself."

We talked about good people who had bad children; we talked about bad people who had good children. Then we moved on to our own children, who, thank God, were good.

"I don't see how that happened, because I can't enforce discipline," said Lara.

I couldn't enforce discipline either, so I told her about the time I tried to chide my son Sergei. "I can't love a boy who misbehaves," I said to him.

"But I love you even when you misbehave," said Sergei, who was three at the time. I apologized to him for saying something that wasn't true.

"I think we are feigning meekness because we don't enjoy punishing," said Larisa.

I asked Larisa if her parents had been worried about Yulik publishing in the West.

"What do you mean, worried? They didn't know."

We laughed; then I told her about my mother telling me to stop associating with the Daniel *kompaniya* after she read the *Izvestia* story about the arrests.

"But I keep showing up at your apartment, and she is so nice to me," Larisa said.

"That's because she doesn't know you are Yulik's wife. Your last name is Bogoraz. Every time you leave, she says, 'I really like your friend Lara. I wish she would come more often.' "

Our chat broke off the instant we saw the first guard tower.

✦

The camp warden decided to involve Larisa in the reeducation of her husband.

"Larisa Iosifovna, first of all I would like to ask if I can be helpful in any way," he said.

"I do have a request. I would like to leave a four-kilo parcel for my husband."

"Certainly," said the warden, and he wrote an order to allow an extra food parcel. "Larisa Iosifovna, I, too, have a request. We have information that your husband and other inmates drink alcohol-based lacquer in the camp furniture plant. Perhaps you could tell him that such things should not be done."

"That's interesting. He never used to drink lacquer when he was in Moscow. Perhaps he is drinking it because there is nothing else to drink."

"Well, there is another matter. He is keeping company with some very bad people."

"That's unusual. My husband has always made a point of associating exclusively with decent people."

"Well, now, Larisa Iosifovna, your husband is associating with people convicted under Article 70."

"Well, I must remind you that, my husband, too, was convicted under Article 70, and I know he is a decent man. I don't think you should worry. My husband would not be friends with anyone who is not a decent person."

While Larisa was in jousting with the warden, I walked around the village. Its highest structures were guard towers. Its only residents were guards and civilians who managed production of cupboards, tables, and chairs at the camp's furniture plant.

As Larisa, Sanya, and I walked toward the guesthouse where we were to spend the first night, someone hollered to us from the camp's work zone.

"Whom are you visiting?"

"Daniel!"

"Oh, Yuli Markovich." Clearly, Yulik was a celebrity.

The guesthouse was adjacent to the camp. The only way to get closer was to climb to a stoop of a nearby peasant hut. It was a high stoop that offered a view of the camp's residential zone.

That was where we saw Yulik and a group of his friends. They were about fifty feet away.

"Lyuda, look at this guy," Yulik hollered, pointing at a friend.

"This is Tolya Marchenko. He is like you. He's read Lenin from start to finish. He's getting out in three months."

The following morning, we walked up to the gates of the residential zone. At 7:00, the guards strung two wires across the road to the gates of the work zone. The gates swung open and, under guard, the convicts, about two thousand of them, were brought out to work.

Lyonya Rendel was in the first row, on the end. He walked as slowly as he could, which gave us about fifteen minutes to talk. He looked jaundiced, like Alek Esenin-Volpin when I first met him. Earlier, in a letter, he had asked me to look up his mother. I told him that I had and that she looked reasonably well and could hardly wait for him to get out.

Meanwhile, hundreds of men with shaved heads filed past us, wearing identical pea coats and rubber boots. The procession went on, and I stood there, trying to catch shreds of their conversations. I heard few Russian words. The prisoners were speaking Ukrainian, Lithuanian, Latvian, and Estonian.

Yulik, Larisa, and Sanya were now at the camp's family barrack, which left me with nothing to do but wait for prisoners to cross the road that connected the work zone to the residential one. I sat down on a bench near the barbed-wire fence.

"Lyuda," I heard. Three convicts were being taken to the work zone.

I ran toward them. "I am Tolya Futman," said one convict. "I am Valera Rumyantsev," said the second. "And I am Tolya Marchenko." There was something heroic about their looks and their introduction.

I couldn't sleep that night. The guard dogs barked incessantly. The night glowed with searchlights. I thought of the lights, the barbed wire, the machine guns and German shepherds. I also thought of the Decembrists, of Herzen, of Rendel, of Daniel and Sinyavsky.

Awareness of prisons had been with me since childhood. The world of barbed wire was never far away; it was where my neighbors disappeared to in 1937. It was also where Yulik and Andrei were sent to after their trial. They had gone into another world, and, ultimately, it did not matter how sad or outraged I was by their passage. I knew nothing of that new world, and no witness account, not even a stack of samizdat manuscripts, could describe it to me. To begin to understand it, you had to see the guard towers and hear the yelping dogs. All the while, you had to keep in mind that the people being moved from zone to zone were not different from you; if anything, they were better.

The following Thursday, when I returned to Moscow, a copy editor stopped by my desk. We had discussed a project just before I left. Now she had a few questions. She talked as if we had just interrupted our conversation. I stared at her. My God, it's just been one week; Friday through Thursday. So why did I feel as if I had lived a lifetime? I felt as if I was not in Moscow. I was still in the camps. I was part of that other world, the world where justice is not even an issue.

◆

My sons' interest in politics picked up a bit after Daniel's arrest. They wanted to know what Yulik had written. I handed them a book.

On the first day of the Daniel-and-Sinyavsky trial, eighteen-year-old Seryozha asked if he could cut classes and go to court instead. I said it would be fine. After realizing that friends of the defendants would not be allowed inside, Seryozha went to school.

Sometimes, the boys brought their friends over to read samizdat at my house. It was dangerous. The friends could have said something to their parents, and if the parents regarded such reading as offensive or simply imprudent, there could be problems. Still, I trusted my sons' judgment, and I wasn't mistaken.

During Sergei's final year at school, I was summoned by his principal, who informed me that he was outraged by Sergei's paper on *The Young Guard*, Aleksandr Fadeyev's fictionalized story in which Komsomol members wage a heroic struggle with the Nazis.

It was a short paper: "I cannot describe my feelings about the book because I found it so boring that I was unable to finish reading it."

"Do you realize what this means?" the principal bellowed.

"What do you want me to do? The boy was just being honest."

I couldn't do much about that paper, and neither could the principal. Expelling a student required too much paperwork, too many explanations; and in the end, the school collective would have to share the blame for Seryozha's poor upbringing.

"Now I understand where such views come from," the principal said, and he was not too far off the mark.

The boys understood what was going on around them but turned their attention to matters other than politics. Sergei was interested in engineering; Misha, in mathematics.

A few years later, in tenth grade, Misha came to me and said apologetically: "Mother, you probably won't approve, but I have joined the Komsomol. I felt left out, and I think it would make it easier to get admitted to the university."

"Why should I mind? It's your decision," I said. And I really did not mind.

✦

On July 20, 1966, at my birthday party, after everyone but a dozen closest friends caught the last trolley home, Sybarite Lyovka Malkin made a feeble attempt to analyze Tertz and Arzhak from a literary standpoint.

As in the past, I refused to discuss Yulik's and Andrei's use of metaphor while they sat in Mordovia.

Malkin's response was astounding: "So they sit in Mordovia. The whole world worries about them, the *New York Times* covers their trial, and everyone's running around collecting warm things and money. Now where were all of *you* when they jailed *us*?"

Malkin was making his speech from the green chair that concealed within its upholstery the typewritten manuscript of *The White Book*.

Six

Tolya Marchenko was getting out. "Don't bother buying him a half-liter bottle," a letter from Daniel warned us. "He doesn't drink. But he does have a sweet tooth."

Here is all we knew about Tolya: He grew up in a Siberian railroad town, got thrown into the camps at nineteen, broke out, tried to cross the border into Iran, and got thrown back in, this time as a political prisoner. When I saw him in Mordovia, I noticed his deep-seated eyes, which seemed to radiate an otherworldly glow.

I picked up a box of twenty eclairs and went to Larisa's to wait. Larisa, Natasha, and I sat up till midnight, but Marchenko didn't arrive. Yulik had given us the wrong date.

Marchenko arrived two days later, in his camp-issued rubber boots, dark blue pants, and a pea coat. The distinctive odor of the camps held its own against the smoke of Larisa's cigarettes.

He bit into a pastry. There was no reaction, no sign of pleasure on his face — hardly what you would expect from a man with a sweet tooth who had spent six years living on camp grub. He reached for another pastry. Still no reaction. In later years, I realized that for days after their release *zeki* are unable to taste food.

Up close, I could detect an unhealthy, glassy glow in his eyes. He had to be ill; very ill. He looked as though he needed rest, but we couldn't stop asking him questions, and he didn't want to stop answering. Fatigue had pushed him into the psychic plane where speech flows without effort, independently of the narrator.

We sat up past the time the trolleys stopped running, past the time the metro closed for the night, past the time you could reasonably expect to catch a taxi, then past the time the trolleys started running again.

Tolya's sense of Soviet history was so much better than mine, mostly because so many primary sources could be found wearing camp-issue pants and pea coats. He learned about Soviet imperialism from inmates from the Ukraine and the Baltic republics. He learned about Stalin's terror by observing the prison cells of Beria's secret-police operatives.

I asked Tolya why he began to read Lenin.

"I wanted to learn to think for myself," he said.

With just eight years of schooling, he felt intellectually inferior to virtually every *zek* he respected. Besides, every Thursday, *zeki* were forced to listen to "political information" sessions led by corrections officers.

"I didn't want that semiliterate telling me what to think," Tolya said. "So I read Lenin from top to bottom."

His conclusions were remarkably similar to mine. Lenin was a spineless politico who was not above telling a lie and who was too preoccupied with historical fantasies to feel any concern about the well-being of his countrymen. As we talked, Tolya showed me a thick stack of notebooks in which he had documented those inconsistencies.

Tolya's stories invariably returned to the same two themes: the conflict between the government and society and the conflict between the individual and the state.

+

"If he had gone untreated for two more weeks, he would have been dead," a surgeon said to Larisa when she came to visit Tolya in the hospital.

Four months before his release from the camps, Tolya had suffered an acute inflammation of the ear, which another prisoner, a physician, diagnosed as meningitis. The surgeon told us that the pus had shot up from Tolya's left ear the instant he made an incision.

"I have never seen a patient go untreated for so long," he said.

Tolya's head was bandaged and shaved even closer than before. He had a shooting pain in his ear, but his otherworldly gaze was now gone. What I'd mistaken for a look of spiritual intensity was actually a symptom of advanced inflammation.

I brought Tolya a volume of *The Count of Monte Cristo,* thinking that it would be easy reading and a good diversion from the pain. He took the book without enthusiasm.

"Why don't you take the Count home with you?" said Tolya as I got ready to leave.

"Why? It's good reading."

"It's all right; the guys in the camps have retold it to me."

"I can imagine what that sounded like."

"It was good enough. There's so much to read, and I've read so little that I don't have time for this."

"It's a good book. I promise."

"I have no time for such books."

Next on the reading list was *The Master and Margarita,* the long-banned novel that had just been serialized by *Moskva* magazine.

In the 1920s, a reviewer called its author, Mikhail Bulgakov, "a literary garbageman picking the morsels out of the vomit of a dozen dinner guests." Another critic called him a "son of a bitch," and yet another a "neo-bourgeois creature spraying its venomous yet impotent saliva at the working class and its communist ideals." Bulgakov died in poverty (but of natural causes) in 1940.

The Master and Margarita, a mystical tragicomedy, begins with the Devil suddenly materializing at the Patriarch's Ponds in the center of Moscow. The Prince of Darkness is a likable character if only because the targets of his fury warrant no sympathy.

For Tolya, the book was an introduction to Moscow. Bulgakov caught the spirit of the city, its intelligentsia, its fools, its lore — and its scoundrels. Bulgakov himself is in the book, cast as the Master, a writer driven to madness by reviewers. The Master burns his unpublishable book about Jesus of Nazareth, but in the end, the Devil retrieves the manuscript.

"Manuscripts don't burn," he explains.

After *The Master and Margarita*, Tolya read *The White Book*. On January 22, we gathered at Larisa's to celebrate Tolya's twenty-ninth birthday. He sat quietly, taking in the intelligentsia ruckus. An uninformed observer would have thought that it was Alik Ginzburg's birthday. Everyone wanted to come up and talk to Alik personally, to say something like: "A fascinating book. It will live forever."

Ginzburg sat at the table, calmly accepting the compliments. He, as well as everyone else at the table, knew that three other Moscow samizdat activists had been arrested in the preceding four days. We also knew that Ginzburg had delivered a copy of *The White Book* to the KGB, and that it looked as if he would be arrested next.

The compliments were our way of saying good-bye to the author.

✦

Marchenko's problems weren't limited to poor health. He couldn't find a job or a residency permit.

A permit to live in Moscow, being one of the most valuable commodities in the USSR, was out of the question for a released political prisoner. Finding a place outside Moscow was also a problem. Whenever we managed to find him a room, the local militia refused to issue a permit. "We've got enough of your kind as it is," they said. One town refused to issue a permit because the room Tolya found was too close to the Leningrad-Moscow highway. (Who knows, a "political" could blow up a bus.) In another town that turned him down, Tolya was told that in accordance with the comprehensive plan, the street where he'd found a room would be razed by the year 2000.

A Soviet citizen was not allowed to go without a job for more than four months, and Tolya's grace period was running out. By February, he'd become vulnerable to prosecution on two criminal charges: "parasitism" and violation of residency laws.

In late spring, he decided to go to his parents at the depot town of Barabinsk, on the trans-Siberian railroad. There, he was certain to find a job and a residency permit. After a few months, he would save up some money and return to look for work in towns around Moscow.

My parents, Mikhail Slavinsky and Valentina Yefimenko, in 1926, shortly after they were married. They were nineteen-year-old Komsomol members and true believers in communism. In fine revolutionary fashion, they wore similar shirts.

At eleven, I believed that I lived in the best country in the world, led by the wisest man in the world, Comrade Iosif Vissarionovich Stalin.

This 1936 photograph became the official symbol of Comrade Stalin's love for children. Years later, in graduate school, I was stunned to learn that my acquaintance Gelya Markizova was the girl in the photograph. Shortly after she posed with Stalin, her father was executed and her mother died under suspicious circumstances.

My contemporaries would later refer to their marriages as "escaping into family life." In 1947, I married Valentin Alexeyev, an air force officer.

My sons, Seryozha (*left*) and Misha, in 1958.

During the thaw, Moscow intellectuals gathered into *kompanii,* which met to recite poetry, drink, dance, sing, and swap manuscripts and stories. The *kompaniya* above, called the Brotherhood of Impoverished Sybarites, was formed by Moscow students who were later convicted as members of a subversive organization. After serving prison terms, the young men continued to call themselves Sybarites. In 1968, I married one of them, Nikolai Williams (*front row, third from left; and below*).

COURTESY VLADIMIR FRUMKIN

Bard Bulat Okudzhava performing at a party in 1980.

COURTESY BORIS FILIPPOV

My friend Yuli Daniel. In 1965, he and another writer, Andrei Sinyavsky, were arrested for publishing their works in the West. Their trial in 1966 marked the beginning of the dissident movement.

Aleksandr Esenin-Volpin, the first man to use the word *glasnost* as a political slogan. Esenin-Volpin, the son of one of Russia's most adored poets, Sergei Esenin, was an eccentric poet and mathematician who paid for his candid statements on politics by serving time in internal exile and in psychiatric institutions.

GEORGE KRIMSKY

In 1965, to protest the arrests of Daniel and Sinyavsky, Esenin-Volpin organized a demonstration by the statue of poet Aleksandr Pushkin in Moscow. (I was one of the people who attempted to talk him out of the idea.) The demonstration later became an annual event: Human Rights Day, December 10. Above, the Human Rights Day observance in 1976.

COURTESY JERROLD SCHECTER

A 1967 photo of Anatoly Marchenko, a Siberian laborer and political prisoner who taught himself to write and became the premier chronicler of life in the camps after Stalin.

Marchenko's future wife, my friend Larisa Bogoraz (*right*), with Pavel Litvinov and his future wife, Maya Kopeleva (*far left*), on the way to Marchenko's trial. A KGB tail is partly visible behind Larisa. On August 25, 1968, four days after this snapshot was taken, Bogoraz, Litvinov, and five others staged a Red Square demonstration to protest the Soviet invasion of Czechoslovakia.

Sentenced to four years in internal exile, Larisa was taken to the Siberian town of Chuna, where she did hard labor at the lumber mill shown here. She lived in the peasant hut below, which was bought for her use by her Moscow friends. The hut was later resold and the proceeds were used to buy huts for other prisoners.

Aleksandr Ginzburg, the author of *The White Book,* an account of the trial of Daniel and Sinyavsky that led to Ginzburg's own prosecution and a sentence of five years in the camps. Ginzburg's trial, in 1968, was covered in a new, unofficial publication, *Khronika tekushchikh sobytiy* ("The Chronicle of Current Events").

Pyotr Yakir, the son of an executed Civil War commander, challenged the "re-Stalinization" that marked the end of the thaw. But after his arrest in 1972, Yakir recanted, gave testimony against more than two hundred dissidents (including me), and called for the end of *Khronika*.

Former general Pyotr Grigorenko, a champion of the rights of the Crimean Tatars, victim of punitive psychiatry, and, later, member of the Moscow Helsinki Watch Group.

Some members of the first Moscow dissident organization, the Initiative Group in Defense of Human Rights. *From left to right (closest to foreground):* biologist Sergei Kovalyov, philologist Tatyana Khodorovich, mathematician Tatyana Velikanova, physicist Grigory Podyapolsky, and religious writer Anatoly Krasnov-Levitin.

Attorney Sofya Kallistratova, a leading practitioner of "dissident law" who later became a dissident herself by joining the Moscow Helsinki Watch Group.

Right: Khronika activist, Initiative Group member, and mathematician Aleksandr Lavut.
Below: Physicist Yuri Orlov, founder of the Moscow Helsinki Watch Group.

LYDIA VORONINA

Andrei Sakharov (*far left, in dark coat*) trying to attend Orlov's 1978 trial.

KIRSTEN GOLDBERG

Larisa (*right*) and me at Washington's Dulles Airport in 1989. As chairman of the revived Moscow Helsinki Watch Group (of which I am a member), she had come to the United States at the invitation of the New York–based Helsinki Watch. She stayed with me for a month.

The next problem was finding a way to keep in contact. Larisa's correspondence was monitored by the KGB. My letters may have been opened, too. We needed a third address.

"I need to get letters from a man," I said to a friend, an artist. She asked no questions.

Marchenko's first letter was inordinately thick, about twenty pages. Larisa asked me to look through it. The letter was filled with heavy-handed accusations hurled at camp authorities. Every other sentence ended with an exclamation mark. But I could still detect some semblance of the stories Marchenko had told with such unassuming grace at Larisa's kitchen table.

I asked if Tolya was trying to write a book.

He was.

✦

Shortly after Ginzburg's arrest, the House of Scientists posted an announcement: "An informational program about the work of investigational organs of the Committee for State Security." The lecture would be read by Investigator Pakhomov of the KGB. The announcement did not specify that he had led the preparation of the Sinyavsky case.

Larisa had a plan. Through her network of friends, she asked academy member Mikhail Leontovich to come to the lecture and ask a question about the Ginzburg case. Leontovich, a physicist who made little secret of his sympathies, sent word that he would be delighted to come.

Now all Larisa and I had to do was get inside the House of Scientists. The club was closed to everyone except scientists and their families. We needed to enlist the help of my former husband.

The divorce had taken all the tension out of our relationship. Valentin stopped by regularly, to visit the boys or to tell me about his amorous conquests. The subtext was the same: "See, there are a lot of young, attractive women who want me." I still felt some guilt. I had left him through no fault of his own. In some ways, he was a victim. So, if he enjoyed telling me about his exploits, I obliged by hearing him out.

"Valya, a friend and I want to go to the House of Scientists. Can I have your pass?" I asked when he came to visit.

"Of course," Valentin said. I would show his House of Scientists membership card, then Larisa and I would sit silently at the meeting, watching academy member Leontovich make the KGB squirm.

✦

Had the announcement made a mention of Investigator Pakhomov's role in the Daniel-and-Sinyavsky case, the House of Scientists auditorium would have been packed. As it was, the announcement brought out only those interested in the work of our heroic guardians of state security. About fifty people, mostly old ladies, bunched in the front rows. Most of them got in by virtue of being someone's mother-in-law.

Investigator Pakhomov was a stocky man. His massive, red face towered over a snazzy, white, nylon shirt (the height of fashion in Moscow of 1967). He handled the lecture with a certain aplomb.

Foreign intelligence services had devoted enormous resources to ideological warfare, he said. In such-and-such a year, the CIA budget was estimated at so-and-so million dollars, a substantial share of which was used as bait for subverting the ideologically unstable among Soviet citizens.

"And, comrades, there are times when Soviet people do take that bait. Like the recent case involving two writers."

I squirmed. Pakhomov did not come out and claim that Daniel and Sinyavsky had been paid by foreign intelligence services. That charge was not made even by the prosecution. Knowing acceptance of money from foreign intelligence services would have constituted treason, not "anti-Soviet propaganda." Unable to make that allegation directly, Pakhomov resorted to crude innuendo: foreign intelligence services had allocated funds to subvert Soviet citizens and Daniel and Sinyavsky merely "took their bait." The word *bait* was more vague than the word *money*.

Larisa and I looked around. It was the right moment for Leontovich to raise his hand. "Do you know what he looks like?" Larisa whispered.

I had seen Leontovich once, years earlier, at the dacha of Sybarite Slava Grabar. There had not been a formal introduction. Leontovich, whose dacha was adjacent to Grabar's, had said something to Grabar, then gone inside the house.

"I don't think I see him here," I said.

The meeting went into a question-and-answer session. It was up to Larisa and me to make a move.

Lara raised her hand; Pakhomov nodded in her direction. Though he'd led the Sinyavsky case, he had to have been able to recognize Mrs. Daniel.

"My name is Larisa Bogoraz. My husband, Yuli Daniel, is one of the two writers you have referred to. There are two parts to my question.

"First, you implied that the two writers got some form of financial gain from their work. I know for certain that neither of them has received anything from any intelligence service. They did not even claim the royalties from their works. They published their works in the West because they could not publish at home. So, if you have any evidence that was not presented at the trial, I would like to hear it.

"Second, you have just mentioned that the Soviet penal system is humane and that prisoners receive meals with sufficient calorie-and-vitamin content. Would you please tell us, what is the calorie-and-vitamin content of a prisoner's diet?"

"I'll tell you right away, a prison is not a resort," Pakhomov said through a rising wave of hissing and heckling. The elderly people who had come to hear a speech about our heroic guardians of state security did not approve of Larisa's presence.

"Vitamins!" someone shouted. "Give them a bullet each! That's the vitamins!"

We got up to leave, but the crowd surrounded us. The heckling grew more intense. "Just look at them. Vitamins, they want. Fruits and vegetables. How did they get here, anyway? Who brought them in? Let's find out. Get someone from management to take their documents." Presumably, one of the old folks had gone out to get the House of Scientists administrator.

I clutched my purse. Valentin's membership card was in it. A colonel in the Soviet air force would not be given much leeway. If the crowd went after my purse, his career would be over. Larisa was pale. It was her question that had caused their outrage. One unthinking moment, and the life of an innocent man hung in the balance.

"Yes, yes, let's check. Let's check." The voice was familiar. It was that of a scientist whose book I had edited. He was an older, distinguished man who wore an elegant, dark suit and exuded authority. "Please, let me through. Thank you."

He got through the crowd, moved in behind Larisa and me, put his hands on our shoulders, and ordered the crowd to disperse. Seeing that justice was being done, the crowd parted.

"Lyuda, let's go quickly," he whispered. "I'll walk you to the hallway. There is an open door at the end. Then, you run."

When we walked out onto the cold Moscow street, I reached into my purse, pulled out Valentin's membership card, and put it in my coat pocket. We went up a dark street. The danger had passed.

"Excuse me! Wait up!" boomed a voice behind us.

I shuddered. They had caught us.

"I'd like to ask you something." Behind us was a young man; he was slightly out of breath.

"I just heard you ask a question back there," he said to Larisa. "Please, tell me, how did your husband get the courage to do what he did? How could a Soviet person get the resolve to publish in the West?"

From the way he asked the question, I could tell the young man was neither a detractor nor a sympathizer. He was just interested.

By then, I had become an expert at taking that question. "What's wrong with publishing abroad? Herzen did it. Does that make him a traitor?"

The young man stopped. He looked at me, and I recognized the expression in his eyes. The answer was so obvious; how could it have been so elusive for so long?

I had answered his question completely.

✦

On an August morning in 1967, I got a call from Captain Mirolyubov of the Committee for State Security. (KGB officers rarely divulged their first names or even their real last names.) He asked if I would be able to come over right away.

"We called you because your name was in Ginzburg's address book," the captain told me as I seated myself across the desk from him that afternoon.

That was a lie. The day Alik gave me *The White Book,* he told me that he had left his address book with a safe person.

"Of course. Alik's name is in my address book, too. We are acquainted."

"Ginzburg is being very cooperative with us, and he has told us everything," said Mirolyubov.

That didn't sound right, either.

"All I will ask you to do today is confirm what I already know."

I nodded.

"Alik told us about one particularly important conversation you had at his apartment at noon, December 27. Do you have any recollection of it?"

"No. Not offhand."

"Well, let me remind you. You came in and asked, 'Is it ready?' Ginzburg said, 'No, it's still drying.' You said, 'Have you gone crazy? She's got her bags packed.' Ginzburg: 'How about another hour.' You (with a sigh): 'Fine.' Ginzburg: 'Good-bye.' You: 'Good-bye.'"

Nice work. Ginzburg had told them that I had said fine "with a sigh"? The apartment had been bugged, and I was being confronted with a transcript.

"I have no idea what this is about." Of course, I did. Ginzburg had been developing film taken in Mordovia by Nina Strokata and Nadya Svitlychna, another Ukrainian. There were photographs of guard towers, of a prison convoy being led across the road from the residential zone to the work zone. Some shots were taken from the stoop where I stood when Yulik introduced me to Marchenko.

The person "ready to leave" was Strokata. She was going to take the film back to the Ukraine. Alik was a good phototechnician, and, of course, he could be trusted with that kind of work. The only problem was getting him to do the work on time. For all his good points, Alik was not one of the most organized human beings on earth.

The photos were eventually developed, but soon after returning to her home in Odessa, Nina sent me a message that her apartment and her office in Odessa had been searched. At subsequent interrogations, she was asked about some "manuscript." She had no idea what that was about, and neither did I.

"I have told you, Ginzburg has told us everything. We just want you to confirm this to us," repeated Mirolyubov.

"I am sorry, but I just can't recall. The conversation you are asking about would have taken place in December, and this is August." What could he do? Open up my skull and see that I knew precisely what the conversation was about, and that I also knew that he was on a fishing expedition?

"What is your maiden name?" Mirolyubov now stood over me, shouting.

"Slavinskaya."

"What is your father's name?"

"Mikhail."

"Where is he?"

"He was killed in the war."

"I have told you that we know everything!"

"You have. And I am answering your questions."

"Did Ginzburg ever give you any film?" In Russian, the same word denotes "film" and "tape."

"Yes."

"What was on that film?"

"Songs."

"Was there a song by Aleshkovsky?" So, they had Alik's tape recorder, too.

"I don't remember; it was a long time ago."

"Do you remember the song about the herring that marries a whale?" I remembered that song. A herring marries a whale, and at first the marriage is viewed as a form of bestiality, because in our country herrings must marry herrings and whales must marry whales. Punitive measures are taken by the authorities, but then are called off by the Central Committee, which concludes that if the couple manages to produce whale offspring that taste like herring, there will be more foodstuffs to satisfy the needs of the toiling masses.

I held off answering, hoping to hear Captain Mirolyubov describe that song to me.

"The herring marries a whale, and the matter is treated as a sex offense," he said, stopping short of the Central Committee.

"I recall something like that. Is that not allowed?"

"Ludmilla Mikhailovna, you disappoint me. I have told you that

Ginzburg has told us everything. We know everything. All we expect you to do is confirm it."

"I don't know what you want me to confirm. That a herring married a whale?"

"What is your maiden name?" Not that again.

"I have told you, Slavinskaya."

"Do you know where your father is?"

"He was killed in the war."

"Are you married?"

"Divorced."

"Do you have children?"

"Two sons."

"You do know about legal sanctions for giving false testimony?"

"I do."

"Are you employed?"

"Yes."

"Where are you employed?"

"At the Nauka Publishing House. As an editor."

"Is it a good job?"

"Yes, it's a good job."

"What do you think they would do if I picked up the phone and told them that you are refusing to give truthful testimony to the Committee for State Security?"

"They wouldn't like it. They might even fire me. But if you have to call, go ahead."

"What is your maiden name?"

"Slavinskaya."

"Where is your father?"

"He died in the war."

"Ludmilla Mikhailovna, you have refused to confirm what Ginzburg has already told us. It's bad for you, bad for your children, bad for Ginzburg. Go home and think about what happened here."

What in the hell did he want of my dead father? What could he possibly want to find in my communist youth? It was as clean as Zoya's.

That evening, I told Larisa what had happened. She asked me to repeat it at least twice.

"Did he take down your name, date of birth, nationality, all that, before the interrogation?"

He hadn't.

"Did he take notes?"

He hadn't.

"Lyuda, that was not a formal interrogation. It sounds like you were being questioned by someone in operations. It's not an existing case, and it sounds like it could be a new case against you."

✦

The "Red Cross" was becoming increasingly active. The wives of Ukrainian prisoners were constantly in and out of our apartments, Lara and I had been summoned to interrogations on the Ginzburg case, and, both of us agreed, it was quite possible that at least one of us would wind up behind bars.

I was divorced. Lara's husband was in the camps. Neither of us had siblings. What would happen to Lara's son? What about my children? And who could attend the trial and tell our friends what happened?

I don't recall whether it was Lara or I who offered the solution. I just remember how outrageous it seemed at first: we would tell everyone we were cousins. Then, if one of us got arrested, the other would invoke our familial rights and drag our fraudulent family tree all the way to the Committee for State Security. It would mean telling a lie, and it must be told that I subscribed to the truth ethic of Alek Esenin-Volpin with one exception: lies concocted for the KGB. I saw nothing improper in attempting to deceive that organization. Unfortunately, lies have a way of being followed by other lies.

To make the "cousins" story stick with the KGB, we had to begin by deceiving our friends. At some party we went to, I addressed Lara as "*sestrichka*" (my "dear little sister") and she responded with something in the same vein.

"I didn't know you were sisters," said someone in the *kompaniya*.

"Cousins," Lara said. Now we had witnesses who could confirm that Lara and I were first cousins and that we called each other "*sestrichka*."

✦

In the summer of 1967, I found Tolya a place to live in the town of Aleksandrov, about two hours by train from Moscow. It was a one-room peasant hut, which he shared with its owner, an old woman everyone called Aunt Nyura. The room was partitioned off with a cupboard and a curtain, and Tolya's corner was just big enough for a bed with a straw mattress, a small cabinet, and a chair. Tolya also managed to get a residency permit and a porter's job at a liquor-and-vodka plant.

On most Saturdays, Larisa left Moscow for Aleksandrov. I had guessed that she was helping Tolya with his writing, but I didn't really know. By that time, Lara and I had an understanding: we did not ask each other about sensitive matters unless either of us needed assistance. Much of what we did was punishable by law, and if one of us were to be arrested and the other summoned to an interrogation, she would be able to say "I don't know" without lying. It is always easier to tell the truth than to make up a credible story.

In September, Tolya took a leave of absence from his job and moved into a room at a country retreat for writers and journalists. A friend had made the arrangements. Lara took a two-week vacation and spent it editing Tolya's book.

One day in October, half a dozen of us gathered in a two-room Moscow apartment. Between us, we had two typewriters, and in the next three days we were able to type up two hundred notebook pages covered with Tolya's tight handwriting. It was the first time I saw the magnificent book called *My Testimony*.

Those who could type (there were four of us) worked in shifts, till our minds went dim. Those who couldn't type dictated or stacked the pages and corrected typos. Two people with a typewriter worked in the kitchen; two more worked in one of the rooms. The hosts' child slept in the room between them. Heaps of paper, carbons, and manuscript pages were stacked all around. In the kitchen, someone was constantly making coffee and sandwiches; and at any given time, at least one of us was asleep on the couch or on the cot.

Despair would often descend upon me in the Vladimir prison. Hunger, illness, and, more than anything else, defenselessness and inability to stand up to evil would drive me to the point where I was ready to lunge at my jailers. To lunge at them and perish. Or else, to find another form of suicide. Or to maim myself, as others had done before my eyes.

But something stopped me; it was the hope that one day I would get out and tell everyone what I saw and what I lived through. I vowed to myself that I would survive and live through anything. And I made that promise to my friends who still had many years to spend behind bars and behind barbed wire.

I thought of ways to carry out that mission. I thought that it would be impossible to accomplish it in our country, where the KGB attempts to control every uttered word. It seemed senseless even to attempt it. Everyone is so paralyzed by fear and overcome by the hardship of life that no one is interested in the truth. Therefore, I thought, I would have to cross the Soviet border. Then, at the very least, my testimony would become a document, a source for historians.

My prison term ended last year. I was freed. I understood that I was wrong, and that my testimony is needed here, at home. The people want to know the truth.

The point of this book is to tell the truth about today's camps and prisons, to tell the truth to those who want to hear it. I am convinced that glasnost is the only effective weapon in the battle with evil and lawlessness around us.

The stories I had heard in Lara's kitchen were now on paper, told in the same unmistakable voice. It was an honest voice, a voice devoid of any pretense. It was Tolya's voice.

Tears welled in my eyes as I typed Tolya's anecdotes. The book worked. It worked! There wasn't a gratuitous story, not a single runaway condemnation. It was a book only Tolya could have written. Only he could remember so much detail.

"If Galina Borisovna knew what's being typed here, she would bring a division and surround the whole square block!" exclaimed our host as soon as he started proofreading. Galina Borisovna — initials G.B. — was his code for the KGB.

By dawn of the third day, the work was done, and Tolya and Lara left with a suitcase filled with rough drafts and final versions. One copy remained with the hosts, another was taken to friends who were beyond suspicion, the third was dispatched to the West, and three more went into samizdat.

This was followed by months of waiting for word from Western publishers.

"So, author," I said to Tolya once. "I hear you are ready to receive your royalties."

"Not really," he said. "I will be paid in years, not rubles."

Seven

The government's pogrom had not stopped. On September 16, 1966, a ukase of the Supreme Soviet of the RSFSR amended the Criminal Code of the Russian Republic to include Article 190. The new article imposed imprisonment for up to three years for "slandering the Soviet social and political system."

The proposed law was broader than the existing Article 70, which punished anti-Soviet propaganda. Article 70 required the prosecution to demonstrate that the accused acted with intent to undermine the Soviet state. To convict under Article 190, the state had to demonstrate only that a "slanderous" statement had been made. Whether the statement was intended to incite a riot or to entertain friends was irrelevant. The language of Article 190 could be interpreted to include speeches made at public meetings, distribution of samizdat, or even a casual dinner conversation.

Before the new law was ratified, a petition signed by twenty-one prominent writers and scientists warned the Supreme Soviet that the proposed Article 190 contradicted "the Leninist principles of Socialist democracy" and threatened to "infringe on liberties guaranteed by the Constitution of the USSR." Dmitry Shostakovich was among the petitioners. So was Andrei Sakharov, a nuclear physicist living in the shadows of the Soviet hydrogen-weapons program. The Soviet elite had risen to demand that the Supreme Soviet be guided by the Soviet Constitution. The ideas of Alek Esenin-Volpin were acquiring a life of their own.

The law went into effect in late December 1966. On January 17, four samizdat activists were arrested and charged with anti-Soviet propaganda under Article 70. On January 22, about twenty people gathered on Pushkin Square to demand freedom for the four and the repeal of Article 70. Four of the demonstrators were arrested and charged with slander under Article 190.

The demonstration was organized by a group that called itself SMOG, an acronym for the Youngest Society of Geniuses. Most *SMOGisty* were students who had been expelled from the universities for gathering in front of a statue of poet Vladimir Mayakovsky to recite defiant poetry — their own. In SMOG lingo, the poet's name was shortened to "Mayak," a word meaning "lighthouse," and that term was used to refer to the statue. In untamed verses that routinely mixed profanity with the symbols of Christian faith, *SMOGisty* demanded purity of art and threatened to "deprive Socialist realism of its virginity." Since gathering at the Mayak usually involved getting into scuffles with the militia, respectable, middle-aged people rarely attended. One exception was Alek Esenin-Volpin.

Two of the arrested demonstrators, Viktor Khaustov and Vladimir Bukovsky, were sentenced to three years in the camps under Article 190. The other two recanted, thereby avoiding the camps. After the conviction of Bukovsky and Khaustov, the samizdat journalist who had compiled the transcripts of the trials was summoned to the KGB and warned that he, too, could be prosecuted under Article 190.

Political trials have a way of leading to more political trials.

✦

Pavel Litvinov, the samizdat journalist in question, was not stopped by the KGB warning. Instead, he sent *Izvestia, Literaturnaya gazeta, Komsomolskaya pravda, Moskovsky komsomolets, The Morning Star, Humanité,* and *l'Unita* an open letter: "On September 26, 1967, I was summoned to the Committee on State Security, to the Committee official Gostev (2 Dzerzhinsky Square, room 537). Our conversation was witnessed by another KGB official who did not identify himself." This was followed by the transcript of the conversation.

"Pavel Mikhailovich, we are not going to debate now, we are merely giving you a warning," the KGB official said. "Imagine what would happen if the entire world found out that the grandson of the great diplomat is involved in such affairs. That would mar his memory."

"I don't think Grandfather would take offense. Am I free to leave?" answered Pavel Litvinov. Pavel's grandfather, Maxim Litvinov, was no stranger to conflict with the authorities. As the people's commissar of foreign affairs, he incurred Stalin's wrath by recommending against making the pact with Hitler's Germany.

The transcript of the KGB warning to the younger Litvinov didn't make it to the pages of *Izvestia, Literaturnaya gazeta, Komsomolskaya pravda, Moskovsky komsomolets,* or even *The Morning Star, Humanité,* and *l'Unita.* But I did hear it broadcast over the Voice of America, Radio Liberty, the BBC, and the Deutsche Welle. It seemed the open letter was being read every other night, with its author being identified as Dr. Litvinov, a prominent physicist and the grandson of the late people's commissar. To the KGB's chagrin, the world found out that the grandson of the great diplomat was indeed involved in "such affairs."

Pavel was neither a prominent physicist nor Dr. Litvinov. He was a tall, sandy-haired young man who had grown up enjoying the benefits of good looks, money, connections, a famous name, and the good life in the high rises for government officials. That was his birthright, but Pavel wanted something more. Through friends, he was introduced to the *SMOGisty.* They were his age, and it would seem that he should have been comfortable gathering at the Mayak, shouting defiant verses, and fighting with the militia. Still, Pavel kept looking.

Sometime in 1967, Aleksandr Ginzburg introduced him to Larisa Bogoraz and her circle of middle-aged scholars, scientists, and literati. Pavel was twenty-seven; most of us were forty. He had been a teenager at the time of Stalin's death, which meant he did not bear the scars and confusion the Great Leader inflicted upon us. By the time Pavel joined our circle, we all had concluded our painful questioning of the Soviet system. We knew who we were and what we wanted. By joining us, Pavel was spared our lonely search. He could simply accept our answers.

✦

Pavel had his own circle of friends, some of whom followed him into our movement. One such newcomer was Andrei Amalrik.

"He is a good man to know," said Pavel as he led me off to meet him. "He knows lots of foreign reporters." From that, I assumed that Amalrik was also involved in sending appeals and manuscripts to the West.

Amalrik lived in a communal flat in the Arbat. Half of his tiny room was taken up by a grand piano, which neither Andrei nor his wife, Gyuzel, knew how to play. Gyuzel's paintings were being used in place of curtains and room dividers. There was also a large bookshelf, apparently made by Amalrik himself. On the shelf stood dozens of books published by émigré presses in the West. At the time, such books were still rare, and the few people who happened to have them usually refrained from displaying them.

Later, when Amalrik and I became better acquainted, I realized that he was a rebel by nature. During his first year at Moscow University's history department, he wrote a paper challenging the official view that the Russian state evolved from the Slavic tribal order; instead, Amalrik sided with prerevolutionary historians who argued that Russia's governance was set up by the Scandinavians, whom the Slavs invited to rule them. Saying that the Slavs were unable to govern themselves and that they knew it struck at the heart of the Russia-the-Motherland-of-Elephants patriotism being taught at the department of history. For his dangerous thoughts, Amalrik was expelled from the university.

After expulsion, he wrote plays and made a living as a middleman, selling avant-garde art to foreign reporters. In 1964, Amalrik was convicted for parasitism and sent to work at a Siberian collective farm. He returned to Moscow in 1966.

After internal exile, Andrei did not end his contacts with foreigners. On the courthouse steps during Ginzburg's trial, Amalrik met the future publisher of his essay *Will the Soviet Union Survive till 1984?* (At the time, the Soviet empire seemed a mighty monolith, but Andrei's book prophetically predicted its disintegration.) Later, he would start referring to himself as "the communications officer" for the human-rights movement.

Amalrik was close to the *SMOGisty,* but he was not one of them. Pavel, Larisa, and I could count on him, but he was not part of our circle, either. Brash, fearless, and abrasive, Andrei had a way of telling you precisely what he thought. ("Lyuda, you've grown older and fatter," he said to me once.)

Even his friends in the Western press corps couldn't count on his benevolence. He attacked them in a particularly stinging and brilliant essay, "Foreign Correspondents in Moscow." Behind his back, friends current and former called Andrei "the lone wolf." Some even considered him a KGB agent. Only his second arrest, in 1970, convinced the skeptics that they were wrong.

✦

It was hard to imagine a debut more dramatic than Pavel's. His coverage of the Bukovsky and Khaustov trials was in the tradition of *The White Book* and Frida Vigdorova's reporting on the Brodsky trial. He worked in the open, calling his sources on the phone and making no secret of his intentions to complete the manuscript. He acted as if law ruled supreme in the state, as if the judicial process was not held subservient to the political needs of the Communist party. Just as the Decembrists had denied the existence of tyranny, Pavel refused to acknowledge the KGB. He acted as a citizen in a situation where citizenship, heroism, and defiance were one and the same.

Despite the KGB warning, Pavel completed the transcript of the Bukovsky and Khaustov trials. As the manuscript was being prepared for publication in London, Pavel was getting ready to cover another political trial, that of *samizdatchiki* Yuri Galanskov, Aleksandr Ginzburg, Aleksei Dobrovolsky, and Vera Lashkova.

If the Daniel-and-Sinyavsky case was about the right to publish abroad, the case of the four *samizdatchiki* was about the right to self-publish. The attack on samizdat came at a time when the intelligentsia could no longer imagine life without it.

It was not yet clear what the government was trying to accomplish. Two contradictory trends were emerging: one, toward Stalinism, the other, toward continued liberalization. On the one hand, the government had imprisoned Daniel and Sinyavsky; on the other hand, it had exiled Valery Tarsis, a lesser writer who also had published in the West. The authorities had scrapped plans to publish Solzhenitsyn's *Cancer Ward,* but they did publish Bulgakov's *Master and Margarita.* They didn't arrest Alek Esenin-Volpin after the Pushkin Square demonstration, but they did arrest the *samizdatchiki* Galanskov, Ginzburg, Lashkova, and Dobrovolsky.

These inconsistencies showed that the course had not been set. Our actions could still make a difference. It was the time to fight for samizdat. It was the time to come out in the open, for samizdat could not be defended in secret.

✦

The intelligentsia struck back with a barrage of petitions.

I guess if we had been a few years younger, we would have preferred demonstrations. But when you are forty, the act of shouting slogans in the streets loses its allure. Besides, what we had to say could not be reduced to slogans.

The concepts of *glasnost* and the rule of law are not easy to explain to a government that chooses to ignore them. Nonetheless, hundreds of us decided to tell the Brezhnev clique that we took exception to its new policies. We expressed our disagreement in a manner appropriate for people of our age and social status: in writing. Some of our epistles to the authorities were lengthy, restrained, and legalistic. Others were short, punchy, and sharply worded. If you liked a letter, you signed it.

Over the course of a year, petitions were fired off to the Supreme Soviet, the procurator general, the KGB, the ministries of health and internal affairs, the Chief Administration of Corrective Labor Camps (Gulag), the unions of writers and journalists, the institutes of health and nutrition and of state and law, the presidents of the Academy of Sciences and the Academy of Medical Sciences, the rector of Moscow State University, the patriarch of all Russias, *Pravda, Izvestia, Literaturnaya gazeta, Rudé Právo, Liteárni Listy,* the BBC, *Pratze, Humanité, l'Unita, The Morning Star,* and the Congress of Communist Parties in Budapest.

Sometime in 1968, the word *podpisant* was coined. It means, literally, "the person who signed" and rhymes with the word *diversant,* a commando. Altogether, about a thousand people took part in the petition campaign.

For me, the first petition was the hardest to sign. Associating with Larisa and Marya, standing outside the courthouse, observing the Pushkin Square demonstration, hiding *The White Book,* visiting Daniel, and typing Marchenko's manuscript did not amount to open defiance of the system. There was still a chance that "they" wouldn't find out.

What would happen to me if I did sign? And what about my sons? And my job? What would I do if I lost it? I thought of a sign I had seen on a bulletin board: "The Bolshevichka Clothing Factory Seeks Seamstresses." Then I recalled that someone had told me that a seamstress, if she is fast, could earn as much as 240 rubles a month. At the Nauka Publishing House, I was earning 280 rubles, bonuses included.

Now, what if I didn't sign? Even my youngest, fourteen-year-old Misha, was old enough to ask, "Aren't you friends with those people? There are lots of petitions going around. Why didn't you sign?" What would I say? That I valued 40 rubles a month, my job, and his future? If I said that, how would I be able to tell my sons that they should always act in accordance with their conscience? How would I teach them not to be cowards? Did I want them well fed or did I want them decent? Both would be nice, but there are times when a choice has to be made.

All of this may sound heroic and Zoya-like, but as I write this, I wonder if my sons would have ever challenged me had I decided to remain silent. And I wonder if I really had reasons to fear their challenge. It could well be that I manufactured their potential questions as justification for coming out in the open. I could no longer resist the urge to say what I thought. This way, whatever the consequences, I could say to myself that I was taking a stand for the sake of my sons.

The following morning, I signed a letter in which 118 people demanded to attend the upcoming trial of Galanskov and Ginzburg.

From that point on, letters became easier to sign. A month later, Alek Esenin-Volpin asked me if I would sign another petition demanding an open trial for Galanskov, Ginzburg, and the other defendants. I signed, then suggested: "Alek, tomorrow I am going to be in a *kompaniya* where everyone will be interested in signing. Why don't you let me take a copy?" Most people in that *kompaniya* had written letters in defense of Daniel and Sinyavsky two years earlier. It seemed certain that they would sign.

Later that evening, the cold, hesitant stares of the four couples around the table told me that my prediction was wrong. "Look at it this way, Lyuda," one of the guests said. "If you took a stand on every form of injustice in this country, where would you start and where would you stop? How would you choose?"

"We wrote letters in defense of Daniel and Sinyavsky because they are our friends," someone added. "We were defending our friends. That's all. Getting into this fight would mean getting into politics. We don't want to do that; we are private people."

I, too, was a private person. And I wasn't eager to get into politics. But defending samizdat was not politics. We were defending our liberty to choose what we read, our way of life. If anything, it was self-defense. But these people had made their choice: they decided to wait out this moral dilemma. I must have looked crushed.

As I was leaving, the host gave me a peck on the cheek and said, "Lyuda, this is a promise. If those sons of bitches ever arrest you, we will write a whole stack of letters. You know why? Because you are our friend."

The choices of the times were not as simple as principles versus career. For some, retaining the career was also a matter of principle. Yura and Marina Gerchuk, husband-and-wife specialists in Russian architecture, were involved in preserving historical and architectural monuments. They were also part of Daniel's *kompaniya*. After signing a letter in defense of Daniel, Yura was expelled from the Union of Artists. After that, the Gerchuks remained friends with Larisa and Yulik, but took no part in the petition campaign.

"These structures are falling apart. If we don't work to preserve them, who will?" Marina used to say.

✦

A couple of days before the start of the Galanskov-and-Ginzburg trial, I stopped by the judge's chambers and dropped off my formal request to attend the trial. "There will be a seat for you, don't worry," Judge L. K. Mironov assured me. "The trial is open."

Both of us knew he was lying.

✦

On January 8, 1968, about two hundred people gathered outside the Moscow City Court. It was even colder than during the Daniel-and-Sinyavsky trial.

We stood outside, watching the designated spectators come in and the witnesses come out. We saw Aida Topeshkina exit in tears. She had testified in behalf of her friend Galanskov, then refused to leave, saying that under Soviet law witnesses are obligated to remain in the courtroom for the duration of the day's session. Judge Mironov ordered her out of the courtroom, after which she was forcibly removed by the KGB to the heckling of the audience.

At the end of the fourth day, Pavel and Larisa seemed to be in a rush to get someplace. They tried to hail a taxi, but none would stop. Finally, Pavel approached the driver of one of the black Volgas that followed him everywhere.

"How about a ride?" Pavel asked.

"Against the rules," answered a startled operative.

"What if you lose us?"

"Don't worry. We won't."

Three hours later, when I turned on my shortwave radio, a voice from London read the "Bogoraz-Litvinov letter." The letter had a peculiar address: "To the World Public." It called for disqualification of Judge Mironov and release of the defendants pending a new trial that would be held in accordance with Soviet law and in the presence of international monitors.

"We are sending this appeal to the progressive Western press and request its prompt publication and broadcast over the radio," Larisa and Pavel wrote. "We are not approaching Soviet newspapers because that would be futile."

The following morning, a crowd of two hundred once again gathered outside the courthouse.

"What was the verdict?" someone asked as the spectators, some of them wearing KGB uniforms, began to file out.

"Not enough," said one. His aggravation made us repeat the question.

"What's the verdict?"

"Should've been more."

"What's the verdict?"

"Not enough! Not enough!"

Galanskov got seven years. Ginzburg got five. Lashkova got one. Dobrovolsky, who cooperated with the prosecutors, got two.

When the trial was over, one of the foreign reporters came up to Larisa and said in Russian, "Please tell me if there is anything I can do to help you."

"Thank you, but you have done enough," she said.

"No, I am asking if there is anything I can do for you personally."

"It's very kind of you, but everything is fine."

The reporter walked away. "Who is that?" I asked.

I knew that anything might happen to Larisa, and a foreign reporter offering assistance seemed like a godsend.

"Anatole Shub," she said.

"Whom is he with?"

"The *Washington Post,* the *New York Times,* something like that. I can't remember."

I remembered that name — thank God.

✦

On January 18, six days after the verdict came down, a colleague at the Nauka Publishing House told me to take a look at a *Komsomolskaya pravda* story about the trial. The first few paragraphs had the familiar feel of a libelous diatribe. Then I stumbled across the name of a French citizen who had received the manuscript of *The White Book:* Mikhail Slavinsky.

I sat back. My head slumped against the back of the couch. Time slipped by — an hour or a second; I don't know.

Father was in France. He had published the same book I was concealing in the upholstery of my overstuffed chair.

He must have been captured. He must have gone through the Nazi camps. He was living in a new country, wondering what had happened to Mother and me, yet not daring to contact us. Russia was still his interest, his obsession. He had his *Kolokol,* and I was part of it.

But what about Mother? She had remarried. Should I tell her what I know? Or should I contact him first? How would I do that?

The KGB interrogation . . . "What is your maiden name?" "Where is your father?" The investigator kept coming back to the same questions. Naturally, the KGB would know more than I. And what about their transcript of my conversation with Alik Ginzburg?

"Is it ready?"

"No, it's still drying."

"Have you gone crazy? She's got her bags packed."

The search at Nina Strokata's apartment in Odessa. What were they looking for? *The White Book?*

It's clear. Looking through the dossiers, they stumbled across Ludmilla Mikhailovna Alekseyeva, maiden name Slavinskaya. Ludmilla Slavinskaya. The daughter of Mikhail Slavinsky, the publisher of *The White Book.* Ludmilla knows Aleksandr Ginzburg. She must have been in contact with her father; she must have carried out his assignments; she must have asked Ginzburg to photograph the pages of *The White Book,* then sent the film to Odessa with Nina Strokata. Then Nina handed the rolls to a French sailor; the sailor brought them to Marseilles and forwarded them to Mikhail Slavinsky.

It was so elegant, so tempting in its simplicity. But how do you prove it? By scaring me into a confession.

Hence: "Ginzburg has told us everything. We know everything. All we expect you to do is confirm it."

How could I confess to something that didn't take place? I didn't even know my father was alive — if, indeed, he was alive.

That night, I saw him in a dream.

We meet. He hasn't aged. We talk. He is sad that he hasn't made an attempt to contact us. He could have tried, but that would have put us in danger. They would have accused us of being spies. His spies. I agree. He says he has a new family.

I wake up, but our dialogue goes on in half-slumber. I tell him about his grandsons. I tell him about my life, my views, my friends. I tell him about Larisa Bogoraz, Yulik Daniel, Pavel Litvinov, Tolya Marchenko. I tell him that I am trying to be what I thought he had been, a citizen. I speak quickly, without words. He nods with understanding.

I tell him that Mother doesn't know what's going on in my life.

She is not as emotional as he. She is correct. She is decent. As much as I love her, I cannot share my thoughts with her. She knows half of me, the half that is correct, the half without sin — her half. Again I speak without words; again he nods. Could he be dead?

What do we do now? I cannot visit him in France. They won't let me. He cannot visit me here. They won't let him. I must find his address. Then we can write to each other.

He appeared again the following night. We talked. I woke up. We kept talking.

◆

To get in touch with Father, I contacted a French student who was going to school in Moscow and dating the nephew of Slava Grabar. The woman had just returned from her Christmas vacation, and now I would have to wait till summer. Four months.

Meanwhile, I decided to say nothing to Mother. If I reached him, I would tell her immediately. If not, there would be no need to stir up old memories.

In June, I received a postcard from Paris: "I saw him. He is four years older than you."

The KGB was wrong. Father had nothing to do with *The White Book*; he never saw France. He had died in Myasnoy Bor after all.

I wondered how the KGB could have thought their suspicions credible enough to question me about my maiden name and even try to scare me into a confession. Of course, I was bitter about losing Father again. But mostly I was angry at the incompetents who had given me hope that he was alive. If I, a Soviet citizen, managed to check out a KGB hunch in less than six months, they should have been able to do it in a day. Instead, they kept building a conspiracy theory that eventually involved Aleksandr Ginzburg, the Ukrainians, foreign sailors, and Russian émigrés.

They were just as incompetent as every other Soviet bureaucracy. Granted, their bureaucrats were paid better than the rest of us; but that didn't mean they worked better. It just meant they drank more.

◆

In the third week of January, Boris Shragin, Natasha Sadomskaya's husband, had shown me a petition he had addressed to Roman Rudenko, the procurator general. The petition reiterated the demands set forth by Larisa and Pavel in their letter to "the World Public." I signed the letter and offered to take it to a few of my friends.

One of the first to see the letter was "R," a mathematician. "If you can omit the last line, I would be happy to sign," he said. "I could also have a few of my friends sign it."

The last paragraph informed Rudenko that if he failed to respond, the petitioners would appeal to "the world public." The change he suggested didn't strike me as significant. I asked Shragin if I could take it out, and he agreed.

R signed the letter. A couple of days later, he returned with the signatures of eight of his friends.

Next, I canvassed the Sybarites. Kolya Williams signed first. Then I went to see Slava Grabar and his wife, Lena Kopeleva. They signed, and our conversation went on as if nothing of significance had taken place.

Then I called Les Tanyuk, a theater director at Moscow's Central Children's Theater. Tanyuk, a Ukrainian, had been living a gypsy existence. Around 1960, in Kiev, he started a "club of creative intelligentsia." The club, organized by the local Komsomol, included the Ukraine's progressive writers, critics, and poets. It functioned just long enough for the Komsomol to realize that when Ukrainian patriots get together they recite poetry and discuss the true history of the Ukraine. The club was disbanded, and Tanyuk moved to Dnepropetrovsk. He took the director's job at a dying little theater and talked the local Komsomol into letting him start another "club of creative intelligentsia." There, too, the club was disbanded. He moved to Odessa, took a job at a dying little theater, started a club, and waited for history to take him up on the dare to repeat itself. It did.

After exhausting the supply of dying little theaters and gullible Komsomol bosses in the Ukraine, Tanyuk had moved to Moscow. "Let's meet tonight at ten-thirty at the park by the Bolshoi," he suggested when I contacted him.

As we sat on a bench under a streetlight, Tanyuk looked over the document as if skimming a familiar text. He signed the letter, and that was it. Of course, he knew that he would lose his job again; such things had been routine for Les Tanyuk.

The following evening, I went to see "X," a friend of Larisa's who had helped Tolya when he was writing *My Testimony* and had given books and money to the "Red Cross."

X read the letter with great care.

"I will not sign it," he said. "Furthermore, I would advise you to withdraw your signature."

"Why?"

"Because there is a major difference between doing something useful and acting like an idiot. Sending this letter is no different from going to the KGB and saying: 'Here we are. Here is where we work. Here are our addresses. Dispatch the Black Marias at your convenience.' These people get paid to find us. It's idiocy to do their work for them."

X was intelligent enough to anticipate my response: "How can you have *glasnost* without the KGB knowing?" But taking this argument further would have constituted proselytizing, which is an unacceptable practice in matters of conscience.

✦

On January 26, Larisa tromped in unannounced.

"Are you the one who crossed out the last line?"

"I suggested it."

"You had no right to change the author's text!"

"I checked with the author first."

"Why did you cut it?"

"R said he could get more signatures this way."

"What about the people who had signed the letter with the last line? How do you know they would have signed without it?"

"As I said, R's friends wouldn't sign it with the last line."

"So who needs them!"

She slammed the door, and for at least two days we turned into ideological opponents.

✦

On February 14, a month after the Galanskov-and-Ginzburg trial, the militia, accompanied by a psychiatrist, entered the apartment of Alek Esenin-Volpin.

When Alek was ordered to come along, he said simply, "*Ne poydu*" — "I won't go" — leaving it up to the militia to carry him out of the apartment. He did not kick them or fight back. The law was being broken by the authorities charged to uphold it, and Alek was not about to become an accessory. He simply went limp and allowed himself to be carried out. At first, he was placed in a psychiatric institution for the chronically ill and criminally insane.

In a matter of hours, hundreds of Alek's friends were repeating his words: "*Ne poydu.*" A petition demanding his release was signed by ninety-nine mathematicians; two members of the Academy of Sciences appealed to the minister of health; and in a matter of days, Alek was transferred to a less notorious institution. He was released on May 12, after three months of confinement.

The petition campaign did not help Galanskov and Ginzburg, but it had helped Alek: at least in his case, the authorities had backed down under pressure from the public.

Eight

I was a little surprised to receive a summons to appear before the Party Committee of the Bauman Region of Moscow.

I called Natasha Sadomskaya.

"Borya got a summons, too," she said.

I liked that even less. I scanned over the events in my recent past that could make me vulnerable to party sanctions. Could they have found out about my role in the typing of *My Testimony*? Could it have anything to do with the "Red Cross"?

The next day, Boris Shragin went to his regional committee, and I went to mine. At the committee offices, I ran into Moisei Tulchinsky, Natasha's first husband and a colleague of mine at the Nauka Publishing House. The plight of the Jewish people had imprinted itself on Moisei's long face. Now, sitting in the antechamber of the Party Committee of the Bauman Region, he looked his saddest.

Tulchinsky didn't even know about *My Testimony,* so why were we called in together?

I was called in first.

A green felt cloth covered a long table. A jug of water stood in its center. A dozen of them sat around the table.

"Ludmilla Mikhailovna, please tell us what you have been doing in the past three years."

"Working as an editor at the Nauka Publishing House."

"And what have you been doing outside work?"

"Being a mother."

"What else?"

"I like to read books."

"What else have you been doing?"

"Nothing."

"Please tell us, have you signed any letters?"

"What kind of letters?"

"Like the letter to the procurator general."

I had signed that letter as "L. Alexeyeva, editor." There are many L. Alexeyevas in the USSR. Some of those L. Alexeyevas are named Ludmilla. Others are named Lydia, Larisa, Lubov, Leokadia, Lukerya. Some Elenas abbreviate their names as "L.," for Lena, and some Elizavetas like to be called Liza. There is also a chance of encountering a Luiza or even a Lenina, a name that means "she-Lenin." No doubt, many of those women are employed as "editors," which means they edit newspapers, poetry, prose, scholarly papers, scientific data, or film.

By their faces, I could see that they thought they were questioning the wrong L. Alexeyeva. They had to have looked over my files. They knew I was the daughter of two party members, one of whom died in the war. Mine was the biography of an upstanding Soviet citizen. Surely, it had to be someone else.

I could have lied. I could have told them they had the wrong "L.," the wrong "Alexeyeva," and the wrong "editor." Instead, I said, "Yes, I signed it."

"Why did you sign it?"

As officials of the regional committee, they were responsible for the "moral-political education" of every Communist in the Bauman District of the City of Moscow, and since one of those Communists had gone bad, there would be reports to file and authorities to notify.

"I agreed with everything contained in the letter, so I signed it."

"What was it that made you think that the letter was factually correct? Didn't you read the newspapers that stated plainly that Galanskov, Ginzburg, and the other defendants were, in fact, lackeys of foreign intelligence services?"

"What the press published was simply untrue. Just as in the Daniel-and-Sinyavsky trial, evidence was either suppressed or falsified."

"Did you sign any other letters?"

"Yes. I signed three."

"Who was the author of the letter to Procurator General Rudenko?"

"I don't know."

"How could you sign a letter whose author you didn't know?"

"Easily. I agreed with every word, so I didn't care who wrote it."

"Who brought you the letter to sign?"

"I don't want to answer that question because that would be indecent."

"What's more important to you, your relationship with the person who brought you the letter or your relationship with the Communist party of the Soviet Union? Have you forgotten that you are a Communist?"

"Not at all. But I have always thought that a Communist should first and foremost be a person of conscience and high moral standards. And it is a matter of decency not to inform on others."

I talked, looking at the green felt, trying to concentrate on every word, paying no attention to them, as if I were reciting a monologue.

I was alone among the enemy. I knew that I stood to lose everything I had accomplished in my forty years. It was a Zoya situation, except I no longer wanted to be like Zoya. Now I had another role model: Larisa Bogoraz. I thought of her cool self-control at the KGB interrogation in the case of Daniel and Sinyavsky. A few months earlier, before signing the petitions, I would have fallen short of my new role model. But I had made my choices, and now it was just a matter of following through, even if that meant becoming a seamstress at the Bolshevichka sewing factory.

As I listened to my own answers, I realized that I was not playing Larisa. I was being myself. It wasn't Larisa, it was I who was delighting in the opportunity to tell them that I would not wag my tail in their presence, that from now on I would not defer to them to tell me what's right, that from now on my soul would be my own and that nothing they could do would hurt me.

I knew that after standing up to them I would not be able to bow my head to the collective again. And I was not alone. As other *podpisanty* were being dragged to personnel offices and their regional committees, *glasnost* was taking its next step. It was spilling out of *kompanii* and into the offices of party officials.

It was not just an emotional outburst that made us tell them what we thought. It was the subconscious realization that real change would come only through them. Political power was in their hands, and it would have taken a revolution for us to take their place. We were too disillusioned with the results of the past revolution even to contemplate another one. So, instead of taking arms or organizing underground cells, we were inviting the authorities to start a dialogue with us. To initiate that dialogue, we had to announce who we were and what we wanted.

At the end of my discourse on conscience and decency, I looked up at the inquisitors. I saw a sea of green felt and over it a dozen faces ranging in color from raspberry to fuchsia. It seemed every other one of them was about to have a stroke.

They said I was free to leave.

✦

While I was inside, another millennium of plight had imprinted itself on Moisei's face.

"Mos'ka," I said, "they are asking about the letter. They want to know who wrote it." We had a couple of minutes to talk while the inquisitors were sipping water and taking valerian drops.

Moisei didn't want to get expelled from the party. He didn't want to be fired. He didn't have the luxury of saying it was another Moisei Tulchinsky who had signed the letter. Nor did he want to say that Boris Shragin, the second husband of his former wife, was the man who had written the letter. It was a sad situation all around.

"I'll just tell them I wrote it," he said.

I could picture it: Mos'ka confessing, sadly, very sadly. "I did it." It would make it difficult to keep asking to name the real author. The adversary would be disoriented.

✦

That evening, Boris Shragin told me that two of his closest friends, Yuri Davydov and Piama Gaidenko, a husband and wife, had recanted their signatures. To keep their jobs, they concocted a story about Shragin coming to their apartment late one night and pressuring them to sign some letter he had written. Since they trusted Shragin, they signed the letter without analyzing its content.

Now Davydov and Gaidenko argued that they were not responsible for their actions because they were sleepy. It was all the fault of Boris Shragin, the author of the letter to the procurator general. Absurd as their explanation sounded, the two were forgiven. They had done precisely what the authorities wanted: they had repented and they betrayed a friend.

Just fifteen years earlier, with or without repentance, people like Davydov and Gaidenko would have found themselves in the camps of Magadan. But the times had changed, and as much as the Brezhnev circle longed for the law and order of Stalinism, it lacked the historical opportunity to resort to mass terror. Even in the midst of the political turmoil of 1968, Moscow intellectuals could not vanish in the middle of the night. In Brezhnev's Russia, the authorities were obligated to do the paperwork, produce a semblance of a legal cause for arrest, and stage something that had the appearance of a fair trial.

Political trials, especially those held in Moscow, triggered considerable public outcry. Each wave of repression had created an increasing number of disenfranchised intellectuals, people who had lost their jobs and social status and who now made it their life's work to protest political persecution and demand *glasnost*. These people weren't great in number — a few dozen activists and about a thousand vocal supporters. But in Russia, the land of the Decembrists, it didn't take many people to bring about social transformation.

We would have kept up our work even if we were completely ineffective; however, we were remarkably effective. While our own authorities ignored our calls to dialogue and reform, the West wanted to know all about us. As a result, our struggle received sustained, detailed coverage from Western reporters.

Over the next fifteen years, political arrests and political trials in Moscow, Leningrad, Vilnius, and Kiev received coverage by virtually every Western news organization in the Soviet Union. Those dispatches were then broadcast back into the USSR over the Voice of America, Radio Liberty, the BBC, the Deutsche Welle, and other shortwave radio stations. Their listeners in the USSR numbered in the tens of millions.

Thanks to those broadcasts, thousands of wronged and disaffected people nationwide learned that a loosely knit network of Muscovites had systematic access to foreign journalists and shortwave radio stations. The Ukrainians, Lithuanians, Latvians, Armenians, Crimean Tatars, Meskhetians, Volga Germans, Jews, Baptists, Adventists, and Pentecostals learned that it was possible to use our Moscow samizdat and our Western-press connections to bring *glasnost* to their struggles.

✦

Following the canons of party discipline, the case of Ludmilla Alexeyeva and Moisei Tulchinsky was forwarded to the party bureau of the Nauka Publishing House.

That was bad news for Nauka. Just a month earlier, Mikhail Samsonov, head of the publishing house, and Yevgeny Eskov, the party organizer, had been called to the Central Committee and chastised for publishing a history of the first days of the Great Patriotic War. The book, called *1941,* by Aleksandr Nekrich, said that Stalin ignored repeated warnings and failed to prepare for war with Germany, making it possible for the Nazis to advance toward Moscow and nearly crush the Red Army during the first months of the war.

The first printing of the book virtually evaporated from stores. As a Nauka employee, I was able to get my hands on two copies. If given a chance, I would have bought a crateful.

Nekrich's *1941* would have been a great success — if it hadn't scared its editor. Afraid of being called an accomplice to publication of a revisionist tract, the editor "alerted" the head of her department but was ordered to keep working on the book. Then she alerted Samsonov, with the same results. As she was going up through the channels, the book was getting closer to publication. It was in stores by the time her complaints reached the Central Committee.

The Central Committee, however, determined that continued distribution of *1941* did not serve the interests of the party. The book was taken out of stores and destroyed, and the Nauka top officials, Samsonov and Eskov, were given a "strict reprimand with a warning about expulsion," the highest sanction short of being thrown out of the party. They escaped stiffer penalties by agreeing to admit their "political mistake" at a public gathering.

That admission was made at a Nauka party meeting. I sat in the back of the room, playing tic-tac-toe while watching two serious scholars admit to political errors. As historians and *frontoviki,* they knew that Nekrich was right about 1941; as Communists, they had to feign being sorry.

Now Eskov and Samsonov had to sit at a green felt-covered conference table, presiding over the special meeting of the party bureau called to consider the misdeeds of Moisei Tulchinsky and Ludmilla Alexeyeva.

I was seated at the center of the table, directly across from Samsonov. I was ordered to open up before the party and name the author of the letter to the procurator general. This was repeated several times. Each time I declined, Samsonov let out a deep sigh or gave me a quick look of sympathy and warning. With all the might of his body language, he was trying to tell me to change my strategy, to compromise, or, at the very least, to show regret.

"Lyuda, I don't think you understand the situation," Eskov whispered to me in the hallway during a recess. "The question being decided is whether you stay in the party. Why don't you think of ways to help yourself? Otherwise, you will be expelled." I thanked him and said I would give the matter some thought.

Eskov and I had known each other since the university. He had sat on the Komsomol committee that considered the case of Stella Dvorkis, and he was there serving on the presidium at the meeting where I was reprimanded for singing about an Australian pioneer and reciting the frivolous poetry of Anna Akhmatova.

When the meeting resumed, I was offered a compromise: I would say merely that I regretted that the letter had been read by foreign radio stations and thus had hurt the prestige of our country.

I couldn't say that, either. "That would be confusing cause and effect," I said. "The cause is the unlawful trial of four citizens. If not for that, there would have been no letters for foreign radio stations to broadcast, and our country's much-valued prestige would still be intact. If this lawlessness is corrected and Ginzburg and others are released, I would write another letter to repair the damaged international prestige of the Union of Soviet Socialist Republics. But the initiative has to come from the judicial organs."

Moisei Tulchinsky was next.

SAMSONOV: Did you sign the letter to Roman Rudenko?
TULCHINSKY: Yes, I did.
SAMSONOV: Who was the author of that letter?
TULCHINSKY: I was.
SAMSONOV: We know you aren't telling the truth.
TULCHINSKY: No, I am telling the truth. I wrote it.

Later, the Moscow rumor mill spewed out a story that explained why I had been expelled from the party while Tulchinsky got off with a reprimand. According to that story, Tulchinsky had confessed and repented at a closed-door party meeting.

Tulchinsky neither confessed nor repented. He just looked sad, and that turned out to be sufficient grounds for Samsonov, Eskov, and the rest of the party bureau of the Nauka Publishing House to treat him with lenience.

✦

A couple of days after the meeting, Samsonov sent down word that he wanted to see me.

He came out to greet me in his reception room. "If anyone calls, take messages," he said to his secretary as he led me in and closed the door.

"You do know that I am very disappointed with your conduct at the party bureau," he said. "There was a way to prevent your expulsion from the party, but you made no attempt to stay in. Now there is no hope of keeping you in your job. I see you have been a model employee. You get bonuses regularly. I see you are divorced and have two children. It makes me very sad. I have invited you here because I would like to hear your reasons for making no attempt to stay in the party. Do you like your job?"

"Yes."

"So why didn't you try to keep it?"

"Because that would have meant going against my conscience."

He pondered that for a moment. Then he turned to the subject he must have considered many times: "Naturally, you know that I was in a very difficult situation because of the Nekrich book. But I am not sorry that I acted the way I did. I am not sorry I repented. I suppose you could say that it was because I have a good job, a big office, a secretary, a car with a chauffeur, and enough money not to worry about spending an evening in an expensive restaurant. I guess you might say that I went against my conscience to preserve these privileges. I can't deny it, that was part of it. But there were other reasons. What would have happened if I had walked out and slammed the door, just as you are doing? We can see what we would forgo. Jobs, privileges. But what would we gain? What if all the people who want to tell the truth, all the people with a social conscience, walk out and slam the doors behind them? Can you tell me what we would accomplish?"

"I can only tell you what I have accomplished. I have a clear conscience. It's nice to have a car, a chauffeur, a secretary, a big office. These are great comforts. I have some great comforts, too. I am well paid, and I am able to work at home. That's why I will be sorry to lose this job. But there is also the comfort of being able to say to yourself: 'I am a decent person and I do not take part in indecent games. I behave in accordance with my concept of what is right.' "

"Ludmilla Mikhailovna, you and I work for a publishing house. For us, the concepts of free speech, the historical truth, and freedom to publish are of primary importance. But the majority of people in our country are concerned about other problems. They are engaged in a struggle for survival. They are concerned about finding food and being able to buy shoes for their children. They are not concerned about the pursuit of historical truth and freedom to publish. These are our intelligentsia excesses. Now, if you had been given a chance to face the workers at the Likhachev Automobile Plant, I don't think they would have supported you. I don't think they would have understood you. Don't you agree?"

"Absolutely. I am certain that I would not be a great success at a meeting at the Likhachev auto plant. But you and I aren't auto workers. We are historians, and as historians we know that the majority isn't always right and that until our country becomes democratic, there will not be enough food and enough boots for the children."

Samsonov did not relish putting his signature on the resolution to fire me. He wanted me to understand that.

"Tell me something else. Why do you, personally, need freedom of expression? What do you want to say?"

"Nothing. I just want to hear what intelligent people want to say."

"I am afraid there is just one thing I can do for you," said Samsonov. "If you submit a resignation and leave quickly, your work record will not reflect that you have been fired."

"What would that accomplish?"

"It would be easier for you to find another job."

It was a good-hearted offer. By accepting it, I would have made it look as though nothing had happened: there were no unjust trials, no protests, no petitions, no battles at the regional committee of the party or the Nauka party bureau. I couldn't accept. Nor could I expect Samsonov to understand that I was not posturing. He had reason to be irritated. I was denying him the opportunity to do something decent for me, to help me, to ease his own conscience. He and I were in the same situation: we were fighting for our souls.

"No, it's better if you go ahead and fire me," I said. "I don't want to leave my job and you have no legal grounds for firing me. And when you do fire me, I will sue the publishing house, and the publishing house will have to stand before a judge and argue that I was the wrong person for the job."

"You do understand that you would lose that suit."

"I do."

"So why do it?"

"A few of us decided that we would sue, so we would not stand still while they shoot us. The firing would be illegal, and the trial would make it obvious."

"How will you live? You have two children to feed."

"If it comes to it, I will take a job as a seamstress. The Bolshevichka Clothing Factory pays 240 rubles a month."

"I hope it doesn't come to that."

"We'll see. There are worse things in life."

✦

Kolya Williams and I had been dating for about a year, and he had heard all of my pronouncements on the institution of marriage: that it was a no-win lottery; that I knew of no marriages I wanted for myself; that children are the only reward of marriage and, since I had two sons, I'd done my part. Williams had been married twice, both times unhappily. He took great comfort in knowing that I had no intentions of making permanent, legal claims on his persona or his famous name.

Now I was in danger. There was no way to tell how long it would take me to find another job, and as an unemployed, divorced woman, I was open to prosecution under antiparasitism statutes. This made Williams propose.

It was the least romantic proposal imaginable: "Look, if we get married, you can tell them that I support you, and they can go to hell. You need that paper saying that you are married. We don't have to live in the same apartment. We would not have to have joint finances, and you would not have to change your name. Everything will stay the same between us. That little piece of paper will be for them, not for us."

That was a nice offer, something you would expect from a friend. In March of 1968, we went to the Office of Registration of Deeds and Conditions of Citizens (those conditions include birth, death, marriage, and divorce) and filed an application for a marriage license. Since such applications take a month to process, the "marriage registration" was set for April 19.

There would be no flowers, no reception, no band. We would just return to my apartment and toast the occasion. It would be an early evening. The procedure required two witnesses, so I invited Natasha Sadomskaya and Kolya invited Slava Grabar.

On April 18, I mentioned to Larisa Bogoraz that Kolya Williams and I were going to register as a married couple.

"When is the wedding?"

"What wedding? We are just inviting two witnesses. It's all a formality."

"When is the registration?"

"At five tomorrow."

At four-thirty the following day, Larisa and Tolya Marchenko showed up with a big bouquet of lilac. I told them they were crazy. Then the two prearranged witnesses showed up. We got on a bus that took us to the Office of Registration of Deeds and Conditions of Citizens. Through the rear window of the bus, we watched two dark-colored Volgas that were following Lara and Tolya.

The registration was completed, the papers were stamped and signed. Lara and Tolya left, and the invited witnesses came back to the apartment. Slava reached into his coat pocket and pulled out a bottle of vodka.

I went to the kitchen to cook dinner. The doorbell rang. It was Ada Nikolskaya. With flowers. The bell rang again. It was Kolya's mother. "I know there is no reception. I just stopped by to congratulate you."

They drank while I cooked. Ada and Natasha helped themselves to the linen cabinet, pulled out white lace bedspreads, and threw them over their heads. When I walked out of the kitchen, they were dancing. One of them attempted to throw a veil on me as well. I told them to stop it and escaped into the kitchen.

A few minutes later, Grabar ran into the kitchen, red-faced and sweaty. It looked as though he had been dancing and drinking. "Just ran into some great girls!" he announced.

He had known those great girls for a decade.

◆

The following morning, a phone call from the Bauman regional committee notified me that pursuant to a vote of the party organization of the Nauka Publishing House, I had been expelled from the Communist party of the Soviet Union.

According to procedural guidelines, it is the local party meeting, not the regional committee or the party bureau, that has the final authority to expel a party member. It's a dramatic procedure: the party member is ordered to put his identification card on the table, after which his fellow Communists decide about whether he should be allowed to reclaim it. If the party member in question is not present at the meeting, he cannot be expelled.

I didn't want to go to that meeting. Samsonov and Eskov, too, didn't want to see the unrepentant Alexeyeva address the full audience of her fellow Communists. The decision to expel me was made in my absence, which made it invalid.

"I am calling you from the regional committee," said the voice on the phone. "We would like you to return your party identification."

"Why should I?"

"Because you have been expelled."

"But if I have been expelled, why do I still have my party identification?"

"Because you have not turned it in."

"I didn't turn it in because I was not present at the meeting where I was expelled, which means my expulsion was invalid, which means I am entitled to hold my party identification."

"In that case, you are being ordered as a party member to come to the regional committee and turn in your party identification."

"But I no longer have to take orders from the party. You've expelled me."

"Under what conditions would you be willing to turn in your party identification?"

"You could send your Leonid Ilych Brezhnev to fetch it for you."

The phone went dead.

✦

I was fired on April 23, 1968. The reason: "not answering the demands of the position" — incompetence. On the last day of the month, Kolya said: "I know our marriage is just a formality, but I am here a lot. I eat here. So why don't I let you have my salary this month." He kept about twenty rubles for pocket expenses.

In the first week of May, Kolya was called in by his supervisor, Sergei Ivanovich Strizhenov, head of the mathematics department at the Institute of Light Chemical Technology.

"Nikolai Nikolayevich, I am afraid I have bad news. I understand you have signed something."

"I have."

"That's bad. Very, very bad. You know, just about everyone on our faculty is Jewish. You and I are among the few Russians."

"I don't see how the Jewish people have anything to do with it." Then Kolya explained that Galanskov and Ginzburg were guilty of no crimes, and that he had signed the letter out of solidarity with his friends. It was in no way a political statement.

Kolya was not in the party, so it seemed there was a chance that he would get off with a reprimand. The mathematics department considered the case without anyone calling for his dismissal.

The meeting of the entire faculty was next. "People with such views should not be allowed to teach; we don't want another Poland," said the institute's party organizer, referring to the 1956 student uprising in Poland.

Then one of the professors raised a question: "I understand there was a letter from ninety-nine mathematicians protesting the decision to commit Aleksandr Esenin-Volpin to a psychiatric institution. Did you sign that letter as well?"

Naturally, Kolya Williams had signed that petition.

"Why did you sign it?"

"I signed it because he is my friend." It was all over.

"Why, it seems all your friends are ideologically unreliable."

"I don't know, I guess it just happened that way."

♦

A group of students was waiting outside the auditorium where the meeting was held. Kolya came out and told them that he had been fired. Then they all headed off to some dive.

Meanwhile, I waited for Kolya's call. He was to have been back at two, no later. At three, I became worried.

Kolya should not have been fired; and if he had been, it had to have happened because of me, I concluded. Kolya's dissertation was nearly completed. Parts of it had been published in a scholarly journal. If he'd lost his job, he would not be able to defend his thesis. His career would have suffered an enormous setback — all because he was stupid enough to propose and I was selfish enough to accept.

At five, I realized that I could no longer stay in the apartment berating myself. I went out and walked along Leningradsky Prospekt, looking in store windows. I hadn't even noticed that some of these stores existed; I was always in too much of a hurry, rushing from the bus stop to the apartment and back. There was never a chance for a leisurely stroll.

I stopped to inspect a pair of black boots from France that were on display. They had low heels, they were lined with fur, they looked well made and comfortable; but they cost 120 rubles, which would have been almost half of my monthly salary — back when I had a monthly salary.

"I need winter boots," I thought. It was late May. "If I walk in and they have my size, I will buy them." They had my size, and I bought them.

Kolya came home around eleven that night. The following morning, after he sobered up, we assessed our situation: he was living in my apartment, he had turned over his salary, and our friends had begun treating us as a married couple.

Was it possible that we were indeed married?

Nine

Now all of us, the thousand *podpisanty*, were in a precarious situation. Would we become paragons or pariahs? Twelve years after the Twentieth Congress, was Soviet society ready to understand what we were trying to accomplish? What would happen to those of us who had chosen to walk away from their careers? Could such people survive outside the collective? Would society turn away from *podpisanty* or would it find ways to support them? Was it ready to disobey the government?

It was obvious that we were neither extremists nor political renegades. Our views were typical of the entire intelligentsia. The novelty of our action lay in the fact that we chose to defend our right to get up and walk away from the collective.

We broke the code: we disobeyed, and our disobedience cost us the privileges that came with membership in the collective. Now we were learning just how difficult it was to survive on our own. Yes, many of those who chose to remain silent were in agreement with what we had said. But would those people think of us as their vanguard? Would they help us survive? Or would they turn away, leaving us in our new helplessness?

In those days, Moscow buzzed with stories about *podpisanty*; reputations were created and destroyed. Since most *podpisanty* had to face party bureaus and public meetings, there were several sources for every story. Everything was public and verifiable.

Late in the spring of 1968, Larisa asked me to phone her friend Lev Kopelev, a writer and editor, former *politzek*, and, most recently, a *podpisant*. I had seen Kopelev at the birthday parties of his daughter, Lena, who was married to the Sybarite Slava Grabar. Though we were in the same crowd, we had never been formally introduced.

"Lev Zinovyevich, Larisa asked me to relay a message to you," I said.

"Who is this?" Kopelev asked.

"You don't know me," I said.

"Still, I'd like to know."

"My name is Ludmilla Alexeyeva."

"Oh, Lyuda. Of course I know you. You were having all those problems at the Nauka Publishing House. How did it end? And how is Kolya Williams? Has he found another job?"

✦

The four couples around the table seemed tense; I thought it was because Kolya Williams and I were late. We drank a couple of toasts and exchanged some jokes, some gossip, a few pleasantries. The tension lingered.

"How are things?" someone asked me.

"Funny you should ask," I answered. Some stories beg to be told with a Yiddish accent. "Vell, Kolya, too, has been thrown out of his job, can you believe such a thing?"

Silence. They had something to say, all of them. But none dared say it first. Finally someone managed: "What did you expect when you signed that letter?"

It was a *kompaniya* Kolya had been part of for decades. I, too, had known those people, as Kolya's girlfriend. Now I could tell that they had been discussing us before we walked in. It was as if I had heard them talk: Lyudka's a good woman, but nutty. She keeps drifting into politics. Now our Kolya's got himself married to her and he's got problems. That's too bad.

"We expected that matters of employment would be decided on merit rather than on ideological reliability," I said. Kolya said nothing.

"Have you forgotten where you live? If you like being such a hero, don't go around complaining about being fired or about your husband being fired."

What they really meant to say was: "You self-centered lunatic, you've ruined our friend's life."

"What we did had nothing to do with politics," I said.

"So what do you call your samizdat?" *Your* samizdat, as if they had forgotten about all the books they had borrowed from me.

"What do you mean, *my* samizdat? Don't *you* enjoy it?"

"It doesn't reach us." Now they were angry at me for hogging samizdat, too.

"You know where to find it. I didn't expect such a reaction here. At the party committee it was no surprise, but I didn't expect my friends discussing Kolya's and my problems in such a tone."

"It's precisely because we are your friends that we can tell you what we think. We are concerned about you dragging Kolya into all that."

I got up. "Kolya, you are welcome to stay if you want. I can't see how I would be able to sing and dance here after this conversation."

Kolya left with me. A couple of days later, I asked him to call back and reconcile, but many years passed before I returned to that *kompaniya*.

◆

"Payday is coming, but Kolya and I won't get paid," I lamented to Ada Nikolskaya.

"Why are you whining?" Ada said sharply. "You knew what you were doing."

I knew that if we began to starve, Ada would be the first person to offer ten rubles and a kilo of sausage. I was Ada's friend. In the previous couple of weeks, I had become her hero, and heroes, as everyone knows, don't whine. They say: "Everything is under control. We shall prevail."

That was a valuable lesson. I have not whined since.

◆

By late spring, the pattern of repression against *podpisanty* became clear. There was no doubt that the whole operation was being coordinated by the party rather than by the KGB. Naturally, the party began with its rank and file. Those who named names were left alone. Those who didn't name names but expressed regret or at least looked as if they were sorry got "strict reprimands," but stayed in the party and in their jobs. The unrepentant were expelled, fired, and blacklisted. It took years for most of us to find other work.

There was a certain logic to these sanctions: by joining the party, we had made contractual obligations. Now, in the view of party leaders, we had reneged.

After the rank and file, the party went after students, school-teachers, and professors. Teachers and professors were not black-listed. They were allowed to find jobs outside education. I took some solace in the fact that all of them lost their jobs: it meant that Kolya's firing had nothing to do with our marriage.

Kolya's new job, at a computer center, paid half his old salary. His marriage proposal had been quite timely. A few months after I was fired, I was officially asked to provide proof of earning an income. "I am supported by my lawful husband," I said.

Sybarites Slava Grabar and Yura Gastev also lost their jobs. Gastev never found another permanent position. Slava, a born teacher, had to take a research job at the Academy of Pedagogical Sciences. But his wife, a proofreader, was never even called in to personnel about her signature on the letter to the procurator general. Apparently, her position was not deemed important enough for anyone to care about her citizen valor.

Theater director Les Tanyuk was fired from the Children's Theater, but quickly found another directing job. *Podpisant* Leonid Pazhitnov, a philosopher colleague of Boris Shragin's at the Institute of Art History, was asked by the institute's party chief to sign a prepared statement of regret. "Tell you what," Pazhitnov told him. "I am not going to sign it. If I sign, I'll lose the respect of my friends, and you aren't going to like me anyway. So I'll stay with my friends and we'll see whose side comes out ahead." He ended up writing movie scripts.

Sasha Morozov, a literature scholar who had helped compile the samizdat anthology of Osip Mandelshtam, ended up learning to drive a truck. To my knowledge, he was the only *podpisant* to resort to manual labor.

✦

The story of Moisei Tulchinsky keeping his job because he looked sad inspired Natasha Sadomskaya to practice sadness in front of a mirror. "Look, girls! How's this?" she said, demonstrating the look to a *kompaniya*. "When they ask me questions, I'll do this." Since her husband, Boris Shragin, had been fired, the feigned sadness was all that stood between her and poverty. Fortunately, Natasha's acting ability was sufficient to satisfy her boss, Yuli Bramley, a classmate of ours from the university.

There was an abundance of stories about sympathetic bosses and party bureaus. Some administrators tried to limit sanctions to "strict reprimands," which allowed them to avoid firing their employees. Others attempted to get by with sharply worded speeches or simple shouting. Some of those sessions had strong overtones of comedy.

"Have you gone crazy, girls? Signing that letter to the procurator general!" yelled Timur Timofeyev, formerly Tim Ryan, as he was working over Veta Faleyeva and Marina Feigina (formerly Rosenzweig), my close friends at the university and his subordinates at the Institute of the International Labor Movement. "Did you know that same letter was signed by Ludmilla Alexeyeva? Do you know who she is? She runs a political salon for foreigners! Did you know that there were two black foreign limousines in her wedding procession?"

Moscow stories improve with repetition. Someone had said that two KGB cars followed Larisa and Tolya to our wedding. Someone else made the cars "black." Then someone changed the black cars from a domestic make to foreign. Then the black, foreign cars turned into black, foreign limousines. Then the person whose wedding included the ominous cortege of black, foreign limousines became the hostess of a diplomatic salon.

"Timur, we aren't the crazy ones," said one of the girls. "Do *you* know who Ludmilla Alexeyeva is? That's Lyudka Slavinskaya."

Tim regained control, told Marina and Veta that they were free to go, filed an appropriate report, and that was the end of it.

✦

In those adrenalin-filled months, news traveled faster than political jokes; news about Pavel Litvinov, the author of the transcript of the Bukovsky and Khaustov trials and the coauthor of the Bogoraz-Litvinov letter, traveled faster than any other news.

"How is Pavel?" someone asked Tatyana Litvinova, his aunt.

"I don't know. My shortwave radio isn't working too well," she said.

Pavel's fame had begun to rival that of his grandfather. Hence, the remark by Mikhail Maximovich Litvinov, Pavel's father: "I am used to being known as the son of a famous father. Now I am getting used to being known as the father of a famous son."

✦

Lida, my friend from graduate school, tried to keep in touch, but that was becoming increasingly difficult. She and her husband were on the way up; I was on the way out. Without actually saying it, she made it clear that she didn't want me to talk to her about my other friends, political trials, and political prisoners. Her views weren't different from mine. She just couldn't afford to act on them.

After I lost my job, Lida found typing for me to do and made an attempt to keep me in her social circle. One evening in the summer of 1968, Lida and her husband were entertaining two Hungarians. They were "kosher" Hungarians, probably Communists. I did my best to keep from saying anything that would embarrass my hosts. That meant concentrating on small talk, which was dutifully translated by Lida's husband.

When the subject drifted onto political matters, the Hungarians were careful, too. "Your government behaved quite wisely," one of them said about the course of the Communist party of the Soviet Union in agriculture, foreign affairs, or whatever. There was no way to tell if the word "wisely" was being used in jest.

"So you think they have it in them to behave wisely?" I said. It was a faux pas. The remark didn't get translated. When Lida and I went into the kitchen to fetch dessert, she whispered, "Lyuda, please watch what you say. They understand a little Russian."

Lida remained my friend. She kept an eye out for free-lance writing, editing, and typing jobs. She called regularly, and every now and then we met at some restaurant for lunch. But I was never invited back to her house.

✦

Lyonya Ziman called to offer me a free-lance job typing mathematics problems for extension students at a Moscow institute. "The pay is dismal, but the amount of work is unlimited," he said.

Not only did he make the effort to find me a typing job, he also went out of his way to find my telephone number. Ziman and I had met only once, outside the courthouse during the Galanskov-and-Ginzburg trial.

Soon after Kolya reported to work at the computer center, his boss, Igor Ovsyannikov, made a valiant effort to hire me as an English translator. I spoke no English, but Kolya assured me that since the computer was always down, he would be able to do the translations for me during work hours.

Unfortunately, someone up high, probably the KGB, blocked my hiring. I called Ovsyannikov with a suggestion that he hire Vadim Meniker, the economist who had monitored foreign newspapers for us; he had been unemployed for over two years, ever since writing a letter in defense of Daniel and Sinyavsky. That hire went through.

Sometime in the fall of 1968, Vladimir Matlin, a writer Kolya and I had never met, called to ask Kolya to consult on a documentary about some mathematician. Matlin didn't know much about mathematics, and "consulting" would entail Kolya and me coming to Matlin's apartment, reading a short script, staying for dinner, and getting paid the equivalent of a month's salary. Kolya picked a date, the session went well, and a little later Matlin called to arrange another consultation.

"We have to warn him," I said to Kolya on the way to Matlin's apartment. "He could be getting himself in trouble." It's one thing when people choose to take risks. It's something else when they act without knowing about the danger. Kolya agreed.

After the work was done — I think it took all of fifteen minutes — I started to deliver my warning: "We have to tell you something —"

"No, you don't," Matlin interrupted.

"I really think you should know —"

"No, no, I shouldn't."

✦

There were others who didn't want to know, among them an Azerbaijani party official who asked me to help him write a doctoral dissertation on national problems in Azerbaijan. He never told me where he got my name or how he knew that I might be available to help him. Nor did he ask where I worked. I suspect that he knew everything.

His dissertation was quite enlightened: national identity is not necessarily a bad thing, and since the party strives to encourage "friendship of all ethnic groups," it should not portray the Russians as "the elder brother" of other ethnics. The dissertation was classified, but the party official did not have native command of Russian and needed someone to edit his work and help him invoke enough quotes from Marx, Engels, and Lenin to give the work a noncontroversial appearance.

Ghostwriting in Russian is called "Negro" work. The allusion is derived from Negro slaves toiling anonymously for the master. Besides the dissertation, my "Negro" jobs included a scholarly paper on wood carving in the Vologda region in the Russian North and a report for a designer who was trying to bring elements of folk costumes into modern clothing.

✦

Even "Y," my boyfriend from the last year of school, came up with a job offer. Y had graduated from the Military Institute of Foreign Languages, a place that trained military translators as well as spies. He studied French.

Sometime back in 1952, he called to invite me to dinner. "Can you line up a girl for our dinner companion?" he asked. It was an odd request, but I obliged.

The dinner companion Y had mentioned was a Cambodian who spoke no Russian. It was an expensive dinner, and after we finished dessert, Y picked up the check.

"Why did you spend so much money?" I asked Y later, as he walked me home.

"I need him for work."

"I didn't hear any business discussed. Why did you invite me and ask me to find another girl?"

"It wasn't my money."

"Whose was it, then?"

"The people's. Why not invite some girls if it's the people's money?"

"You are writing reports on him?"

Y nodded.

"How can you?"

"It's no problem. He's a monkey; he isn't one of us."

I told Y never to call me again.

Y had once been a nice, intelligent boy worthy of sympathy, love, understanding. But he had determined that success required a few little compromises. So he had written a few reports. I don't know if he ever stopped. All I know is that it didn't help. His translating career didn't lead to an embassy post; all he did was ply Cambodians with vodka in Moscow restaurants. The KGB must have sensed that he was just a guy making little compromises and that he wasn't entirely theirs. But he wasn't ours, either.

After he found out that I had been fired, Y gave me a call and asked if he could stop by. "Lyuda, I have lined up a job for you," he said. "It pays so well that you'll praise Holy Jesus those numskulls at the Nauka Publishing House threw you out. Can I come over and tell you about it?"

The following day, he outlined the project: a deputy chief of the Ministry of Foreign Affairs needed a "Negro" to write a pamphlet about Africa liberating itself from colonialism. "The deputy minister doesn't need the money," Y said. "The entire honorarium goes to the Negro. The research is done. It will be brought to you in a black Volga. You'd be able to write it with your rear left paw."

Then he handed me a folder with the first installment of research materials. It was all about the Soviet Union aiding the progressive forces of colonial Africa while the sinister imperialists, with their monopolies and their CIA-funded saboteurs, lurked in the background, looking for a way to stop the victorious march of world socialism.

I thanked Y for his concern.

✦

Poverty hit Misha harder than us. At least, we didn't absolutely have to buy new clothes. But he was growing out of his. By September 1969, when he started tenth grade, he had grown out of his old school uniform, but I could not afford to buy him a new one.

His hands and feet stuck out by three or four inches, and all I could do was add "cuffs" made out of strips of the uniform he'd outgrown three years earlier. I was as careful as I could be, but the alterations were quite visible.

Misha didn't ask for anything. He knew we were broke and that we weren't buying anything for ourselves, either. Still, I was hurt by this. It's hard for a boy to be the worst dressed in class.

The following year, when he was about to start at Moscow University, we faced staggering clothing expenses. He needed new shoes (about 40 rubles), a suit (at least 100), two or three shirts (12 to 15 rubles each), a coat (at least 100), and a winter hat (20). Altogether, I needed about 300 rubles to pay for Misha's wardrobe.

I knew of only one way to raise that much money: typing samizdat. Some of our better-paid friends wanted to have samizdat books of their own, and they were prepared to pay. At the prevailing market rate of 10 kopeks per page, I needed to type 3,000 pages to raise 300 rubles.

The books I picked for retyping included the memoirs of Nadezhda Mandelshtam, *Only One Year* by Svetlana Alliluyeva, and three other books I can no longer remember. Now, a few words about my typewriter: it was a turn-of-the-century Mercedes that stood about a foot off the table, weighed about sixty pounds, and had the tightest keys I have ever encountered on any typewriter.

I never typed at my apartment. It was safer to use the apartments of people who were beyond suspicion. So, on a regular basis, I had to wrap the typewriter in a blanket, slip it into a large, vinyl bag, and lug it to some less dangerous place.

By the end of the summer, Misha was fairly well dressed.

✦

Mother knew nothing. If I had told her, she would have had to confront her Stalin-era fear that expulsion from the party would be followed by arrest. Then I would have had to explain that, unlike Father, I had no plans to petition to rejoin. And then I would have had to give her my reasons.

I thought she was past the age when she could alter her life or her view of the world. She was a faithful party member, and finding out that her daughter was one of the renegades the newspapers were writing about would make her choose sides. All of it would hit her if I got arrested, but until then she didn't need to worry.

When I'd worked at Nauka, I had gone to the office once a week, on Thursdays. So, to keep Mother from calling Nauka some Thursday and asking for Lyuda Alexeyeva, I called her every Wednesday night.

This worked for a year and a half, until Mother moved in with me for a month in the winter of 1969. It was one of her selfless acts:

while Sergei was studying for exams, she let him have her apartment so he could cram in peace.

While she was staying with me, Mother happened to take a call from Larisa's father.

"Lyuda is at work," she said. It was Thursday.

"Oh, she has found a job! She never told me!"

"What do you mean, she's *found* a job?" Mother didn't even know that my friend Larisa was Larisa *Bogoraz*. She called Nauka and asked for me.

"Lyuda," she said when I walked into the apartment. "I understand you were fired more than a year ago."

"Since you already know, I was fired for signing letters protesting political trials. I didn't want to tell you because that way you could say honestly that you knew nothing about it. Kolya was fired, too, but he has found another job."

She was silent for a while.

"Oh, now I understand why you always seem to have no money." She had been wondering why I had been wearing badly worn clothes and subsisting on vegetable soup. She thought I had suddenly become a spendthrift.

All through the night, I listened to her tossing on a folding bed in the adjacent room. In the morning, after Kolya went to work and Misha went to school, she returned to the subject of my firing and my political views.

"I have thought about what you said to me last night. And I think you were right not to tell me. Let's keep it that way."

Ten

Had they been released after their trial, Daniel and Sinyavsky would have been unable to recognize their old freewheeling *kompaniya*. It had changed in tone and focus. With the petition campaign, the *kompaniya* changed once again, and no less profoundly.

The remnants of other *kompanii* joined the remnants of ours. We were just a handful, but a more diverse handful. Our circle now included twenty-five-year-old *SMOGisty* and eighty-year-old Bolsheviks crusading for the return to the "Leninist principles" of the revolution.

With a few exceptions, we were too busy to run from party to party. Instead, we remained in small groups that knew of each other and, when necessary, called on each other.

One group, the Marxists, were our forefathers. They were older men who had challenged the system a generation before we did. Among them was Pyotr Grigorenko, a general who had been placed in a mental hospital for distributing leaflets that called for the return to true Leninist principles. At the hospital, Grigorenko learned about *glasnost* from Vladimir Bukovsky. (Bukovsky had learned about it from Alek Esenin-Volpin.)

Grigorenko's friend Sergei Pisarev, too, had been committed to a mental institution, after writing to Stalin that the alleged "doctors' plot" had the appearance of a hoax played by the enemies of socialism. After Stalin's death, Pisarev wrote a letter demanding an investigation of the use of psychiatry for punitive purposes. An investigative commission formed by the Central Committee in response to his letter found that abuses had indeed taken place.

Another friend of Grigorenko's, Aleksei Kosterin, devoted his golden years to crusading for the rights of the Crimean Tatars, an ethnic group that had been accused of collaboration with the Nazis and, in its entirety, deported to Central Asia. Kosterin spent seventeen years in the camps, and after his release his Moscow apartment became the place for the Tatars to get legal advice and editing help on appeals and petitions demanding permission to return to their homelands. After Kosterin's death in 1968, his crusade for the Crimean Tatars was taken up by Grigorenko.

✦

Viktor Krasin and Pyotr Yakir were united by opposition to what they called "re-Stalinization." Krasin, my contemporary, was first carted off to Stalin's camps for joining a Marxist cell. (One of the cell's four members turned out to be an informant.) After prison, Krasin managed to earn a degree in economics. Yakir was the son of Yona Yakir, a Civil War hero and the commander of the Kiev military district, who had been executed by Stalin.

Yakir the younger was arrested at fourteen. He grew up in the camps, met his wife in the camps, fathered a daughter in the camps. After being released, he graduated from the Historical Archives Institute in Moscow and got a job at the Academy of Sciences. Still, he had the manners, the look, the walk, and the lexicon of a man who'd been formed by association with young criminals.

He talked like an adult, he drank vodka like an adult, but to me he was always a boy whose emotional growth had stopped the instant the operatives slammed the door of the Black Maria.

✦

Sergei Kovalyov, an internationally acclaimed biologist, was part of a group of liberal scientists who would later form the core of the human-rights movement. In 1969, after learning that his boss at Moscow University was being dragged to KGB interrogations because of him, Kovalyov did the decent thing: he quit the job he loved.

"Why would a man like you, someone who does not believe in God, face certain imprisonment in a fight against evil?" a Pentecostal activist once asked him.

"It's a matter of conscience," Kovalyov said. "And conscience is all that separates us from the animals."

Aleksandr Lavut, a mathematician, was a quiet man who usually sat in the corner, chain-smoking. You had to strain to hear his voice. The quiet Sasha Lavut spent over a decade helping the Crimean Tatars and producing samizdat. In his final statement to the court that was about to convict him under Article 190, he said, "I liked the first line of the prosecutor's speech. 'Soviet laws must be observed.' If they had been, we would not be here today."

Tatyana Velikanova, also a mathematician, had lost two jobs in her profession, then became a practical nurse at a Moscow hospital. "I'll get back to mathematics in my cell," she used to say. Between her work, samizdat, and caring for her three children, it's a wonder that Tatyana ever slept. Tatyana refused to acknowledge the KGB. She even remained silent throughout her trial. Only after being sentenced to five years in the camps and five in internal exile did she comment: "The comedy is over. It's all there is."

✦

Valery Chalidze, a physicist in his early thirties, started out as a follower of Alek Esenin-Volpin. He was precisely the kind of legal scholar the Soviet system did not want: a critical thinker. He studied laws for loopholes and wrote lengthy analytical tracts.

Chalidze opposed demonstrations, public brawls, and fiery declarations that could be used by the authorities to prosecute under articles 70 or 190. "Going to prison is unprofessional," he used to say. "My mission is to keep people from putting themselves behind bars."

Chalidze became the leading "legalist." Others were Esenin-Volpin, Yulius Telesin, and Boris Tsukerman. The four shared a curious characteristic: none was ever imprisoned.

✦

Sofya Vasilyevna Kallistratova in 1967 decided that as a defense attorney she was obligated to consult and represent participants of the emerging human-rights movement. "All too often, an attorney has to help people who are not decent," she said. "I like to help decent people."

Kallistratova found the dissenters through her friend Dina Isaakovna Kaminskaya. Over the next decade, they became the leading practitioners of what might be called dissident law. Kallistratova and Kaminskaya weren't just attorneys; they were very much a part of our circle.

✦

Thanks to letters from the camps, we were learning about religious prisoners and about "nationalists" from the Baltic and the Ukraine. Since their families stayed with us in Moscow before taking trains to Mordovia, our network kept expanding. Through those new connections, we could keep track of new government repressions taking place thousands of miles away.

The volume of information we were receiving had begun to overwhelm our ability to record and exchange it. It was simply impossible to keep track of the thousand *podpisanty* as they were being dragged through the KGB's inquisition. That information was no less important than what was in *The White Book,* and it had to be collected systematically. We needed a samizdat way of sharing news of what was going on — a bulletin that would record the information that came our way. It would offer no commentary, no belles lettres, no verbal somersaults; just basic information. Natasha Gorbanevskaya, a professional editor, agreed to take the job.

The name of the bulletin was borrowed from a BBC Russian-language news roundup: *Khronika tekushchikh sobytiy* ("The Chronicle of Current Events"). Natasha typed up one copy with seven carbons, then handed the carbons to friends for retyping. We typed a few more copies and handed them out to friends; they, too, made additional copies.

Instead of an epigraph, Natasha typed in the text of Article 19 of the Universal Declaration of Human Rights:

> Everyone has the right to freedom of opinion and expression; this right includes freedom to hold opinions without interference and to seek, receive, and impart information and ideas through any media and regardless of frontiers.

The first issue, dated April 30, 1968, led with a report on the Galanskov-and-Ginzburg trial and a cascade of brief items describing the outrages that followed the trial. Events were described in a wooden, impersonal style.

> Simultaneously with expulsion of the participants in the protests, officials also expelled BORIS ZOLOTUKHIN, the defense attorney who represented ALEKSANDR GINZBURG. The expulsion from the party was motivated by ZOLOTUKHIN's "un-Party and un-Soviet line of defense." In his closing statement, the defense attorney convincingly countered all the arguments advanced by the prosecutors and — for the first time in the long history of political trials — demanded complete acquittal of his client. After his expulsion from the party, ZOLOTUKHIN was removed from the post of manager of a legal-consulting office.

As did most of our works, the issues of *Khronika* eventually ended up in the West and were broadcast back to the USSR over shortwave radio.

In the first issue, the majority of stories came from Moscow and Leningrad. Only one news item came from the Ukraine. A later issue suggested a method for sending information to the bulletin: "Tell it to the person from whom you received *Khronika,* and he will tell it to the person from whom he received *Khronika,* etc. Whatever you do, don't try to get through that chain on your own; if you do, you may be mistaken for a [KGB] informant."

While the first issue contained just a single news item from the Ukraine, issue number 7 contained eight such news items, issue number 13 contained ten, and issue number 28 contained twelve. *Khronika*'s second issue included a news item on the Crimean Tatars. News from Lithuania first appeared in August 1970. News from Georgia started appearing in July 1974. Baptists found their way to us in December 1968, the Adventists in July 1970, Jehovah's Witnesses in June 1971, and the Pentecostals in July 1974.

A decade after the appearance of *Khronika*'s first issue, I tabulated that the journal had covered 424 political trials, which netted 753 convictions. Not a single defendant was ever acquitted. There were also news items about 164 people who were found insane and involuntarily committed to mental institutions.

Thanks to *Khronika* and our press conferences, the authorities had to assume that news of every arrest would echo in the West, end up on a shortwave-radio program, and become known throughout the USSR. From the start of the 1968 crackdown, the arrests became part of international *glasnost* and, as a consequence, diminished the Soviet Union's cherished international prestige.

✦

Sometime in June 1968, Pavel Litvinov asked me to type a few pages from a manuscript by Andrei Sakharov. I had heard the name, but I didn't know much about the man.

"He is a physicist who became an academy member very early in life because of the H-bomb. Now he is doing a lot of thinking," Pavel explained.

From the disjointed pages, I couldn't tell which direction Sakharov's thoughts were taking. All I could see was that the author had toned down harsh statements made in the rough draft. Later, I learned that the bulk of the manuscript had been typed by a secretary at his institute, who then took one carbon to the KGB. Now Sakharov needed a dependable samizdat typist to make revisions. I had no idea that I was typing abstracts of what would soon become one of the most celebrated essays of our time.

The essay, "Progress, Coexistence, and Intellectual Freedom," included a conspicuous caveat that the author's views were "deeply socialist." I did not find that off-putting. In early summer of 1968, there were few antisocialists among the Moscow intelligentsia.

Most of us evolved in a similar pattern: we were socialists in 1953; we were still socialists in 1956; we had few thoughts about socialism for the twelve glorious years of the thaw; then, in 1968, we believed again.

Ours was an informed, cautious optimism. We recognized that Stalinism represented a fallback position for the governments headed by Khrushchev and, later, Brezhnev. In 1968, we knew that more and more people were ending up in the camps, that free expression in official publications remained a fantasy, and that samizdat could lead to a prison term. But we also thought that the Stalinist past was so horrifying that our leaders would not dare to return to it. We were hoping that they would at least attempt to move forward, and "forward" to us meant the way of Prague Spring. We were hoping that Czechoslovakia's reformers would develop — and that our government would import — a form of socialism that people like us could accept.

Sakharov wrote that war in the nuclear age is suicidal and that some sort of a compromise between the socialist and capitalist worlds represented the only chance for survival of mankind. The essay outlined something Sakharov called "optimistic futurology," a plan for the peaceful convergence of the opposing systems:

Step One: Democratization of the Soviet political system and economic reform encouraging initiative. This process should begin in 1968 and be completed by 1980.

Step Two: Four years after the Soviets begin reform, the United States takes a convergence measure, instituting controls on its economy to shrink the private sector while expanding the public sector. This begins in 1972 and is completed by 1985.

Step Three: In 1972, the USA and the USSR lower arms expenditures and divert the resources previously spent on arms to alleviating poverty around the globe. This is accomplished by 1990.

Step Four: By the year 2000, social structures would become so similar that world government becomes feasible.

In later years, the author of "optimistic futurology" refined his ideas to arrive at something more feasible: achieving an atmosphere of trust between nations, which, he argued, would be the first step toward disarmament.

In Western democracies, Sakharov wrote later, all international agreements were in effect monitored by the legislatures and citizen groups. In the USSR, such monitoring was punished by imprisonment. Consequently, the West could not trust the Soviets to live up to their international promises. This observation led Sakharov to his central recommendation to the Soviet leaders: give your citizens greater political freedom, thereby building trust with the West as a way to assure disarmament.

✦

In those days, I was a socialist by default. I wanted democracy; it didn't matter whether it was socialist, capitalist, or some mixture of the two. It seemed there would be less of a leap between Soviet socialism and democratic socialism than between Soviet socialism and bourgeois democracy. It seemed more feasible for the Soviet democracy to evolve within a socialist framework.

Thus, in the spring and summer of 1968, as the Soviet leadership was yearning for the law and order of Stalinism, the entire Moscow intelligentsia was preoccupied with Prague Spring.

Natasha Gorbanevskaya could read Czech, as could a friend of Williams's, an electrical engineer. Because of them, we were able to keep abreast of the latest polemics in *Literární Listy* and *Rudé Právo*. We could see that the ideas of Prague Spring were a lot like our own, and there was something captivating about reading newspaper polemics identical to midnight debates in Moscow kitchens.

The political and economic system Czechoslovakia's reformers were trying to transform had been created as the mirror image of ours. Therefore, Czechoslovakia's experience with reform would be transferable to our country. My best-case scenario went something like this:

After reforms, Czechoslovakia's workers would be given incentives to produce, factory managers would suddenly see value in innovation, writers would be allowed to publish. As labor, management, and the intelligentsia united, economic indicators would shoot up.

Impressed by the Czech economic miracle, Soviet leaders would attempt similar reforms. Naturally, Brezhnev and his clique would be interested in revamping the economy rather than in democratizing the society. But from the Czech experiment, they would be able to see that democratization was an essential condition of economic renewal.

We found a peculiarly Russian way to express our solidarity with the Czech reformers. We drank to them. After the traditional toast to those who could not be with us, we drank to Comrade Dubček, Comrade Mlynář, Comrade Černík. Some of our admirers of Prague Spring aimed to honor every one of the dozen or so comrades on Czechoslovakia's politburo.

One evening in July 1968, Williams and his electrical-engineer friend got politicized on vodka and staggered out onto the Arbat screaming, "Long live Comrade Dubček! Long live Comrade Černík! Long live Comrade Mlynář! Long live democracy! Long live economic incentives!" They were stopped, taken to a police station, then released. To the consternation of the authorities, public expression of support for members of the politburo of a fraternal socialist state did not constitute an unlawful act.

✦

Our letter campaign, coupled with the reform movement in Czechoslovakia, may have been too much for the Kremlin to bear. A Moscow rumor held that in early spring of 1968, at a meeting with the Moscow Communist-party leaders, Brezhnev set aside his prepared speech and screamed, "Don't you see, everything is falling apart!"

By the summer of 1968, as Czechoslovakia's newspapers were brimming with enthusiasm for reform, Soviet coverage of Prague Spring reached new levels of viciousness. Newspaper attacks began in June, with criticism of Alexander Dubček. By July, Soviet journalists claimed that enemies of the revolution had endangered the conquests of socialism in Czechoslovakia. The tone of the stories suggested that Comrade Brezhnev and others on the Soviet politburo were not going to stand by idly while Czechoslovakia was moving away from the Soviet model. But what would they do?

As a former *politzek*, Tolya Marchenko was conditioned to assume the worst. On July 27, Tolya sent a letter to *Rudé Právo, Literárni Listy*, the BBC, *Izvestia, Pratze, Humanité, l'Unita*, and *The Morning Star*:

> Are our leaders indeed distressed by the events in Czechoslovakia?
>
> I think they are more than distressed. They are frightened. That's not because these changes represent a threat to socialism or to the security of the Warsaw Pact countries. They are frightened because these changes have the potential to undermine the authority of the leadership in those countries and discredit the methodology of governance that currently prevails in the socialist camp.

Tolya was arrested on July 29, 1968.

✦

Larisa asked if I would sign a letter protesting Tolya's arrest. Seven of Tolya's friends were getting together to write it.

"Look, Lara, I have something else to do, so why don't you sign my name to it," I said. "I'm sure all of you will write something intelligent."

When I looked through the letter a day later, I realized that I had made the wrong move.

"Citizens!" the letter began. It read as if its author was standing atop an armored car in a crowded square. It was didactic, it was bombastic, and it sounded like a political manifesto rather than a letter signed by Marchenko's friends. It gave no sense of the real Tolya, no sense of the young man who could have started his life anew but chose to put everything on the line for the "politicals" still doing time in Mordovia.

When I read the epistle, I realized that someone could go to prison, and that it could be me. I should have taken part in the writing. It's one thing when they imprison you for something you agree with; it's entirely different when they get you for signing a document you don't even like.

I told Larisa what I thought of the letter.

"It's been mailed," she said. "What can you do?"

♦

Unfortunately for all of us, August 7 was not one of the better days for Irina Belogorodskaya, Larisa's real cousin and a human-rights activist. In the late afternoon, Belogorodskaya stopped over at my apartment to assemble copies of the letter she had picked up at a typist's. (Belogorodskaya couldn't type, but she could find reliable typists.) I helped her collate. When we were done, we discovered that one of the copies had come out a page short, so we threw that copy out.

The following day, a KGB major and a search team of three plainclothesmen showed up at my apartment with a search warrant. Behind the couch, they found the missing page. It must have fallen as Irina and I were collating.

"Where did this come from?" one of them demanded.

"I am one of the authors," I answered. "It's natural for me to have a copy."

"Where are the rest of the pages?"

"I don't know."

They left. Thus ended my first search. The place had not been ransacked. All of my books had been opened, thumbed through, shaken over the floor, and put back on the shelves, though not exactly where I had placed them. The framed photographs were left slightly out of place. So were the clothes. So were all my papers. Everything was back in its place — *almost*. And that meant not at all.

I wanted to burn that apartment. It was no longer my own. I wanted to be rid of it, to start anew. In later years, there would be a second search, and a third; five searches in all. Each of them left me with the feeling that I had been violated.

The following morning, Larisa told me that Irina Belogorod-skaya had been arrested and charged with distributing a document containing slander against the state. The document in question was our letter in defense of Marchenko. Irina had inadvertently left the bag containing the copies of the letter in a taxicab. The cab was then stopped by the KGB operatives who had been tailing her.

Since Irina had been arrested even though she did not sign the letter, conventional logic dictated that those who had signed would be next on the KGB list.

✦

On August 10, I went to have a molar pulled. The dentist was surprised.

"It can still be saved," he assured me.

I didn't want to explain that I expected to be arrested, that there are few things worse than having bad teeth in the camps, and that I didn't have time for fillings, caps, and root canals.

I don't expect anyone who hasn't had a tooth extracted in the USSR or a Third World nation to understand just what that process involves. The anesthetic lasted for forty minutes; the tooth hung on for two hours.

There's no way to tell how long I sat on the bench outside the clinic trying to gather my wits. It must have been another hour. I sat in a dizzy haze, thinking about going home, or at least calling Kolya Williams. Kolya, an expert on incarceration, had asked me to call home every hour on the hour. That way he would know that I had not been arrested.

He had been walking around half-crazed, muttering, "The camps are no place for a woman." I kept asking him to stop, but he didn't. I had intended to call him, but I felt dizzy, short of breath.

At home, Kolya informed me that I had failed to call for three hours in a row and that he was furious. I said that in my condition I had no tolerance for his juvenile complaints. He walked away, grumbling something about the camps being no place for a woman. I dropped onto the bed.

Pavel Litvinov called and said he had to come over. "Fine," I said.

It had to be a letter in defense of Irina Belogorodskaya. I lay in bed, thinking through the events of the previous few days: Marchenko was arrested for writing a book and letters of protest; I allowed someone else to sign my name on a letter protesting his arrest, then regretted it after seeing the letter; Irina left the letter in a taxi and was arrested. Now the eight people who signed the original letter had to write another letter in Irina's defense. All this was compounded by the agony of tooth extraction and my fear of prison. Williams and I were scheduled to leave on vacation the following morning — a delayed honeymoon. Would I be arrested during the night? Or would they grab me at the airport, the way they had grabbed Yulik Daniel?

"I am really scared, Pashka," I said to Litvinov when he arrived.

"Do you want to sign it?" he asked, handing me the letter.

I signed it.

✦

In Kiev, we spent three days with Ivan Svitlychny, a writer, translator, and literary critic who had been at the center of the cultural renaissance in the Ukraine. I had met him a few years earlier, through Yulik Daniel and Larisa. Svitlychny and his wife, Lyolya, came to Moscow once every six months, mostly to buy books, and sometimes they stayed with us.

The Svitlychnys' Kiev apartment was an unofficial center of the Ukrainian intelligentsia. These people were nothing like the Moscow intelligentsia. They didn't use foul language; they drank in moderation; and, I suspect, most of them slept exclusively with their spouses.

While the Russian intelligentsia suffered great losses in Stalin's purges, the Ukrainian intelligentsia was decimated. Consequently, most of the writers, poets, and historians who gathered at Svytlychny's were *intelligenty* of the first generation. Most of them were children of peasants. They were united in opposition to official efforts to reduce the teaching of the Ukrainian language and gradually replace it with Russian.

In many ways, the Ukrainian intelligentsia was ahead of us. They were more politicized and better organized. In the early 1960s, they were able to gather thousands of people for public rallies, poetry readings, and "evenings of Ukrainian culture." For that reason, they became the first target of the Brezhnev clique. Arrests in the Ukraine began months before the arrests of Daniel and Sinyavsky. Our host was among those arrested. He was held in prison for eight months, then set free.

If nothing else, the experience had shown Svitlychny who his friends were. On one of our evenings together, he told the story of a young poet named Vitaly Korotich. In 1965, when the KGB started arresting his friends, Korotich decided to lie low. Around that time, by accident, Korotich took a bus seat next to Svitlychny, who had just been released from prison. Throughout that bus ride, Korotich looked down at his feet, saying nothing.

The times had changed. It had become dangerous to look up.

✦

After three days in Kiev, Kolya and I went to the country. We stayed in a Ukrainian peasant hut that belonged to a country schoolteacher, a friend of Svitlychny's. During the summer, the teacher left for another village, where her husband, also a country schoolteacher, had a bigger house.

Having nothing else to do, we spent the first half of each day picking mushrooms. Cleaning mushrooms can take an eternity. Since there was only one hot plate and one small skillet, the cooking took over an hour. By the time the last batch was done, the first needed reheating. My jaw stopped hurting and Kolya stopped muttering about the camps being no place for a woman. Our life acquired a healthier focus.

On August 21, the local newspaper carried the following wire story:

Tass has been authorized to report that the party and state officials of the Czechoslovak Socialist Republic have appealed to the Soviet Union and other allied nations with a request for urgent aid to the fraternal Czechoslovak people, including assistance by military forces. That appeal was caused by the threat to socialism and the constitutional form of government in Czechoslovakia posed by counterrevolutionary forces that had banded with outside forces hostile to socialism.

On August 21 Soviet military units entered the territory of Czechoslovakia. The actions being undertaken are not aimed against any state. They serve the cause of peace and are dictated by concern over strengthening peace.

I wasn't present when the politburo decided to "strengthen peace" by invading a sovereign country. I wasn't even a Communist any longer. The crimes of the party were not my crimes. Yet I felt shame in its purest, strongest form. I was ashamed of my Soviet passport, I was ashamed of being Russian, I was ashamed of being part of a barbarian country that had clubbed its enlightened neighbor. Everyone I talked to felt that intense shame.

What was going on in Moscow? Were Black Marias circling the city, rounding up the "ideologically unreliable," my friends? What about Larisa and Pavel? Had Tolya been tried? There was no phone in the village. There was no shortwave radio. Any attempt to change our plane tickets in late August would be futile. We would have to return no earlier than August 26, and that meant five more days of reading Soviet newspapers, listening to a local radio station, and guessing.

On August 25, we got on a bus to Kiev so we could spend an evening with Svitlychny before catching the first flight out the next morning. It was a depressing evening. Most phrases were short and muttered, as if someone had died and everyone else was on Librium. Finally, Svitlychny turned on the shortwave radio.

The first news item was from Moscow: "At least four people took part in a demonstration on Red Square. One of the demonstrators reportedly brought a baby carriage." According to the report, the demonstrators were arrested. No names were mentioned, but I knew of at least three. Larisa had to be there. Pavel, too. The baby carriage was Natasha Gorbanevskaya's.

The following day, Kolya and I walked into our Moscow apartment. I dropped the suitcase, walked to the phone, and stood there. I knew that I would call, Sanya would answer, I would ask for Lara, and he would say, "Mother has been arrested." I was afraid to dial.

The phone rang. It was Sanya. "Mother has been arrested," he said.

✦

When you are insulted by your inferiors, when you are humiliated so deeply that your entire being rebels, when you want to stand up and do something — anything — to separate yourself from that thing called "the masses," you turn to the Decembrists. And if you happen to be a poet and a citizen, you will be unable to keep your shout trapped in the confines of your throat.

Now, meet Aleksandr Galich, the author of screenplays with such titles as "A Criminal against the State" and "Taymyr Is Calling." He lives in a writers' compound, in a large apartment furnished with Scandinavian furniture, and eats off imported china.

He is always sick; death is not at the doorstep, but it is near, watching from across the street. Would it please the Creator if Aleksandr Arkadyevich Galich squandered his gift in order to put vodka and caviar on the table?

When he isn't writing commercial screenplays, he writes poetry that censors don't see. It is magnificent poetry; he sings it for friends, they record it; then their friends copy it off cassettes and reel-to-reels, the friends of their friends do the same, and so it continues, on and on and on. Galich spends the summer of 1968 in Dubna, a town outside Moscow, working on a screenplay with director Mark Donskoy. Galich despises Donskoy; he despises the screenplay; he despises his life.

All through August, he picks the strings of his guitar to the emerging verses of "The St. Petersburg Romance," a song he is composing about the Decembrists. On August 22, 1968, the day after the invasion of Czechoslovakia, the music and the verses merge into one.

> We repeat their whispers,
> We repeat their steps.
> No one has been shielded
> By experience, yet. . . .
>
> Just the same, no simpler
> Are the tests of our times:
> Can you come to the square?
> Dare you come to the square?
> Can you come to the square?
> Dare you come to the square
> When that hour strikes?

Could anyone come to the square, be it Senate or Red? The hour had struck, announced by the chills that went down our spines. If there had ever been the hour to become a Decembrist, that hour had come.

✦

On August 24, in the Moscow apartment of Lev Kopelev and Raisa Orlova, Galich sang a new cycle of songs. He sang about a large, bronze statue of Stalin marching through nighttime Moscow, followed by pieces of smashed and discarded plaster likenesses of the generalissimo: a parade of arms, legs, a chunk of mustache, preparing once again to feast on human flesh.

> And the drums are beating,
> The drums are beating,
> The drums are beating, beating, beating.

He sang of another parade, a parade of rogues that turned out for the funeral of Boris Pasternak:

> Wreaths recycled as brooms,
> We are sad for the whole half-hour.
> How proud we are, his contemporaries,
> That he died in his own bed!

What an odd source of civic pride: a poet dies in his own bed at seventy; not shot, like Nikolai Gumilev; not driven to insanity, like Osip Mandelshtam; not driven to suicide, like Marina Tsvetayeva. He lives to see old age, and the philistines who had once condemned and banished him from the Union of Writers make up the funeral procession.

Galich sang about a tall, graceful young woman walking down Leningrad's Prague street to the blind, red prison wall of Kresty.

> To feast and execution
> She walks as you once walked
> Through Prague, past Pryazhka River —
> She seeks her own Kresty.

She seeks Kresty in August, Akhmatova's month of doom; the month of Gumilev's execution; the month of their son's arrest; the month Soviet troops were deployed to render assistance to the fraternal people of Czechoslovakia.

Finally, Galich sang his "St. Petersburg Romance."

Pavel Litvinov, who had just married the Kopelevs' daughter Maya, was among the guests.

> Can you come to the square?
> Dare you come to the square
> When that hour strikes?

"Galich glanced at me, and my wife and I felt the urge to tell about our plans to stage a demonstration on Red Square," Pavel recalled years later. "We were afraid that if we told them, then some of those people — those people of the older generation, the generation of Galich and Kopelev, who were then nearing sixty — would feel compelled to join us. We didn't want to put moral pressure on them. Still, when Galich sang, 'Dare you come to the square' the impact was direct. I will never forget it."

✦

On August 25, just before noon, a young woman with a baby carriage rounded the corner from Aleksandr's Garden to Red Square. Along with the baby, the carriage held a homemade flag of Czechoslovakia and two banners written on strips of cloth. One was in Czech: *"Ať žije svobodné a nezávislé Československo!"* ("Long live free and independent Czechoslovakia!"). The second slogan — "To Your Freedom and Ours!" — originated with Aleksandr Herzen, as he sided with the Polish rebels who had fought for independence from the Russian Empire a century earlier.

I don't like slogans. They rob political thought of its inherent complexity. "To Your Freedom and Ours!" may be the only exception. Freedom of the Poland of a century before was inseparable from freedom inside Russia. Freedom of Czechoslovakia was inseparable from freedom inside the USSR. The Moscow thaw was inseparable from Prague Spring; the Moscow trials were inseparable from the invasion of Czechoslovakia. Freedom, as slavery, recognizes no national boundaries.

Natasha Gorbanevskaya, the woman with the baby carriage, reached Lobnoye Mesto, the stagelike stone platform built in 1534 to render grandeur to beheadings during the reign of Ivan the Terrible. Larisa Bogoraz and Pavel Litvinov were waiting. So were Vladimir Dremlyuga, Konstantin Babitsky, Vadim Delone, and Viktor Fainberg.

The clock on the Spasso Tower struck twelve; the seven demonstrators unfurled their banners and settled down on the warm cobblestones. Less than twenty minutes later, they were carted off by the KGB. The following day, the still-uncensored *Literární Listy* newspaper in Prague editorialized: "Those seven people on Moscow's Red Square are at least seven reasons why we will never be able to hate the Russians."

✦

It was 6:00 PM, Sunday, August 25, and defense attorney Dina Kaminskaya was waiting for Larisa Bogoraz and Pavel Litvinov to show up at her Moscow apartment. But the doorbell didn't ring, and Kaminskaya grew increasingly upset. It seemed inexcusable for Larisa and Pavel to miss that meeting. It was far too important.

Just four days earlier, on the day of the invasion, Kaminskaya had gone through the frustration of defending Anatoly Marchenko on trumped-up charges of violating residency requirements. He got the maximum: a year in the camps. And while that was bad enough, Kaminskaya went through the trial fearing that her client would learn about the invasion and make some pronouncement that would open him to additional charges, this time under Article 190.

On Monday, August 26, Kaminskaya would be meeting with Tolya at the Butyrki prison. If Larisa and Pavel had any messages for him, she was prepared to pass them along.

Finally that Sunday night, through the static of a shortwave radio station, Kaminskaya heard that a small group had staged a protest on Red Square. Now she knew what had happened to Larisa and Pavel.

The following day, Kaminskaya received a note Larisa had written before being taken to the Lefortovo prison: "Don't criticize us as others criticize us. Each of us made this decision for himself because it has become impossible to live and breathe. . . . I cannot even think about the Czechs. As I hear their pleas on the radio, I cannot stay silent, I cannot keep from shouting."

There was also a message for Tolya Marchenko: "Please forgive me and all of us for what happened today. I was simply unable to behave differently. You know what that feeling is like, when you cannot breathe."

◆

"I had no doubt that it would happen this way," Marchenko wrote later.

> I knew it for certain, as if I had been sitting in at the meetings of the Central Committee. I knew Czechoslovakia would be strangled. But now that it had happened, it was as if a boulder had dropped right on top of me. The Czechs weren't treated much differently from us, yet it was a personal insult, personal humiliation.
>
> What were my friends doing on the outside? What would I be doing had I not been locked up here, in prison?
>
> On August 26 I heard about the demonstration of seven people on Red Square.
>
> What did I think of my friends' action? I know, there were many opinions on this. Even I was ambivalent at first. Now the authorities were handed the opportunity to put away seven active members of the Resistance. In that sense, the demonstration benefited the authorities. But I also understood that this act of self-sacrifice had been thought through, that it was anything but a lighthearted gesture. Every participant understood that all the roads from Red Square led to prison. But they couldn't live with their country's shame, feeling it as shame of their own. They found just that one way to express their feelings. That demonstration was the sum total of their lives.

Of course, many Russians were appalled by their country's military invasion of a sovereign state. Members of the intelligentsia were more appalled than others, but not everyone had the courage to stand up and protest in the open.

Seven people did.

Later, members of national-liberation movements from the Ukraine and the Baltic states told me what they thought about the demonstration. It would seem that they, people who had taken up arms to defend their land from the Soviet military machine, would not be awed by a "three-minute" demonstration on Red Square. But awed they were. They told me: "Yes, we took up arms, but when you do battle, not everyone dies. So everyone has hope, at least a glimmer. Who knows, perhaps I'll be the one who survives. But when you go out protesting in the open, without weapons, just seven of you against the world, well, that takes a special brand of courage."

◆

The "cousins" story concocted by Larisa and me worked: my name was not stricken from the list of family members who would be eligible to attend the trial of the demonstrators.

On the morning of October 9, 1968, just before nine o'clock, I entered the courtroom of the Proletarsky District of Moscow Municipal Court. Of the forty or so people in the courtroom, half had the unmistakable features of KGB goons. The rest were family members of the defendants. Since the goons came in first, they took the front rows. Family members sat in the back. I came in last, and the only empty seat I could see was in the middle of the first row, with a perfect view of the proceedings.

Seconds after I sat down, the five defendants were led to the "defendants' bench." (Viktor Fainberg had been declared insane and removed from the case. Natasha Gorbanevskaya was not charged at all, most likely because prosecuting a nursing mother at an internationally covered trial made for especially poor public relations.) Each of them looked around the courtroom. The dynamic was clear on first glance: the KGB in the front, relatives in the back.

I could see Larisa's eyes focus on her son and her parents. She scanned the room, from the middle forward. Lara has an expressive face. It takes little effort to read her thoughts.

Our eyes met. She threw her head back. "What?" She was more amused than bewildered. "How did you get to sit with that slime?" I smiled back.

Larisa sat second from the left.

"All rise, court is in session!" And we stood up for Valentina Lubentsova, a pale, austere Soviet woman. A colonel's wife. A guardian of law. A loyal servant of the state. She was known as a competent, fair judge. And she was respected by defense attorneys. Until now. Until her first political case. Over a decade, her courtroom would be used to convict dissidents Sergei Kovalyov, Yuri Orlov, Tatyana Osipova, and Ivan Kovalyov. She did not sell her robe to the state or the party; the state and party owned it from the start. She understood her role: direct a proceeding that would lead up to the sentence.

JUDGE LUBENTSOVA: Defendant Bogoraz, stand up. What can you say about the charges brought against you?

LARISA: On August 25, around noon, I reached Red Square. With me I had a banner that expressed my protest against the military invasion of Czechoslovakia. . . .

JUDGE: What was the writing on your banner?

LARISA: I refuse to answer that question.

JUDGE: Why?

LARISA: Because it is immaterial what *my* banner said. I consider myself in agreement with all the banners: Hands Off Czechoslovakia. To Your Freedom and Ours. Free Dubcek. Long Live Free and Independent Czechoslovakia.

JUDGE: Who was with you in Red Square?

LARISA: I refuse to answer all questions that involve other defendants. . . .

JUDGE: Did you sit down simultaneously?

LARISA: I don't recall.

The government's objective was to show that the protest had been planned in advance, that the banners were libelous, that the protesters were disorderly, and that traffic had been impeded as a result. Each defendant said he had acted for himself and that traffic was not impeded.

At seven-thirty that evening, when I walked outside, I found myself surrounded by foreign reporters. I had a choice: I could tell them what went on at the trial, forgoing any chance of getting back into the courtroom. Or I could be silent. I chose to speak.

By the time I got home, my quick overview of the first day's proceedings was being broadcast over shortwave radio stations. Since reporters hadn't asked my name, I was not quoted directly.

The following day, however, I was told that my name was "not on the list" of relatives approved for attending the proceedings.

◆

On October 11, the Moscow Municipal Court sentenced Pavel Litvinov to five years of internal exile, Larisa to four years, and Konstantin Babitsky to three years. Vladimir Dremlyuga got three years in the camps and Vadim Delone got two years.

As Larisa's "cousin," I faced a number of problems. The worst was what to do about her apartment. Larisa and Yulik were convicts. Sanya, eighteen, had been rejected by Moscow University; his grades were excellent, but his name and his own record as a *podpisant* made him inadmissible. Now he was about to be drafted. That meant the apartment would stand vacant. And that would give the authorities legal grounds to reclaim it, leaving Larisa, Yulik, and Sanya without Moscow residency permits and without a fixed address.

I asked Larisa's attorney, Dina Kaminskaya, to recommend someone who specialized in residential law. The residential lawyer, an elderly, tired woman, received me at her office. She did not offer me a chair.

Standing up, I explained the problem to her: the father was in prison, the mother on her way to internal exile, the son about to be drafted.

The woman looked up from her desk. "Which article is the father convicted on?"

"Seventy."

"And the mother?"

"One ninety."

"And their names?"

"The father is Daniel. The mother, Bogoraz."

"Oh, sit down, please!" She was one of the Moscow intelligentsia. By the end of the consultation, I had her home address, her telephone, and her friendship.

We decided to try to get Sanya into some kind of a job that offered deferment. Without digging, the attorney knew of only one such job: driving a Moscow metro train.

"I don't know if Sanya could do that," I said.

"We'll keep thinking," promised the attorney.

✦

Next, I had to find a way to consult with Larisa. I coached her father to tell her everything during the half-hour post-trial visit he, his wife, and Sanya would be allowed with her. The meeting would be monitored, so we had to come up with a code that would be understood by Larisa and would go over the head of the prison guard. Iosif Aronovich was a wonderful, wise man, but an incompetent conspirator.

The meeting went worse than I expected. Sanya began by telling Larisa that Carrie, the Daniels' Irish setter, had died unexpectedly. Carrie had been healthy and not very old. The friends who agreed to take care of her until Yulik's release treated her well. But every morning, Carrie would come to her caretaker's bed and put her head on the pillow, her big, brown, intelligent eyes showing her distress. It was deep canine sadness that killed her. The entire half-hour ended up being devoted to Carrie.

I had to find another way to tell Lara about the apartment and the draft. It seemed hopeless — until Judge Lubentsova called. She told me that my cousin Larisa Bogoraz had put me on the list of family members she wanted to see before being shipped out. The cousin myth was still alive.

The amount of information I had to give Larisa was overwhelming. My usual manner of speaking, which is significantly faster than average, was not rapid enough. I wanted to spend twenty minutes telling Larisa everything. That would leave us ten minutes to talk.

✦

We ran toward each other. We hugged, ignoring the guard shouting, "Not allowed!"

After he broke us apart, we sat down opposite each other at a

rectangular table, with the guard between us. Larisa looked ema-
ciated but rested. She had done what she wanted to do — and she
was at peace.

I began to talk in a fast, well-rehearsed, coded monotone. I told
her about Sanya's draft status and the apartment; then I told her
that Tolya had arrived at a camp in Solikamsk, in Siberia. I told her
that I had sent him a package and had enclosed some soap wrapped
in an article from *Moskovskaya pravda* that reported the outcome of
Larisa's case. The code I used was very simple. Sanya was "the
infant," Tolya was "Vasya," and so forth.

When I was halfway through, I noticed that Larisa was glancing
at the guard and fighting off an attack of the giggles. Without
pausing in my monologue, I looked to my right. The guard had not
looked too intelligent to begin with, but now he looked like a
complete idiot. His wide jaw had dropped. His vacant eyes were
bulging. I went on with my rat-tat-tat-tat.

"How are you?" I asked Lara when I was done.

"Rested."

"How's the food?"

"Not too bad for someone who's used to the Lenin Library
cafeteria."

"What do you do all day?"

"Sleep. Mostly sleep. And read."

She was reading *The Two Captains*, by Venyamin Kaverin, an
adventure book about men of courage and pure hearts.

✦

Sanya's problems were soon resolved. A neurologist consulted by
the conscription office diagnosed a nervous breakdown.

I saw no evidence of that breakdown. Sanya struck me as a normal boy. It could well be that the physician simply did his duty as
one of the Moscow intelligentsia and signed a letter that freed
Sanya from military service.

Be that as it may, there was still a lingering question of what
would happen to Larisa in exile. We didn't even know where she
would be going, just that her train had left.

She was not allowed any money. She had no warm clothes. And
she had no place to stay. On the train, she would be traveling with
common criminals.

On January 4, almost a month after Larisa's prison train left Moscow, we received her telegram from Chuna, a settlement near Irkutsk in the taiga of central Siberia.

✦

It was a busy week. Besides having to get the tickets to Siberia and pack the suitcases I was taking to Larisa, I had to prepare for a move to another apartment. I shuddered in anticipation of Larisa's wanting to know everything about Czechoslovakia. I did not have the time to collect samizdat journalism for her. Kolya volunteered to help, and by the time of my departure, he had collected a weighty stack of materials. I left for Bratsk with three enormous suitcases and an equally enormous bundle. In them was everything from warm clothes to bedding to housewares to canned food. There might be no food at the stores in Chuna, and January was not the month to start a vegetable garden in Siberia.

In Moscow, Kolya and Misha helped me get aboard the train. Before we got to Bratsk, I made a deal with the conductor: for five rubles, he would carry my suitcase and the bundle out of the railroad car. But then what? Surely, there would be no porters in Bratsk.

Indeed, there were none. Nor did anyone offer to help. To get the luggage inside the station, I picked up each piece separately and carried it three steps. Then I set it down, backed up and carried another piece, then another. It took an hour to get the bags checked in at storage.

The first train to Chuna would not come till the morning. I decided to look around Bratsk, but found nothing except Khrushchev-era apartment buildings, unbearable cold, and darkness. I did not own a pair of felt boots or even a pair of socks. My warmest boots, the French ones, fit snugly over nylons.

In the morning, after spending the night huddled in the station, I took the bags, one at a time, to another platform. Once again, it took an hour, but now I was almost there. At Chuna, I would be met by Larisa.

But Larisa was not at the station. Nor was anyone else. Yet again, I shuffled my bags to the stationhouse, checked them in, and went looking for the hut where Larisa rented a cot.

It was a sturdy Siberian log house. Even the fence and the gate were made of logs. I pulled on the gate. It was locked. I pulled again. I hit it with my fist. I kicked it with my French boot. It was cold. The house was deep inside the lot. And the logs were thick enough to absorb whatever sound my fist or boot could produce. I began to shout, but felt my voice carried off by the howling wind.

The dogs began to gather around me. They were either huskies or timber wolves. They barked, yelped, howled, but their voices, too, were carried off by the wind.

"Whom are you looking for?" asked a passerby, a woman.

I told her.

"You have the right house."

"Are they home?"

"They are."

"How do you know?"

"The smoke's rising from the chimney. Keep knocking."

✦

Finally, the owner of the house came out to pick up a few logs for the night, heard me and the dogs, opened the gate, and led me inside.

"I wasn't expecting you till tomorrow," said Larisa, who was even thinner than in Lefortovo.

She was renting from an elderly couple known around town as Uncle Sanya and Aunt Zhenya. They were pleasant, hospitable people. Uncle Sanya, a retired railroad worker, immediately saw my arrival as an excuse to descend into the cellar and pull out a bottle of *samogon,* homemade vodka. Aunt Zhenya got four glasses, and Uncle Sanya returned to the cellar to get pickles and marinated *cheremsha,* a garlic-like plant. All the while, he was muttering:

> *Sami gonim, sami pyom,*
> *I komu kakoye delo, gde my sakhar dostayom.*
>
> We distill it ourselves, and we drink it ourselves,
> And it's nobody's business where we get the sugar from.

"I will die if I drink this," said Lara, declining *samogon.* Before her arrest, she had a cast-iron stomach. She was well even in

Lefortovo. Now, after three weeks on prison trains and in transit prisons, she was suffering from acute gastritis. Later, the gastritis would turn chronic. Later still, it would cause an ulcer.

In those days, I could still drink like a horse. I drank up my *samogon,* instantly putting myself in good stead with Aunt Zhenya and Uncle Sanya.

The only place I could sleep was Larisa's cot, which we shared. She spent the night telling me about her three-week journey. She'd heard a thousand stories, and she remembered most of them. "One of my travel companions was a murderer," she said. The woman had killed the husband who fathered her three children. "No," she'd told Larisa, "I am not sorry I killed him. He used to get drunk and beat me and the children." There was also a girl named Valya, who'd celebrated her nineteenth birthday by getting drunk and breaking into a store. Once inside, she and her friends got even more drunk and, eventually, fell asleep on the floor. There was also an eighteen-year-old girl named Lida, who was being transferred from a colony for the underaged to an adult camp. With her was a younger girl, her lover. In transit, the girls found out that they would be sent to separate camps.

At a transit prison in Novosibirsk, Larisa started talking with a girl named Dina who was about fourteen and was doing time for robbery. Dina seemed to have read a lot. She was intelligent and self-assured.

"Why? Why did you do it? You could have stayed at school?" asked Larisa.

"Of course, I could have. But why?"

Neither one of us remembered to bring up Czechoslovakia. The Red Square demonstration had launched Larisa's journey into another world — the world of barbed wire, armed guards, and human lives wasted by cruelty and indifference. That world was more immediate. It needed her compassion more than Alexander Dubček, the Czech people, or Prague Spring.

◆

The following morning, Larisa went to her job at the sawmill and I went out to make arrangements to pick up the bags and to look around Chuna. Fortunately, Uncle Sanya lent me a pair of felt boots.

I wanted to find a good, sturdy hut for Larisa to live in. She could not be trusted with such a task. She would have taken too much time to find a house, and, chances are, it would have been the least expensive and most dilapidated hovel in Chuna.

The place I found looked as if it would easily hold up for another four years. It cost 1,800 rubles, about average in Chuna. I put down about 200 and promised to pay the rest within two months. I knew that Larisa had plenty of friends who would pool their resources and somehow come up with the rest of the money.

That evening, Uncle Sanya and Aunt Zhenya invited us to a friend's hut. We declined politely, but they were so insistent that we had to reconsider. As soon as we got out of the house, Uncle Sanya whispered, "We were told to get you out of the house."

"Who told you to do it?" Larisa asked.

"The militia and some man in plainclothes. I am afraid of them."

"Was he local?"

"No, an out-of-towner."

We followed Uncle Sanya and Aunt Zhenya to their friend's house, sat at the table for about a half-hour, then excused ourselves.

When we returned to their hut and opened the heavy gate, a dark figure emerged from the house and darted toward the fence. The KGB had been trying to rifle through the papers I had brought for Larisa. And while our untimely arrival foiled this operation, both of us felt terrible about Larisa's hosts being forced to become informants. There is nothing worse than seeing decent people co-opted and intimidated into performing indecent acts. Larisa had to have a place of her own.

✦

My phone did not stop ringing from the moment I returned to Moscow. Dozens of people had heard that I was back from my two-week trip and that I had fresh news about Larisa. After a while, I started giving the same answer: Come to my place on such-and-such a day, at such-and-such a time. I will tell everyone at once.

More than thirty people crowded into my room. I got up and told the story of Larisa's journey on prison trains, and about her living conditions in Chuna.

"What?" thundered Pyotr Grigorenko. "I say let's buy that house for Lara. Here's my hat." He grabbed his gray karakul hat and threw 10 rubles in it. The hat started filling up with bills and loose change. After making the rounds, it was still short of the needed balance of 1,600 rubles. A substantial collection like that required more time.

"I have a friend who would be happy to advance the money," offered Vadim Meniker. That was just what I wanted to hear.

We bought the house, and four years later, Larisa sold it for 2,400 rubles. She turned the proceeds over to a public fund for political prisoners, which in turn bought houses for two other political exiles in a small Siberian settlement.

✦

In the winter of 1969, Larisa was taken off her relatively light job of cutting the branch stubs off trees in the lumber mill. She was forced to carry logs instead.

Because of an ulcer, she was having problems digesting food, so she stopped eating.

Both Larisa's foreman and, later, the lumber mill manager, said she could be transferred to a lighter job, but that would require a "certificate" from a doctor. The doctor said something rude and slammed the door in her face. She went back to her foreman. The foreman once again sent her to the manager. The manager once again sent her to the doctor, and the doctor once again refused to give her a release.

I don't know if someone had made the decision to kill her, but obviously, a person who cannot eat and is forced to carry logs cannot survive very long. I had to do something.

I decided to find Anatole Shub, the reporter for the *Washington Post* (or was it the *New York Times*?) I had heard him offer to help Larisa in whatever way he could.

I knew little more than the reporter's name and roughly what he looked like. On May 21, I went to the trial of Ilya Burmistrovich, a mathematician charged with slandering the state — or, more specifically, with distributing works by Daniel and Sinyavsky. I looked at the reporters outside the courthouse, but couldn't spot Shub. I went up to a reporter whose face I remembered from another trial and asked him if he could help me find Shub.

That wouldn't be easy, said the reporter, Lars-Erik Nelson of Reuters. On May 20, Shub had been told by the Ministry of Foreign Affairs that he had forty-eight hours to get out of the country. He would have to leave no later than the morning of May 23.

I explained that the matter I needed to discuss was urgent, that it concerned Larisa Bogoraz, and that I would appreciate hearing from Shub before his departure. I gave the reporter my home telephone number.

"I can promise you that I will get this message to him," said Nelson. It seemed futile. Shub had too many other problems. He had to pack, for one thing.

The following morning, my phone rang.

"Hello, my name is Anatole Shub. I am a reporter for the *Washington Post*. Lars-Erik Nelson tells me that you want to talk about Larisa."

Good God! My initial reflex was to hang up. I didn't expect Shub to identify himself over the phone. I would have recognized him. Everything we were saying was being monitored on both ends, his and mine. They would know where we would meet; they would even know why. But Larisa needed help, so I kept talking.

"Where would you like to meet?" asked Shub.

"Since you are the one who is pressed for time, why don't you pick a place."

Shub suggested a cafeteria near the Aeroport metro station in northwest Moscow.

To identify me, Shub brought Lars-Erik Nelson. The three of us sat down at a small, round table. It was a lot like being onstage. A man who had walked in with Shub and Nelson sat down at a table next to ours. As we talked, he leaned backwards. If he'd stretched a little farther, he would have put his ear on our table. That wasn't monitoring; that was harassment.

I began to tell the reporters about Larisa's problems, but immediately hit a snag. Though both of them spoke good Russian, neither was especially familiar with the terminology of lumbering. I had a hard time explaining the difference between Larisa's old job (a branch cutter) and her new one (a porter). Finally, I drew something on a piece of paper.

On May 26, over shortwave radio, I heard a brief dispatch about Larisa's job and her ulcer. Years later, in Washington, Shub told me that on May 25, after his arrival in London, he gave Larisa's story to the *Sunday Times*. Then he included the story in a package he wrote for the *Washington Post*.

A couple of weeks later, I got a call from Larisa. "Lyudochka, everything has turned out fine after all!" she said. "Yesterday I went back to the doctor, and she was gone. So they sent me to a new one, who gave me what I needed. It's too good to believe. It's simply a miracle."

Yes, I said to Larisa, it certainly looked like a miracle.

Eleven

Each of us had to decide whether to serve the new Communist orthodoxy, confront it, fall silent, or find some means of escape. Choices had to be made urgently. There were still some letters of protest being written, but only a few dozen people were signing. For the most part, they were people who hadn't given up or who refused to acknowledge the new political climate.

Other *podpisanty* decided to draw the line after signing two or three petitions during the Galanskov-and-Ginzburg trial. They returned to the old routine: cursing the regime among friends and being silent in public. Earlier that year, many of these people had demonstrated that they were prepared to put their careers on the line, but their sacrifices had not brought about change. The purge of *podpisanty* and, especially, the invasion of Czechoslovakia demonstrated that the country was moving toward some form of neo-Stalinism and that petitions would not alter that new course. It no longer made any sense to write to the authorities, so most people stopped.

As the society quieted down, the authorities stepped up the offensive. Meetings were called nationwide to pass resolutions in support of the invasion. Such meetings were held at all universities, research institutes, bureaucracies, and industrial plants. Some of the resolutions ended up getting published.

The collective of the I. A. Likhachev Automobile Plant unanimously approves the actions of the Soviet government and the governments of other socialist countries. . . .

Soviet writers, like all Soviet people, enthusiastically support the measures undertaken to strengthen socialism in Czechoslovakia. . . .

Thousands of toilers of the Balkhash Metallurgic Facility showed total support for the timely measures. . . .

Resolutions were adopted in a show-of-hands vote, with management, the local party organizers, and the party regional-committee officials looking for the fearless few who voted against. To escape this show of hands, many called in sick or excused themselves to go to the bathroom just before the vote was taken. Many of them were later summoned to their party bureaus and asked to sign the prepared resolutions.

I was told that just before the vote at the Nauka Publishing House meeting, bathrooms filled with people. Samsonov and Eskov made it look as though they didn't notice.

The predicament of decent people in positions of authority became a hotly debated topic in Moscow kitchens. Was August 1968 the right time for all decent people to leave positions of authority and slam the door behind them? Or did they have the moral obligation to stay in their positions, if only to cover for their subordinates as they escaped to the bathrooms?

It was up to each administrator to answer that question for himself.

✦

Mikhail Samsonov chose not to slam the door. He stayed in his job; but he was also a historian, and in his historical works he didn't take part in falsifying the history of the war. Though he was a leading authority in his field, he was not part of the team of historians who compiled a multivolume history of World War II.

In later years, Samsonov took over editorship of a journal called *Historical Notes*. He also became a corresponding member of the Soviet Academy of Sciences. After *glasnost* began, he published a number of newspaper articles about Stalin's incompetent meddling in military decisions, interference that increased Soviet losses and prolonged the war.

As a scholar and administrator, Samsonov tried to get by with a minimum of half-truths and moral compromises to protect his own position and the positions of those in his employ. Another of my bosses, Lev Delyusin, exhibited uncommon valor — or, as some saw it, recklessness.

Just before the end of Khrushchev's thaw, Delyusin, a scholar of the history of the Orient, was invited to establish and head an institute that would track Western sociology, philosophy, history, and political science. He took the job under one condition: that no one would tell him whom to hire or how to do his work. Delyusin's Institute of Information on Social Sciences filled an uncharacteristically large number of its vacancies with scholars and translators who happened to be Jewish. He still had a few vacancies to fill when other institutes were firing their *podpisanty*. From that labor pool, he took the finest specialists he could find.

His institute found an ingenious way to hire me. First, I was brought in as a typist. After two years of being unemployed, I was glad to take any job. I did my typing at home, didn't show up at the institute, and told no one that I was working again. As soon as my trial period was over, I was promoted to editor and could once again go in to the office when necessary.

At about that time, Delyusin noticed that his personnel department had begun to get involved in hiring decisions and that high-placed officials were starting to offer unsolicited guidance. According to institute lore, Delyusin said simply: "Either I work the way I want to or I don't work." His resignation was accepted.

Before he left his prestigious job, his fine salary, and his chauffeured car, Delyusin transferred me to the Department of Scientific Communism, which was headed by his personal friend Yakov Berger. Despite its hideous name, the department tracked the writings of Herbert Marcuse and Jean-Paul Sartre and the latest pronouncements of Western Sovietologists. These were the sort of materials I would have otherwise read in samizdat.

✦

In Russia, a poet is held to higher standards than anyone else. When he loses courage, he loses his talent.

At the start of Khrushchev's thaw, all of us admired Yevgeny Yevtushenko for "Stalin's Heir," a poem about the removal of Stalin's body from the Mausoleum. I admired his "Babi Yar," and I can still recite his poem about a contemporary of Galileo who, for career's sake, did not say that the Earth turns. ("He thought he was building a career / While he was strangling it instead.")

Yevtushenko was selected to attend the Daniel-and-Sinyavsky trial. "I remember the look of horror on Yevtushenko's face," Daniel recalled in an interview shortly before his death. Yes, Yevtushenko was horrified, but he did nothing about his horror.

In 1968, another official poet of the thaw, Andrei Voznesensky, was told he would not be allowed to travel to the United States. Voznesensky responded with an open letter, which was published in the West and broadcast to the USSR. While the intelligentsia was fighting to keep its brethren out of prison, Voznesensky was trying to salvage his plans for foreign travel.

After hearing of Voznesensky's protest, a friend of mine responded with a Voznesenskian rhyme.

> *Prosti menya, moya strana,*
> *Za to, chto ya kusok govna.*
>
> Forgive me, my country,
> For being a piece of shit.

Yevtushenko and Voznesensky retained membership in the Union of Writers. In later years, Voznesensky wrote a tribute to Lenin, and Yevtushenko wrote a long, nonsensical poem about the Bratsk Hydro-Electric Station. In it a pregnant peasant woman abandoned by her lover decides to jump off a precipice, but reconsiders after seeing the grandeur of the dam below and thinking of her collective-farm chairman and Vladimir Ilych Lenin.

✦

In 1965, on a Kiev bus, Ukrainian poet Vitaly Korotich refused to acknowledge his besieged friend Ivan Svitlychny. In the midst of a crackdown on Ukrainian intellectuals, he took a job as editor of *Dnypro,* the Ukraine's equivalent of *Novy mir.* Later, Korotich was allowed to visit the United States. Upon returning home, he wrote *The Face of Hatred,* essentially a book of "ideologically correct" propaganda.

After two decades of posturing, Korotich was named editor of Moscow's *Ogonyok*. His job was to change the stale magazine into the most daring national-circulation publication in the USSR. He thereupon published Gumilev, Pasternak, Daniel, Brodsky, and Marchenko. After a taste of freedom, I suspect, Korotich would find it difficult to return to the days when he could not acknowledge his mentor.

✦

Bulat Okudzhava managed to stay in the party and the Union of Writers by being careful in composing his songs and in picking the company he kept. But he didn't lie and did nothing indecent.

He spent nearly two decades writing love songs and historical novels. After the advent of *glasnost,* he burst forth with brilliant new songs and poetry. He wrote about his childhood, when he believed that he lived in a world ruled wisely by Comrade Stalin, and about his brother Givi, who died after being released from Stalin's camps. He sang pointedly about the decline of the Roman Empire, and about Brezhnev's officialdom desecrating Moscow's romantic Arbat, displacing its residents, and making the place fit their lifestyle. ("The sauna is across the street, but the fauna's not the same.")

✦

Vladimir Vysotsky, like the characters in his songs, has become a legend. Consider the story about his KGB interrogation in the case of his friend and teacher Andrei Sinyavsky.

"Would you sing for us?" the agents supposedly asked Vysotsky when they were through grilling him.

"I need a guitar to sing," he supposedly answered.

"Oh, we just happen to have one."

Vysotsky sang his song, and they let him go.

As intellectual life around him sank into muck, Vysotsky spent part of each year in Paris with his French wife, Marina Vlady; he also drank heavily, drove his Mercedes recklessly through Moscow streets, played in the Taganka Theater, and sang about mythical escapes from the gulag, mythical war buddies being ripped to pieces, and mythical Moscow characters arguing, drinking, stealing each other's women, and, occasionally, knifing each other.

Vysotsky died in 1980 at age forty-two. A musical epitaph by Bulat Okudzhava invoked — whom else? — Bulgakov:

> These songs don't burn,
> they hover in the air,
> and the more you try to harm them
> the stronger they become.

✦

Aleksandr Galich sang at only one concert in the USSR: in 1968, at Academy City in Novosibirsk. He sang regularly in the apartments of people who liked him. Sometimes interrupted when the bell rang, he strummed his guitar, waiting for everyone to come in. These performances were too intimate to be called concerts. It was just Galich and his guitar. He did not have fans; he had friends.

He eventually was forced to emigrate, and in the West he performed, recorded, and made attempts at translation, but the spirit of Moscow *kompanii* was gone from his records. Galich was electrocuted while connecting a new piece of recording equipment in his Paris apartment.

✦

Even in his early poems, Naum Korzhavin reserved first-person singular for lyrical poetry. In the rest of his work, he wrote "we," referring to our generation.

> We can string our verses, simple, intricate, fair.
> But nobody will summon us to our own Senate Square.
> Wreaths of glory won't crown us.
> And in sleds, through the snow,
> Real women won't follow us to places we go.

He wrote these verses in 1944, when our life was not really life and we were a generation without a mission. Korzhavin had not been given the good looks customarily bestowed upon great Russian poets. He was a short, rotund man with bulging eyes and no neck. But like a large number of great Russian poets, he was arrested. It happened in 1947, the year when a person like him could have easily perished. During the thaw, after serving a term in

internal exile, Korzhavin continued to write about "us," the generation devoid of a Senate Square.

At some point, in a *kompaniya*, I read a copy of his "Tan'ka," a
poem about a Komsomol member who takes part in collectivization
and later ends up in the camps. She emerges from the camps as
an old woman of unshaken faith in communism. Korzhavin lectures
her:

> Evil in the name of good.
> I wonder who made up such nonsense.
> In the harshest of trials, in the bloodiest battles,
> If evil is given its way, if evil is led to triumph,
> Then it will exist for itself, alone, in its own name.

Korzhavin was not the voice of the dissidents; he spoke for the
broader circle of the intelligentsia, people who knew right from
wrong but who were unable to act.

In 1976, after being called to a KGB interrogation, Korzhavin
decided to emigrate. As far as anyone knew, he was in no danger of
imprisonment, but he did not want to risk it. "This is the best
situation possible," he said to me a few months before his departure. "I know that I will be leaving, but I am still here."

In more than a decade in America, he has been unable to learn
English; his psyche refuses to accept it. He sits in his Boston apartment, missing Russia.

✦

Throughout the thaw, Roy Medvedev and his twin brother,
Zhores, ran a salon that brought together the better-educated government and party officials, leading scientists, writers, old Bolsheviks, and Marxist reformers.

In those days, in Roy's Moscow apartment, Andrei Sakharov
could be seen talking to Aleksandr Solzhenitsyn. Roy, a historian
and a party member, studied Stalin's terror against the party.
Zhores, a biologist, had written a book about Stalin's destruction of
genetics. In 1964, immediately after the ouster of Khrushchev, Roy
started a samizdat journal called *Political Diary,* which operated for
six years.

Before 1968, no one was shocked by Roy's belief that democratic
socialism represented the only avenue for development of mankind.

After the invasion, Roy remained loyal to socialism. In his 1972 book *On Socialist Democracy,* he outlined his own version of "optimistic futurology," a ten-year plan for democratic reform that would turn the USSR into a genuinely socialist society. The book also acknowledged that democratic socialism had become the weakest of all unofficial ideologies in the USSR.

At the time, Roy was out of work and Zhores was in a mental institution. A year later, Zhores was expelled from the USSR.

✦

In March 1970, physicist Valentin Turchin wrote an open letter in which he invited the Soviet leaders to establish a dialogue with society.

"We seek a positive and constructive approach that would be acceptable to the party and government," he wrote. The letter, which was also signed by Sakharov and Roy Medvedev, continued: "Democratization, conducted under the leadership of the Communist party and in cooperation with all layers of society, would preserve and strengthen the leading role of the party in the economic, political and cultural life of our society."

Democratization would be the key to solving economic problems, from pollution of the environment to compensation for labor to advances in computer technology. It was a moderate argument for gradual reform. In 1983, economist Tatyana Zaslavskaya offered a similar critique of the system at a closed conference in Moscow. Her mentor, Abel Aganbegyan, has been making similar arguments since the thaw.

The Turchin letter could very well be considered the manifesto of Gorbachev's *perestroika.* But in 1970, the government was not inclined to accept invitations to join in dialogue. Soon after writing the letter, Turchin lost his job. Four years later, he started the USSR chapter of Amnesty International. In 1977, he was told that he would never find work in the Soviet Union and was given a choice between imprisonment and emigration.

He emigrated.

✦

After his brush with the KGB in 1957, when Marxist reformers Lev Krasnopevtsev, Kolya Pokrovsky, and Leonid Rendel cited his figures in leaflets, economist Boris Mikhalevsky became more careful.

He burrowed deeper into mathematical economics, carefully disguising his controversial thoughts in formulas and symbols. Since econometrics was just starting to develop in the USSR, Mikhalevsky had few peers. Still, even they frequently regarded his work as esoteric.

Mikhalevsky abandoned his caution in 1965, when he was asked to write an analysis of the performance of the Soviet economy. For starters, Mikhalevsky wrote that the Soviet Union's "military-totalitarian economy" favored some sectors while producing shortages in others. And since prices of scarce goods were kept stable and did not reflect their market availability, inflationary pressures were being created.

Thus, while the price of a can of sardines remained the same, the number of sardines in each can was being reduced or the same can was being relabeled as a new product and reintroduced at a higher price. Mikhalevsky collected his information by visiting stores once a year and checking the quality and quantity of goods against their prices. Using this method, he calculated that inflation in the real prices of consumer goods accounted for an overall price hike of 20 percent between 1956 and 1965.

For his frank assessments, Mikhalevsky was demoted and kept from going on a business trip to France, which was using one of his planning models. Finally he decided to emigrate, but was told that he should not even bother to apply. He knew too much. Mikhalevsky was fighting battles at home, too. Lena, his wife, wanted a baby. Boris didn't. "Elephants don't multiply in captivity," he said. Finally, Lena prevailed. In 1973, while she was giving birth, Boris drowned while on a canoe trip. He was forty-three.

✦

Natan Eidelman, a classmate of Mikhalevsky's in Moscow University's history department, also ended up on the KGB blacklist because of Krasnopevtsev's Marxist leaflets. After the 1957 case, Eidelman found a job at a museum outside Moscow. Trying to keep his sanity, he began to write. Eidelman wrote about Pushkin, the Decembrists, Herzen. In time, he became a popular historian of the Westernizers in Russia. It is telling that when I was putting together an index to the complete edition of Herzen's London-based publications, the Nauka Publishing House designated Eidelman as the expert for me to consult. Though he had no advanced degrees, taught no courses, and was not working with any institute, Eidelman was universally acknowledged as the leading authority in his field. His books, written for a general audience, leave no doubt that Eidelman, too, was a Westernizer. When he wrote about Pushkin and Herzen, the reader had no choice but to think of samizdat. When he wrote about the Decembrists, he evoked thought of modern dissenters. When he wrote about Pushkin's relationship with the czar, readers couldn't escape thinking of the perils of more recent samizdat authors. By writing about nineteenth-century Westernizers as if they were his contemporaries, Eidelman showed that Russian history had constant themes — themes that have remained unchanged over centuries.

Consider the conclusion from his book *Pushkin and the Decembrists.*

[The years] 1825 and 1826 were the landmark, the borderline that has divided many biographies into before and after.

Of course, this does not apply only to members of secret societies and the participants in the [Decembrist] uprising.

A certain era, its people, and its style were falling into the past.

Did these words not apply to Eidelman's era, Eidelman's generation, Eidelman's "before and after"?

> We repeat their whispers,
> We repeat their steps. . . .
> Can you come to the square?
> Dare you come to the square
> When that hour strikes?

Twelve

A Soviet dissident quickly became a pariah even among people who privately shared his views. He served as a silent, or not so silent, reminder that some people in Soviet society had chosen to act as citizens. By just being there, a dissident could induce guilt. The easiest way out would be to dismiss him as a wild-eyed fighter for justice with a penchant for heroic poses and drastic pronouncements.

Isolated from society, we lived in what amounted to a ghetto. Those who didn't wish us well characterized that ghetto as the place for failures. ("If you lack talent to triumph in your profession, you take it out on the regime.") It was not always easy to explain to outsiders that most of us were successful professionals who had become pariahs by choice, that we had no regrets and few doubts.

Our ghetto had its own traditions, literature, celebrations, etiquette, even institutions. While the rest of the country celebrated May 1, "the day of solidarity of the working masses," and November 7, the anniversary of the Bolshevik Revolution, we celebrated March 5, the day Stalin died.

When our friends spent their birthdays in prison, we celebrated with their relatives. On Daniel's birthday, we went to the home of

Iosif Aronovich Bogoraz, Larisa's father. On Galanskov's birthday, we gathered at his mother's; we called her Aunt Katya. On Ginzburg's birthday, we went to see Ludmilla Ilynichna, his mother; we called her *starushka,* "the old lady." On Andrei Amalrik's birthday, we went to Gyuzel's. On Larissa's birthday, we went back to Iosif Aronovich's. And later, after Galanskov's death, we returned to Aunt Katya's.

At all our gatherings, the first toast was raised to the hostess, the birthday boy, the newborn, or whatever. After 1967, we added a second traditional toast — "To those who cannot drink with us," a reference to *politzeki*. Eventually, it was abbreviated to "Toast Number Two." Everyone knew what it meant. After drinking to those who weren't with us, we raised glasses "to the success of our hopeless cause." That joke was on us.

Whenever you learned that a friend had been arrested, you pinned his picture on the wall, in solidarity. Whenever you found out that a friend's apartment was being searched, you went there and demanded to be allowed in. So, a dozen or so people would congregate on a stairwell while the KGB combed through books, manuscripts, and underwear drawers. In later years, some of us developed the gall to file suits against the KGB after searches or attacks in newspapers. At interrogations, we argued that articles 70 and 190 were unconstitutional because the Soviet constitution guaranteed freedom of expression.

We had work rules, too. If you didn't need help, you didn't tell anyone what you were doing. That was done to protect yourself and your friends. Leaving samizdat at the home of a fellow dissenter was considered unethical. To protect my samizdat from confiscation during searches, I usually piled it in suitcases and took it to friends who were beyond suspicion. I told them what was in the suitcases, then briefed them on what was to be done in the event of a search: "If, for whatever reason, someone opens it, say that I left it without telling you what's inside. I will confirm it."

My favorite hideaway was at the apartment of Nadezhda Markovna Ulanovskaya, widow of Aleksandr Petrovich, the would-be assassin of Hitler and Stalin. As an old Comintern operative with years of underground experience, she was not concerned about the piles of incriminating materials I stored in her pantry. "Go on, dear," she said whenever I showed up. "Hide your little papers. It's fine."

♦

Our movement had no leaders. They weren't needed. Each of us decided what he wanted to do and acted only on his own behalf. In the case of the "Red Cross," that presented a number of problems. Larisa was not born to manage finances, her own or anyone else's. The improvised charitable foundation fell on her shoulders because so many people wanted to help her imprisoned husband. Larisa did the best she could, and, fortunately, there were no standards for evaluating her performance.

With Larisa in internal exile, I found myself in the role of the fund's administrator. I was neither appointed nor elected to head the "Red Cross." Since it was known that I was Larisa's friend and helper, contributors began to show up at my door.

When I looked at the fund's structure and its finances, I was horrified. On the average, the fund collected about 300 rubles a month; but in some months it received 550 rubles, while in others it got only 50. Meanwhile, the single largest expenditure, about 1,200 rubles, came in September, when newspaper and magazine subscriptions had to be renewed for the following year. All publications, from *Novy mir* to *Ekonomicheskaya gazeta,* were in great demand in the camps.

The fund administrator had to spend the whole year praying that there would be enough money left over for subscriptions in September. You couldn't really plan a budget, what with contributions that came in sporadically and no way to predict the number of donors or the amount of their contributions. Projecting the outlays a year ahead was all the more difficult because we were not the ones deciding how many people would be arrested on political charges over the next twelve months.

The insane task was further complicated by accounting difficulties: the administrator could keep no ledgers. The majority of people who gave to our Red Cross didn't want the KGB to find out about their beneficence. Fund-raising, by necessity, involved many people. Some of them were likely to be provocateurs; many were likely to be inexperienced people who talked too much. In either case, information about the fund was bound to reach the KGB, which could then instruct any court to find our relief activities illegal. The administrator would then be open to prosecution for running a financial scam, which meant he risked ending up in the camps for common criminals.

First, I assessed the pattern of giving. Finding none, I drew up a plan. Whenever a contributor — usually someone representing co-workers at some institute or publishing house — knocked on my door, I counted the cash he tendered and delivered a short speech: "Your institute has just brought me seventy-five rubles, but you didn't give me anything last month or the month before. Why don't you give me twenty-five rubles every month. Contribute what-ever you can, just do it regularly. That way I will know what I can count on."

This worked well. Within a year, the fund's monthly take climbed from the average of 300 rubles a month to about 600 rubles a month. But increased giving complicated the accounting. Since the money was kept in my apartment, I lived in constant fear of a ten-ruble bill somehow slipping through my accounting system. So I made a rule: whenever I believed that public money was short, I automatically assumed responsibility and supplemented it from our less-than-plentiful family funds.

After a few months of keeping a ledger in my mind, I began to lose sleep. Around the same time, I realized that administrators of public funds are not universally loved. Stories of my favoring some camps — and some *politzeki* — over others began to circulate throughout Moscow. More specifically, I was accused of favoring my friends Larisa Bogoraz, Tolya Marchenko, and Yulik Daniel. There were also a few people who said with obvious implications: "Alexeyeva's out of work. So you can understand why she is in charge of the fund."

The problems were compounded even further because some do-nors wanted me to give money to particular *politzeki*. One Moscow woman had left 100 rubles of her estate to Marya Sinyavskaya. It was up to me to execute her final wish. And then there was the separate collection for Larisa, the one started by Pyotr Grigorenko to buy the peasant hut in Siberia. Indeed, Larisa was getting more help than the Red Cross beneficiaries, but the money didn't go through the Red Cross. Try to explain that to a *politzek*'s wife.

At first, I was shaken by every story of every wife or mother of every *politzek*. These tired women would sit down at my kitchen table and start telling their tragic stories. Then, with repetition, the stories started to lose their shock value. The elements were the same: the husband, sentenced to ten years, is doing time in Mordovia; he suffers from peptic ulcers but cannot obtain release from work as a lumberjack; the wife has been fired from her job; on the last visit to Mordovia, she was strip-searched and heckled by twenty-year-old prison guards and then not allowed to see the husband; the children have been called "traitors" by classmates and teachers; the *politzek*'s mother is dying of cancer; she won't see the son again. There is uniformity in horror. I began to hate myself for having become so wooden and thick-skinned.

Some of the women asked for a modest stipend for food and other expenses. I wanted to give it to them, but I couldn't. The fund was there to pay the legal fees, to buy food, warm clothes, and newspaper and magazine subscriptions for *politzeki,* and to cover all travel expenses, including food, for family members going to visit them.

These were desperate people. Several had gone first to Arina Zholkovskaya, Ginzburg's wife, who administered a fund similar to the Red Cross. If they played it right, those women could dip into public money twice. I was embarrassed to inform Arina about such cases. Whenever those people knocked on my door, I found that I was unable to look them in the eyes.

Two years after I took over the fund, I made my first attempt to get out. My designated replacement was Irina Belogorodskaya, who had just served a year for having distributed a letter in defense of Marchenko.

I invited Irina to my apartment, gave her a detailed outline of the fund's operation, then asked her if she would be interested in taking over.

"No, thanks," she said.

✦

In May 1970, the KGB came to search my apartment. They found no lists, no ledgers; just 300 rubles in one wallet and 20 in another. (The wallet with 20 rubles was my own.) No lists of fund activists were to be found in our cabinets.

"Where did you get the money?" the KGB investigator asked. She was an attractive woman about my age who came in wearing patent leather shoes, a glistening dress, and liberally applied makeup.

"Are you saying that a Soviet citizen cannot accumulate three hundred twenty rubles through honest labor?" I said. At the time, there was no way we could have accumulated 320 rubles.

Tamara Gnevkovskaya, the investigator, left empty-handed. A few months later, she got drunk in the presence of a man tied into our dissident network. The conversation turned to her work, which Gnevkovskaya said she loved. "I've been in the camps, and I've learned my lesson. It's better to be putting people away than to be put away yourself," she said. It was said that when she was in her teens, she was shoved into one of the cars that cruised Moscow streets in search of sex partners for Lavrenty Beria. The road from Beria's bedroom led to the camps.

A few drinks later, she mentioned her search of my apartment. "They call themselves the intelligentsia," she said. "All they've got is one suit in the closet."

✦

Late in 1971, we moved to a new apartment in southwest Moscow. The phone had not been hooked up; the new address was not yet known to Red Cross volunteers. To keep the fund in operation, I would have had to spend a few days running around Moscow, contacting everyone who needed to know how to find me.

But the morning after the move, I found it difficult to get out of bed. I forced myself to get up, had breakfast with Misha and Kolya, then, as soon as they walked out of the apartment, climbed back in bed, covered myself with a blanket, and surrendered to the sense of heaviness and comfort.

What will happen to the Red Cross if I am arrested or if I die? I thought. I will not be there to fret about *politzeki* not getting their *Novy mir*. The fund will either continue or it won't. So, let's assume I am dead.

This state of depression lasted for two or three weeks. When I returned to my former self, I used up the money I had, but made no attempt to restart the Red Cross. That made Ginzburg's wife Arina's work more difficult, but soon she found helpers. Complementing Arina's work, a foundation to aid the children of *politzeki* was started by Vladimir Albrekht. The committee raised money by organizing benefit concerts at the apartments of fund activists.

✦

Pyotr Grigorenko enjoyed the free spirit and spontaneity of our movement, but thought it needed some sort of an organizational structure. Even after losing his general's stars, Grigorenko craved something to take the place of battle plans, firefights, air support, and matériel. Pyotr Yakir and Viktor Krasin agreed with him.

I belonged to the opposing school of thought. After sixteen years in the Communist party, I didn't want to be anyone's subordinate or anyone's superior. I wanted to reserve the right to pick the people with whom I worked. Besides, though I pitied Yakir, I did not want to collaborate with him on anything. He was unreliable, loud, and unpredictable. Two episodes made me particularly uneasy.

On August 26, 1968, the day after the Red Square demonstration, a dozen of us gathered in the street outside Dina Kaminskaya's office. As we waited for Kaminskaya to arrive, Yakir heard someone whisper that there had been a series of searches in the Ukraine. "Searches!" Yakir echoed in his booming voice. "We have to tell Natasha Gorbanevskaya! Have her put it in *Khronika*!" Everyone fell silent. Natasha's editorship of *Khronika* was not supposed to be advertised.

About a year later, a just-released *zek* stopped by at Yakir's to bring a message from a camp buddy, Vladimir Dremlyuga, one of the Red Square demonstrators. Dremlyuga wanted to thank me for concealing a ten-ruble note in a book I had sent him. I received that message from Yakir, over the phone: "Hey, Lyudka, I have this *zek* here. He says Volod'ka Dremlyuga got the ten rubles you glued into some book. He says thanks. Well done. Keep it up!"

It was a secret that money was being sent to the camps. The method used for sending money was even more of a secret. Broadcasting it from Yakir's monitored telephone into my monitored telephone made it less of one.

Meanwhile, the uninitiated, including the foreign press corps, seemed to be forming the mistaken impression that Yakir was "one of the leaders" or even "the leader" of the democratic movement in the USSR. He was a natural media event: son of an executed commander, a former political prisoner, and a man of many opinions. Those opinions, broadcast over shortwave radio, indeed made some in the Soviet provinces believe that the opposition had a leader and that Yakir was that leader. So they came to his house with their samizdat and their news dispatches for *Khronika*. I wish there had been a way to get him to stop talking, but our movement had not invested anyone with power to censure or excommunicate. Loud and careless as he was, Yakir was one of us because he wanted to be one of us, because he said he was one of us, and because there was no one who could dispute his claims.

The reality of those claims notwithstanding, with every passing day an increasing number of people perceived Yakir as the leader of the opposition. And every passing day increased the likelihood of his arrest.

✦

In the spring of 1969, Latvia's KGB had arrested Ivan Yakhimovich, the Latvian collective-farm chairman who had written a letter protesting the Galanskov-and-Ginzburg trial, then signed a letter applauding Czechoslovakia's reforms.

Grigorenko suggested forming a "committee" that would demand Yakhimovich's release. Yakir and Krasin backed that idea. The committee would have been the first organization ever to be started by the Soviet human-rights movement. I ran into the three of them at the apartment of Ginzburg's mother as they were deciding whom to invite to join the committee.

"Fine," I said when they invited me. "I'll join if you explain what a committee can do that all of us can't do without calling ourselves a committee. We can sign letters as individuals, we can help his family as individuals. The only thing we can do as a committee is go to prison sooner." That opinion was not mine alone. The Yakhimovich Defense Committee was never formed.

After the letter in defense of Marchenko, I vowed to read all epistles before signing them. I read letters thoroughly, and liked very few. Appeals to Soviet authorities had served their purpose in 1968; through them, the society told the government and the entire world that it had opinions that were different from the officially prescribed ones and that the people and the party were not one and the same. The authorities did not respond. It made no sense to keep writing to them. Such letters had become a dead genre. Besides, my *Khronika,* samizdat, and "Red Cross" work required that I keep a low profile. After 1968, I made it a rule to sign only the letters protesting arrests, as a sign of solidarity with those arrested.

In May 1969, outside the courthouse where *samizdatchik* Ilya Burmistrovich was standing trial under Article 190, Pyotr Yakir told me about a forthcoming letter addressed to U Thant, secretary general of the United Nations. "We are writing to the United Nations because over the past several years our protests and complaints addressed to the highest government and judicial authorities in the USSR have received no response," the letter began.

"That's something I would sign," I said to Yakir.

"Wait a second!" he shouted, and raced for a pay phone.

He returned despondent. "It's already been mailed," he said.

Pyotr had neglected to tell me that the *podpisanty* called themselves "the Initiative Group in Defense of Human Rights in the USSR." I would have been less willing to join anything called "group."

The group was nothing other than fifteen people who had in the past signed a great many letters. Yet, when those same fifteen people decided to call themselves an organization, they struck a nerve. As soon as the letter reached the West, shortwave radio stations read it as the lead news item. After that, all the group members were dragged in to interrogations. I had not seen such a news splash since the Bogoraz-Litvinov letter a year earlier. General Grigorenko may have been right. The movement was ripe for an organizational structure.

A few days after the Initiative Group was announced, I told Tosha Yakobson, a group member, that initially I'd been sorry that the group's letter went out before I was able to sign it. "But I am no longer sorry," I said. "Not everyone should come to the square. Some of us must work in the shadows."

Yakobson looked at me with scorn. I knew what he must have

been thinking: I hadn't joined the group because I thought it would be too dangerous. And he just may have been right.

◆

In June 1969, I received a letter from Tolya Marchenko. He had almost finished his one-year term for "malicious violation of passport rules," but was rearrested in the camp and accused of slandering the state in conversations with other prisoners.

Something had to be done, but it seemed to make no sense to write another letter to the procurator general. If you had to complain to anyone, it seemed more effective to let the new group do the complaining.

The only Initiative Group member I could find was Natasha Gorbanevskaya. "Natasha," I said, "don't you think the Initiative Group ought to take a stand on Marchenko?"

"Yes, but where would you find the Initiative Group in the middle of June?" She paused. "But I guess it's such a clear-cut case that no one will object if we issue something."

The signature under the letter we drafted read "Initiative Group." No names were given. The letter was copied, then passed along to the Western press. Soon after it was broadcast over shortwave radio, I was visited by Tatyana Velikanova, a member of the Initiative Group. Velikanova said she was flabbergasted when she heard foreign radio announcers read an Initiative Group document that she couldn't recall signing or even reading. Since the letter was about Marchenko, she concluded that I would know something about it. I told her that Natasha Gorbanevskaya and I had written the letter.

"Please, don't ever issue Initiative Group documents without consent of the Initiative Group," she said.

About a year later, in May 1970, *Khronika* received a copy of an open letter from the Initiative Group that summarized the group's first year of work. Addressed to Reuters and the Soviet press agency Novosti, the letter said:

After the first appeal and the emergence of the name, "the Initiative Group," it remained to be determined whether the group constituted a onetime association organized to make a

single appeal to the United Nations or whether it would continue its work.

It was another conviction of the already imprisoned Anatoly
Marchenko, the author of *My Testimony,* that made us write
the second letter. That letter was signed: "the Initiative
Group." That was how the decision regarding the group's
continued existence was made.

After the letter about Marchenko was broadcast over foreign
radio, the group could no longer claim to be a onetime association.
To make that claim, it would have had to disavow a letter in Tolya's
defense. Natasha Gorbanevskaya and I had unwittingly forced the
group into continuing its existence.

By May 1970, six of the fifteen original members of the Initiative Group had faced the KGB reprisals: Natasha Gorbanevskaya,
Pyotr Grigorenko, and Vladimir Borisov were in mental institutions; Viktor Krasin had been convicted of parasitism and forced to
move out of Moscow; Mustafa Dzhemiliev and Anatoly Krasnov-
Levitin were in the camps. Over the years, all fifteen faced criminal
sanctions.

The group's letters to the United Nations received no reply.

✦

In January 1971, as I was typing *Khronika* issue number 17, I came
across something called "The Principles and Regulations of the
Committee for Human Rights in the USSR."

As I typed Principle One, I started to giggle:

> The Committee for Human Rights is a creative association
> which operates in accordance with laws of the state as well as
> in accordance with Regulations and Principles as stated below.

The document left no doubt that Valery Chalidze, its author, had
outdone even Alek Esenin-Volpin. It was written in impeccable,
almost comical legalese. I laughed at every sentence, imagining the
look on the face of some KGB operative the morning Valery's
Principles and Regulations were placed on his desk. "I have a talent
to write incomprehensibly," Valery said to me once. Here that
talent was revealed in full.

According to its Principles and Regulations, the committee was going to offer:

- Consultative assistance to the organs of state in the field of creation and application of guarantees of human rights, undertaken on the initiative of the Committee or the concerned organs of governance.
- Creative assistance to persons interested in constructive study of theoretical aspects of the problem of human rights and study of the specifics of that problem in a socialist state.
- Legal educational work, including propagandizing of documents on international and Soviet law pertaining to human rights.

Valery had to have read enormous heaps of Soviet legal documents to emulate their language and give them a creative spin.

My God, it seemed they were going to take minutes at their meetings! That was the opposite of the accepted strategy: we tried not to put much on paper, mostly as a way of keeping our KGB dossiers as thin as possible. The committee even had an administrative structure. At the top of the pyramid were the "Committee Members." They were Valery Chalidze, Andrei Sakharov, and Andrei Tverdokhlebov. All three were physicists.

The "Committee Members" were aided by "Experts." An "Expert" was defined as "a person who, while not being a Committee Member, possesses a recognized competence in the field of human rights." (Alek Esenin-Volpin and Boris Tsukerman were the Experts.) The third designation, that of committee "Correspondent," was "a person who is neither a Committee Member nor an Expert of the Committee." That honor fell on the shoulders of poet Aleksandr Galich and writer Aleksandr Solzhenitsyn.

In 1970, it seemed impossible to imagine the KGB arresting Sakharov, Solzhenitsyn, and Galich. None of the three celebrities had joined groups before. It was a real feat to include them. At the same time, Chalidze, Esenin-Volpin, and Tsukerman would insist on strict observance of Soviet law, giving the authorities no cause for prosecution. The committee would be invulnerable.

When I was through typing, I decided to make arrangements to observe the committee's deliberations. I called Chalidze. "This is Ludmilla Alexeyeva. I would like to petition the committee."

"I am sorry, but the committee doesn't hear petitions from the public," Chalidze said.

"Then, under what conditions does the committee receive information from the public?"

"Please, be so kind as to submit your petition in written form." Formality, after all, was the pillar of the teachings of Aleksandr Sergeyevich Esenin-Volpin.

"In that case, I would like to ask the committee for leniency. I have a very important matter to discuss, but lack the time to formalize it in written form. I would like to testify before you and have my testimony registered in your minutes."

"What is the issue you plan to address?"

"The right of political prisoners to correspond." It was an important issue, and it fit into the scope of themes that were to be taken up by the committee.

"If you insist, we will make an accommodation in your case, but, please understand, the committee meetings are not open to the public. Your testimony will be put on the agenda; you will be allowed to address the committee, after which you will be expected to leave the chambers."

I showed up at the appointed hour, but the three Committee Members were several items behind schedule on their crowded agenda. Valery apologized, then courteously showed me to the couch where I was to await my turn to address the committee.

I couldn't cue in to the discussion, so I watched, enjoying the sight of our first legally founded organization. They were an entertaining trio: Chalidze, the tall Georgian prince; Tverdokhlebov, the young, blond physicist, as tall as Chalidze; and Sakharov, the stooped, middle-aged man in a baggy suit. They sat in chairs around a coffee table in the center of Chalidze's enormous, cluttered room.

"The committee has received a request from Ludmilla Mikhailovna Alekseyeva to discuss the right of prisoners to maintain correspondence," Chalidze announced to his fellow Committee Members.

I stood up and made a brief presentation as the distinguished panelists looked up awkwardly from their chairs.

"Thank you, Ludmilla Mikhailovna. The committee will take this into consideration," said Chalidze.

For weeks, I entertained my friends with the story of my wondrous journey into that inner sanctum of Alek-Esenin-Volpinism.

✦

The Committee for Human Rights in the USSR became the first public association in the Soviet Union to join the international human-rights community. In June 1971, it became part of the International League of Human Rights, a nongovernment group that had an advisory status to the United Nations. It also became part of the International Institute of Law, an organization headed by René Cassin, author of the 1948 Universal Declaration of Human Rights.

None of the members, experts, or advisers was ever arrested for work associated with the committee. That alone could be regarded as a major achievement.

✦

On the evening of March 29, 1971, KGB operatives knocked on Vladimir Bukovsky's door. Bukovsky was on the phone with Valery Chalidze. "It's for me," Bukovsky said. Then the phone went dead.

At that instant, I walked into Chalidze's room. I had just finished typing *Khronika* issue number 18, as well as a short document for the Committee for Human Rights.

"It's a good thing you're here," said Valery. "I have to run over to Bukovsky's. There is a search on."

"I have samizdat with me," I said. I wanted to go, too, but my eight copies of *Khronika* could not be left at Chalidze's. His place was just as likely to be searched as Bukovsky's. Leaving the copies in my bag and taking it with me to a KGB search was out of the question. People who showed up at searches were apt to be frisked.

The prudent thing would have been for me to take my *Khronika* and go home. Instead, I cooked up a plan: Chalidze and I would walk to Bukovsky's together, then I would stand outside while he entered the apartment. When the search had ended, he would come out and get me. If Bukovsky had been arrested, I would talk to his mother. If he hadn't, I would ask him directly what had happened at the search.

Before we could leave, one more detail remained to be worked out: I needed the least conspicuous way to carry the samizdat. I asked Valery to wait, went into the bathroom, rolled up my eight copies of *Khronika,* and placed them in my brassiere.

A few minutes later, Chalidze and I were walking down a winding street off the Arbat. Snow creaked under our feet; it was the kind of gorgeous, wintery evening that made me think of black cats, a full moon, snowdrifts, and *The Master and Margarita.*

I don't know how we ended up in a KGB car. All I can say is that we were walking down the street, then, in an instant, we were in the backseat. "Sitting" would not be the right word to describe my position. There were four of us: two operatives by the windows, and Valery and I between them. My choice was between settling on Valery's lap or the *KGBshnik*'s. Naturally, I chose Valery's.

"Valery," I said, "do you suppose we have been kidnapped by brigands? If these were the authorities, they would have identified themselves and shown us an arrest warrant. If we have been kidnapped, do you suppose it would do any good to scream?"

"Well," said Valery, "if you are referring to observance of established procedure, then, certainly, the authorities would not have apprehended us without first properly identifying themselves and showing us an arrest warrant. But, you see, Ludmilla Mikhailovna, in our country, law-enforcement officials have developed a peculiar tradition of circumventing due process. Given those traditions, I would have to conclude that we have been placed in custody by representatives of the authorities."

At that point, the car pulled to a stop at the militia precinct station. Chalidze announced: "You see, my instinct was right. We are not among kidnappers. You didn't need to worry."

The two goons stuffed in the backseat beside us stayed mum.

Inside the precinct station waiting room, a rustling sound emanating from my chest area reminded me about the eight concealed copies of *Khronika.* Onionskin paper can sound very much like dry, crackling onion skin. It struck me that if any of those people had good hearing, I would be searched immediately.

"I have eight copies of *Khronika* in my clothes," I whispered to Valery.

"Ask to go to the bathroom," he whispered back.

Politely, I asked to be excused, but a woman in a militia uniform was sent to the bathroom with me. I returned to the waiting room, concentrating on minimizing the rustling.

At that moment, a man in plainclothes served Chalidze a search warrant. "We are going to return to your apartment, with the lady," he said.

"Why do you need the lady?" Valery protested. "Let her go."

"Look, I am in a hurry. I am expected back at home," I joined in.

"Do you have any documents?"

The militia officer looked through my passport and told me I could go. Ever so gently, I turned to the door.

"Wait a minute, get that woman back here!" This had to be it. The arrest; Article 70; seven years in the camps, five in internal exile; Moscow anecdotes about the unforeseen quirks of onionskin paper. "Give me back your passport."

The official copied down my name, address, and place of work. Then he returned the document to me and with a wave of his hand told me I was free to go. He had simply forgotten to record the necessary information at first.

Later that night we learned that Bukovsky had been arrested. He would be charged under Article 70 with engaging in anti-Soviet propaganda.

✦

A statuesque Ukrainian artist named Stefa Gulyk came to Moscow with bad news: On December 8, 1971, the Odessa KGB arrested Nina Strokata, *Khronika*'s contact in the Ukraine. Since the KGB had raised its hand against a woman, the knights of the Ukrainian opposition had decided to form the Committee to Defend Strokata.

The committee would include my Ukrainian friends Ivan Svitlychny and Vyacheslav Chornovil, a journalist who had served a prison term for compiling a transcript of the political trials held in the Ukraine in 1965. The Muscovites invited were Pyotr Yakir and I. I was not overjoyed by the idea of forming that committee. Any committee formed in the Ukraine was certain to end up in prison without accomplishing anything save for announcing its charter. Nina's situation would not be better for it.

I told Stefa that we must think of rational ways to help Nina, that we must not be guided by our emotions, and that we should, perhaps, consult a legal expert. Then I took her to see Valery Chalidze, who, predictably, advised against forming the committee.

I asked Stefa to communicate Chalidze's opinion to the committee organizers. However, I said, if they decided to disregard his recommendation, I would join the committee.

After that, Stefa went to see Yakir and Krasin, who suggested the opposite: Go to Kiev, tell your people that we will join, and don't worry about what Chalidze and Alexeyeva say.

By the time Stefa returned to the Ukraine, the question of the committee's formation was moot. During the few days she had spent in Moscow, the Ukrainian KGB had arrested eleven activists, including Ivan Svitlychny and Vyacheslav Chornovil. Dissident crackdowns had a way of starting in the Ukraine.

✦

On the morning of January 14, 1972, KGB operatives broke into eight Moscow apartments, including Yakir's. Additional searches were held in Leningrad, Novosibirsk, and Vilnius. Search warrants were signed by the same KGB investigator. The case was identified as Case 24. After the searches came the interrogations. In Vilnius alone, a hundred people were dragged in. On January 17, Kronid Lubarsky, an astrophysicist, became the first to be arrested in the new case.

The KGB was preparing to deal another blow to the public movement, but with *Khronika* in operation, the authorities could be certain that most arrests would become the subject of *glasnost*. News of each arrest would be broadcast worldwide, literally. That would be devastating, especially considering that in 1972, the Brezhnev government was pursuing the policy of détente with the West. Thus, KGB chief Yuri Andropov's assignment was to strangle *Khronika* without making too many arrests, especially in Moscow. Unable to resort to mass terror, Andropov had to find a creative way to stop *glasnost*. His officials had to study our dossiers and our psychological profiles to find our vulnerabilities.

✦

Kolya Williams was away on business on March 5 of that year. That left me looking for another *politzek* with whom to mark the nineteenth anniversary of Stalin's death.

"Come on over," said Pyotr Yakir when I called to ask if I could be invited to his place.

The host, already red-faced, showed me to a chair. I looked around. The walls in the apartment were bare. The table was covered with a dirty piece of vinyl. *Zakuski,* the appetizers, consisted of a pile of large pickles dumped out in the center of the makeshift tablecloth; they were secreting a puddle of green brine. One of the guests was asleep on the couch; two others, a man and a woman with puffed-up faces, were wandering around the table. None of them seemed to be especially well acquainted with Pyotr and Valentina Yakir, their hosts.

Yakir poured the vodka. The guests, except for the one on the couch, returned to their shot glasses. Everyone drank up and bit into pickles; the partially eaten pickles were then placed directly on the vinyl, alongside the shot glasses. After that, the guests and the host wiped their mouths with sleeves. There were no plates and no napkins.

I was ready to leave. But before opening the door to let me out, Yakir launched into a story.

"Lyudka, listen. I want you to look at this corridor." It was a long, dark hallway with a trunk on the floor and a telephone on the wall. "You know, I get back from work at six. Val'ka comes back at seven. So, I come home and there's no one here. Understand? Just me. I don't go inside the rooms. I just sit down on this trunk, pick up the phone, and call people for a whole hour until she comes in. I call people, and I talk, and all the while I keep looking at the door, thinking, 'Here they are, they've come for me, they'll break in the door, and they'll lead me away.' "

I thought of my phone conversations with Pyotr. Most of them left me wondering why he had called. We weren't close enough for him to call me for no reason. Yet he did — usually between the hours of six and seven.

That ravaged fate of his. He had all the reasons to hate them, yet he had no discipline, no self-control; he was dragged into battles, egged on by the visits of provincial truth-seekers, encouraged by the skin-deep stories written by Western reporters who came to regard his voice as the voice of the movement.

Thanks to the press and the people duped by it, heroic stances had become his identity. He lived for them, trying to forget that beneath his pamphleteering surged the total, paralyzing fear of a privileged fourteen-year-old boy taken away from his mother.

◆

When I heard of Yakir's arrest the following June, I surprised myself by sobbing uncontrollably. I cried for hours, asking myself, "Why?" without finding an answer. I felt that something horrible had happened. There was a sense of catastrophe.

On September 12, the KGB arrested Viktor Krasin. Neither Yakir nor Krasin knew much about the workings of *Khronika*. In any case, they'd heard nothing from me. (My main reason for distrusting Krasin was that everything he knew was immediately passed on to Yakir.) On September 28, the KGB came after Yuri Shikhanovich, a Moscow mathematician.

Now they were precisely two steps away from finding out that, at the time, the bulletin was being edited by Tosha Yakobson, a friend of Daniel's and a member of the Initiative Group. From Yakobson, *Khronika* went to me. I typed the first eight copies and, through a volunteer courier, sent it to Shikhanovich, who was in charge of distributing my eight copies to typists. The system was structured in such a way that Shikhanovich would have known that he was receiving *Khronika* from me, but would not have known that I was receiving it from Yakobson.

On November 4 at the KGB Lefortovo prison, Yakir was allowed to see his daughter. In front of two investigators, he told her that materials shown to him during his incarceration had made him change his attitude toward the democratic movement. More than anything else, he said, the investigators had convinced him of the harmful nature of *Khronika Tekushchikh Sobytiy,* and he asked her to pass on his plea that the bulletin be stopped. Each new issue would lead to new arrests, he had been warned, and would also add years to his and Krasin's prison terms. If *Khronika* continued, anyone could be arrested, even those who had nothing to do with the bulletin.

One thing was clear: Yakir was cooperating with his captors. Later, we learned that Krasin had been broken as well.

✦

On the day of Yakir's talk with his daughter, Yuri Galanskov, the poet, died of a hemorrhage in a Mordovian prison camp. He was thirty-three.

Those who gathered at Galanskov's wake in Moscow divided their time between mourning the young man and assessing the new strategy adopted by the KGB. The Committee for State Security was in effect telling the public that it had taken two hostages, and that unless *Khronika* stopped appearing, it was prepared to take more. Any one of us, even those who had nothing to do with publishing the bulletin, could be taken away.

We had two alternatives: give in to terrorism or extend the misery for Yakir, Krasin, and whomever else the KGB decided to arrest.

✦

Larisa and Tolya had returned from Siberia, and after a few months, Tolya found a place in Tarusa, a town about six hours (by train, then bus) from Moscow. By then, Yulik Daniel was out of the camps, too, and Larisa no longer had to play the role of the wife of a *politzek*. She married Tolya and wanted to join him in Tarusa. However, to avoid prosecution under antiparasitism and residency laws, she had to find a job in Moscow.

I offered to hire her as a maid. No work would need to be done, and no money would change hands. But there could be a problem getting such a transparently bogus arrangement past the authorities. Kolya and I did not have small children, both of us were well, and we did not make enough money to be able to afford a maid. Larisa's degree, the equivalent of an American PhD, was bound to raise flags for the bureaucrats who process contracts for employment of domestics.

Larisa and I agreed on the details: we would say that she would be working part-time and earning thirty rubles a month; on the forms, she would neglect to mention her education; and to make the arrangement plausible, Larisa would try to appear less than intelligent.

"How is this?" asked Larisa as soon as we walked into the building of the regional committee. Her mouth was slightly ajar, her tongue on the verge of spilling out. Her eyes showed complete lack of thought.

"A little overdone."

Throughout our interview, I kept my eyes on the bureaucrat who processed our employment contract. Looking at Larisa meant risking an explosion of the giggles. She had become her role. Her overacting even affected her handwriting. The form was filled out with illiterate chicken scratches.

A few days later, I visited Tolya and Lara in Tarusa. After dinner, I spotted a stack of dirty dishes and began to wash them.

"Draw the curtains!" shouted Larisa. "I don't want the neighbors to see my employer doing my dishes."

◆

Irina Belogorodskaya never learned to be careful. She had served a year in the camps after leaving the bag of letters in defense of Marchenko in a Moscow taxicab. In the fall of 1972, Irina was in trouble once again.

This time she had lined up a typist for *Khronika*. The typist was to be paid for the work but, Irina said, she was dependable. It may well have seemed so, but the typist got caught, and under questioning by the KGB, she said that it was Irina Belogorodskaya who had supplied her with *Khronika*. Poor Irina was dragged through a series of interrogations.

"Girls, girls, I don't want to go to prison — not at this time in my life," Irina lamented to Larisa and me.

Just a few months earlier, Irina had married poet Vadim Delone, one of the Red Square demonstrators. Arrest is never a good thing, but an arrest soon after the honeymoon is even worse.

Finally, she struck a deal with the KGB: she promised to end her involvement with *Khronika,* and the KGB promised to leave her alone.

◆

Sometime in October, at work at the Institute of Information on Social Sciences, I was called in to personnel. A young man, about the same age as my older son, showed me a red booklet that identified him as a representative of the Committee for State Security.

"Please follow me," he said.

I didn't want to make a scene at the office. I waited till we got into the black Volga.

"What is this, theater?" I shouted. "Have you been following me to find out when I would come to the office? What do you want from me?"

"No, no, we just happened by, to see if you might be at the office," the young man stammered. There are times when it pays to be a middle-aged woman.

"Why did you need to pick me up at work? If you want to talk to me, send me a summons, like civilized people! Now the people in personnel will start talking about the KGB coming to get me for interrogations!"

"But we didn't tell anyone that you are being taken to an interrogation. They could just think that you are one of our secret employees."

"Is that supposed to make me feel better?" The young man turned pale.

The black Volga rolled into the courtyard of one of the KGB office buildings.

We walked through the corridors, tunnels, and staircases. The walk built up the drama. Finally, the young man, who must have been a lieutenant, led me into an office, saluted, and did an about-face.

"Actually, I am not the one who wanted to talk to you," said the man behind the desk. Judging by the salute of the lieutenant who had delivered me, this one was at least a major.

"Who is it that wants to talk to me so badly?"

"My supervisor."

With these words, the major took me on another walk through the tunnels, dungeons, and stairwells. We walked into another office. The major stretched out in a salute, passed me over to another operative, and departed.

The "supervisor" — a colonel, I guess — took me on yet another brisk walk through hallways, elevators, and annexes, led me up to a receptionist, saluted, and barked: "Ludmilla Mikhailovna Alek-seyeva delivered to you."

The receptionist, whose rank I didn't want to guess, took me into an enormous, posh office. The bespectacled man behind the mahogany desk got up to greet me. He introduced himself as Aleksandr Mikhailovich.

Aleksandr Mikhailovich wore a dark suit, a fresh shirt, a nice tie, and glasses in an elegant frame.

"Ludmilla Mikhailovna, have you noticed that our organization is very nice to you?" he said.

"Why should I think that? Your people have dragged me away from my desk, virtually kidnapped me, had me follow them through these silly corridors and staircases, and I still have no idea what's going on. Next time just send me a summons."

"You mean you really haven't noticed that we are quite liberal, even lenient, in your case?"

"Honestly, I haven't."

"In that case, let me remind you. A few months ago you were at a militia station with eight copies of a manuscript rustling in your clothes." They must have received the story through the Moscow grapevine. I didn't see them being so gentlemanly as to pass up a chance to pull eight copies of *Khronika* out of a lady's underwear.

"Well, what's fallen off the horse cart is gone forever," I said.

That ended the conversation.

✦

As the KGB kept closing in on *Khronika,* I kept getting dragged to interrogations. Sometimes it was because of Yakir and Krasin; other times it was because of the Ukrainians. It got to the point where I worked out a preinterrogation routine. I would get off the metro at the Karl Marx Prospekt, stop at a carryout food store, buy a ham sandwich, an eclair, a slice of chocolate cake, and two oranges, then walk the rest of the way to the KGB building.

As the interrogator repeated his questions, I answered politely that I knew nothing about *Khronika,* Yakir, Krasin, and the Ukrainians. Around noon, without apologies or excuses, I reached into my bag to produce my sandwich. After eating it, I reached for an orange; the scent of an orange peeled slowly can have a hypnotizing effect. An hour later, I reached for the chocolate cake. Then I peeled another orange. The eclair was saved for the end.

I have no doubt that by the time I got to the eclair, the interrogator had to strain to control his salivary glands. That, of course, put me in the position of strength. There was also the matter of the bathroom; the good Lord had given me a remarkably strong bladder, thereby undermining my interrogator's gambit of restricting my access to the toilet.

I don't know precisely how many interrogations I went to that year; it was more than a dozen. One of them, in October, was less routine than the others. In midafternoon, after I had consumed my second orange but before I got to the eclair, the interrogation was interrupted by a man who identified himself as Vladimir Pavlovich.

Vladimir Pavlovich was about my age. He was tall, elegantly dressed, and courteous. He was from operations. Since he was showing interest in me, I concluded that he was my *kurator* ("curator"), the operative given the power to decide whether, or how soon, I would go to prison.

"Ludmilla Mikhailovna, I think you and I need to talk about Irina Belogorodskaya," he suggested.

I couldn't decline to discuss Irina. Though she lived up to her promise not to work on *Khronika*, there was no guarantee that the KGB would live up to its part of the deal. Irina remained a potential target of Case 24.

"You do realize that she is walking a tightrope?"

"I have a feeling that it would be best for her to emigrate," I said.

"Yes, it might be a good idea," Vladimir Pavlovich agreed. "But that would require an invitation from Israel."

"Don't worry about that," I said. In 1972, the Israelis were routinely sending out thousands of invitations. "Are you saying that if she applies she would be allowed to emigrate?"

"I can't tell you with certainty. Just get her an invitation, and act quickly."

I reported the conversation to Irina. She reported it to her husband, Vadim Delone.

"Vadim says he is a Russian poet, and a Russian poet cannot exist without hearing Russian speech," she finally told me.

It seemed to be her last chance to avoid tragedy.

✦

At first, the investigators confronted me with evidence given by Yakir and Krasin: "Ludmilla Mikhailovna, your friends tell us that you are in charge of the Ukrainian section of *Khronika*."

"That's odd. *Khronika* doesn't have a Ukrainian section." They were right. Much of the news from the Ukraine was channeled through me. But the Ukraine didn't have a separate section, so, technically, the testimony of Yakir and Krasin was inaccurate.

Then came the questions about the Ukrainian Committee to Defend Nina Strokata. The committee was never formed, but the KGB had found a draft of its first document in Yakir's apartment.

"I don't know of such a committee," I said.

"Didn't Stefaniya Gulyk come from the Ukraine to invite you to join it?"

"She came to Moscow to get an attorney for Strokata." That was true. Stefa and I indeed had looked for an attorney.

"Ludmilla Mikhailovna, you shouldn't conceal this episode. We know you were opposed to creating the committee."

It would have helped me to admit that it was so; at the same time, it would have damaged the Ukrainians. It was far more prudent to deny it.

Also, at the time, I feared that the KGB was taking Stefa to interrogations and confronting her with statements like, "Ludmilla Mikhailovna Alekseyeva has told us everything. You were the courier for the Committee to Defend Nina Strokata." So as soon as I returned from the KGB, I asked a friend to take a train to Lvov and tell Stefa Gulyk that I was denying everything about the Strokata committee and that she should do the same. My emissary returned with Stefa's response. She had indeed been dragged to interrogations and confronted with my "admission" of her role as a courier. However, instinctively, she kept batting her eyelashes and claiming that my alleged testimony must be mistaken, because she couldn't recall a thing. "They don't call me an actress for nothing," she said to me later.

✦

Vladimir Pavlovich refrained from asking me about Irina's decision on emigration. He was intelligent enough to know that I would bring up the subject only if Irina said yes. If the answer was no, I would say nothing.

"You do realize how serious Irina's situation has become," Vladimir Pavlovich said.

I nodded in agreement.

"I just think that everything would become much simpler if someone would call and give us the address where *Khronika* is produced. The caller need not identify himself. Just dial me directly, give the address, and hang up. Perhaps you could tell Irina . . ."

"Simple and tasteful."

He smiled.

"Vladimir Pavlovich, first of all, Irina doesn't know where *Khronika* is produced. And, second, I cannot present such an indecent offer to a decent person. I cannot ask her to do something I wouldn't do myself — assuming that I knew where *Khronika* is produced."

"I understand," he said, and I thought he could have been telling the truth.

Irina was arrested on January 3.

At an interrogation the following day, Vladimir Pavlovich, my *kurator,* said: "Ludmilla Mikhailovna, I was the one who arrested Irina. She was arrested because *Khronika* editors chose to disregard our warning and published issue number twenty-seven."

✦

The testimony of Yakir and Krasin was being used in more than two hundred cases. Irina Yakir, Pyotr's daughter, was testifying, too, albeit only against herself. She simply told the KGB that she had been the *Khronika* editor and that she was prepared to pay the price. "It's easier this way," she explained to friends.

Shikhanovich did little more than confirm evidence given by Yakir and Krasin. He had devised what he thought was a clever scheme: he would give only one name, that of a typist — a single mother of three children. Since two of the children were infants, Shikhanovich decided that the KGB would balk before arresting her.

He was right. The woman was taken to an interrogation and fired from her office job. After that, she had to take a lower-paying job at a factory. I was the one who had recommended Shikhanovich to her. "Can I trust him?" she asked me back then.

"Trust him like you trust me," I assured her.

Now Shikhanovich had rationalized that he could sacrifice her. He was more charitable with me. He did not expose me as the person who regularly typed the first eight copies of *Khronika,* which would then be delivered to him for distribution to other typists.

The situation was getting worse. Vadim Delone, Irina Belogorodskaya's husband, had joined the KGB in trying to convince her to testify. He made no secret of his stance. "Prison is no place for a woman," he kept saying. He had been there, he had seen it, and he could speak with authority, he said to Larisa Bogoraz and me. About the only thing we could say was: "We know Irka. If she testifies, she will not be able to live with herself."

Since Larisa and I were intimately familiar with male-*politzek* chauvinism, we knew that arguing with Vadim was pointless.

◆

"How would you characterize Irina Belogorodskaya?" the investigator asked me at one of the interrogations.

"I would characterize her as a decent, honest, good woman."

"Would you say you are friends?"

"Absolutely. Close friends." It was customary to say nice things about those under arrest. The accused were allowed to read the transcripts of interrogations before trials, so verbal outpourings were a way to cheer up a friend.

"Did you ever have any reasons for arguing?"

"Never."

"Now, I would like you to take a minute and read her testimony," he said, handing me a couple of sheets. It was a "protocol" — an interrogation transcript. In it, Irina said that I had typed the first eight copies of all issues of *Khronika* and that I had edited issue number 14.

It was all true. On several occasions, Irina and her former husband, Vanya Rudakov, had taken those copies from me to Shikhanovich. Shortly after the arrest of Natasha Gorbanevskaya, Irina had asked me to meet her at the apartment of Irina Yakir, Pyotr's daughter. There I was asked to edit *Khronika* issue 14. We worked through the night.

"No," I said after reading the testimony. "Irina Belogorodskaya could not have said this. She is an honest woman; she wouldn't say something that is not true."

At that point, it was senseless to try to prevent my own arrest. If the KGB decided that it wanted me behind bars, it had ample evidence to put me away. My responses were directed at Irina. I was hoping that when the investigator informed her that I had refused to confirm her testimony, she would be able to understand my real message to her. What I was really saying was: "Irka, stop it. Don't let them break you. Don't give them evidence to use against other people. Don't take this sin upon your soul."

"You mean you really don't believe that Irina is cooperating with the investigation?" I think my interrogator was genuinely surprised.

At the following interrogation I was given a note from Irina. "Lyuda, I really am saying all this. How is Lara? Give her my love." It was unmistakably Irina's handwriting.

"Do you now believe us that she is cooperating with the investigation?"

"No," I said. "This has to be a forgery. Irina would be incapable of giving such testimony."

"What would you say if we allowed you to see her?" the investigator suggested. We would be interrogated together.

After the investigator dismissed me, I went to see Tolya and Larisa. Tolya was incensed. "If you see Irina, tell her that Lara and I are appalled by her behavior," he said. Larisa said nothing. She didn't want to endorse Marchenko's condemnation. Nor did she want to get into an argument with him. By saying nothing, she left the matter to my discretion.

✦

There was a look of bewilderment on Irina's face. She didn't know whether I would give her a hug or treat her with reserved condemnation.

"Oy, Irka," I shouted, and hugged her.

"No hugging!" shouted the jailer. "We will allow you a brief conversation after the interrogation."

We were seated across a small desk, about a foot from each other.

INTERROGATOR: Ludmilla Mikhailovna, do you know this person?

I: Yes, she is my close friend.

Irina's face brightened up. She was visibly relieved to hear that, despite her testimony, I counted her among my close friends.

INTERROGATOR: Irina, do you know this person?

IRINA: Yes, she is my close friend.

INTERROGATOR: Irina, please tell the investigation what you know about Ludmilla Mikhailovna's role in the production of *Khronika tekushchikh sobytiy*.

IRINA: Since I have been assured that no one will be arrested on the basis of my testimony, I repeat that I have seen Lyuda edit issue number fourteen of *Khronika*. I also know that Lyuda typed the first copy of the preceding issues of *Khronika* and that those issues were then taken to Yuri Shikhanovich.

I was doing my best to look surprised.

INTERROGATOR: Ludmilla Mikhailovna, do you confirm this testimony?

I: I deny it.

INTERROGATOR: Do you mean to say that Irina is giving false testimony?

I: I don't want to say that.

INTERROGATOR: Then why do you think she is doing this?

I: That, to me, is a mystery.

After the interrogation, Irina and I were allowed a short conversation. I decided to tell her what I thought: "Irka, I understand that you are saying all this because you have been assured that no one will suffer as a result of your testimony, but how in the world can you trust these crocodiles?"

I heard a snicker from two of the "crocodiles," who were seated behind me and monitoring our conversation. At that point, it didn't matter who heard what.

"No, I really believe their assurances," Irina said.

"Irka, you are doing a crazy thing. I know you, and I know that if you buy freedom by giving testimony against other people, you won't want to live. Think of your soul!" I was sure I would be ejected, but I wasn't.

"Lyuda, tell me about Tolya and Lara."

"Tolya is strongly opposed to what you are doing."

"And Lara?"

"She hasn't said much."

The meeting was over. I got up, hugged her, and as the jailers yelled, "No hugging permitted!" I shouted, "Irka, I hope you change your mind!"

✦

Shortly after the joint interrogation with Irina, I got a call from Vladimir Pavlovich, my *kurator,* who assured me that he was not calling from his work number and asked if we could meet on neutral grounds. It was an extraordinary request: it appeared that Vladimir Pavlovich wanted to meet outside his office, someplace where we would not be overheard. We met at the place he suggested, the gates of Botkinskaya Hospital.

"Ludmilla Mikhailovna, I wanted to tell you that yesterday in Lefortovo we had a meeting about all these cases. We decided that we would refrain from making too many arrests. We want to stop *Khronika;* that's all. We will not arrest anyone, even people who have been very active, as long as we have assurances that they will refrain from such activities in the future."

He paused, waiting for me to ask, "What sort of assurances?" I said nothing.

"When people confess, we consider it an adequate assurance," he continued. "If there are no such assurances, we would have to apply sanctions. I must tell you this: I have reviewed evidence in these cases, and I have looked at the people involved. They are all different people, but most of them want good for our country. It's just that they have taken an incorrect path.

"I sympathize with you personally. I think you really are a decent person, and I want the best for you. You have said from the start, at every interrogation, that you will not give evidence that will harm anyone. That is decent. But, Ludmilla Mikhailovna, I have reviewed your case, and I have to tell you, you have set the course that leads directly to the camps.

"I want you to look at this and see if you might consider writing something in this vein." He handed me a copy of a handwritten confession.

"Do you recognize the handwriting?"

"I do." It was the unmistakable gothic script of Yuri Shikhanovich.

Among other things, Shikhanovich had written that the Communist party of the Soviet Union to him was "the most sacred thing in the world" and that he would never say or do anything that would damage its good name or its prestige.

"Don't say anything right away. Talk it over with your husband and your friends. Then write something like this, and your case will be closed."

"Vladimir Pavlovich, I am touched by your concern. Of course, I will talk it over with my husband and with my friends, and I can promise you that I will get in touch with you the instant I sense that the Communist party has become the most sacred thing in the world for me."

My *kurator* was unable to suppress a chuckle.

✦

In exchange for their testimony, Yakir and Krasin were given reduced sentences of three years of internal exile. In exchange for recanting before foreign reporters, they were promised release in a year.

Yuri Shikhanovich was declared insane and was committed to a regular mental hospital instead of a "special," punitive one. Irina Belogorodskaya and Irina Yakir were never tried. After being released, Belogorodskaya and Vadim Delone decided that they wanted to emigrate after all. They settled in Paris.

In November 1972, Valery Chalidze left for the United States, to lecture at Georgetown and New York universities. A month later, the Soviet consulate in the United States informed him that a ukase of the presidium of the Supreme Soviet had stripped him of his Soviet citizenship.

Earlier that year, Alek Esenin-Volpin had emigrated to the United States. Left without leadership, the Committee for Human Rights went into decline.

Khronika, too, had ground to a halt. Its editor, Tosha Yakobson, had been given a choice between emigration and prison. In hindsight, I wonder if he would have been better off choosing prison. Shortly after emigrating, he fell into a depression, his first. The vivacious Tosha became suicidal, and in 1979, after many thwarted attempts, he killed himself. Israel was not his spiritual home. His Jewish blood notwithstanding, Yakobson was the kind of Moscow intelligent who could not survive outside Moscow.

Meanwhile, the *Khronika* activists who remained could not resolve the arguments that began with the KGB's announcement of the policy of hostage taking. Some kept repeating that we could not negotiate with terrorists; others kept saying that we had no moral right to risk the lives of innocent people; I kept saying that I was unable to make a choice. If *Khronika* were to resume, I would be happy to join it, I said. By not taking sides, I was in effect voting for inaction. We knew that the KGB was playing on our sense of decency to accomplish what threats, arrests, and expulsions could not.

Hundreds of people had been interrogated, and only a handful had cracked. Still, our movement had lost much of its prestige among the intelligentsia. Remarks heard in *kompanii* included: "Some heroes. They step on their tails, and what do they do? They crack, they plead, they name names." Thousands of people suddenly began to feel good about their decision to keep their distance from the democratic movement. Prisons would have provided a less oppressive environment than the Moscow of that time.

✦

If not for Sergei Kovalyov, Tatyana Velikanova, and Tatyana Khodorovich, our debates over *Khronika* would have gone on for years. In May of 1974, eighteen months after the publication of issue number 27, they called a press conference to announce that they had taken responsibility for further distribution of *Khronika.* It was an act of enlightened self-sacrifice: by becoming the first *Khronika* activists to come out in the open, they made the hostage question moot. The circle of arguments was broken: if anyone was to be arrested, it would have to be Seryozha and the two Tatyanas.

At the same press conference, *Khronika* activists released three issues of the bulletin: number 28 was backdated December 31, 1972; number 29 was dated July 31, 1973; number 30 was dated December 31, 1973. The three issues totaled two hundred single-spaced pages, all of which were edited by Seryozha. Typing them gave me a monstrous headache, but the new issues made up for the eighteen-month publication gap. Andropov's victory had come unraveled.

Thirteen

I began to consider emigration in 1973, after my name surfaced in the Yakir-and-Krasin case.

The first suggestion came from Kolya Williams. The second came from Misha. For the most part, Kolya was motivated by his admittedly chauvinistic belief that "prison is no place for a woman." He was also certain that as a mathematician he could find work anywhere.

Misha's situation presented a more serious problem. I could see that he would probably follow in my footsteps. It could not be avoided. He'd grown up hearing conversations around my dinner table. There were times when I'd asked him to run dangerous errands, like carrying a bag full of covertly Xeroxed copies of *The Gulag Archipelago* from a friend's apartment. (It could not be avoided: a hundred copies had been delivered to Moscow, and they had to be distributed quickly.)

Misha was not a dissident by nature. He was a scientist, like his father and his grandmother. He was also more direct than most people. At work, he was known to get into debates that exposed his real views about Brezhnev, the invasion of Czechoslovakia, political trials, or whatever else was being discussed.

At one point, he announced his decision to withdraw from the

Komsomol. I managed to talk him out of taking that step, but I sensed that my victory would be short-lived. It was beyond doubt that sooner or later Misha would join the dissident world. As soon as he did, the KGB would do everything in its power to have him arrested and shipped off to the camps as quickly as possible. With Misha in the camps, the agency would acquire a way to pressure me.

Still, I thought emigration would bring an end to the happiest and most productive time in my life. Ten years had passed since I'd joined my country's human-rights movement. Now, life outside it seemed unthinkable. How would I live? A Russian historian and book editor who spoke no English could not expect to be deluged with job offers in the West. An American I'd met had once suggested that I move to the United States and become a caterer. It was merely an after-dinner compliment, but it did point out a career option. There was also the option of becoming a housewife, learning English, and devoting my leisure to the study of British literature.

Neither option seemed as fulfilling — or as important — as working on *Khronika*. Besides, the West was foreign to me. Moscow was home.

✦

I knew that my son and my husband were right and that they would prevail. But I couldn't just get up and leave, even if the authorities permitted it. I got involved in a series of residential exchanges aimed at leaving Mother in our apartment and switching her old apartment for a better place for Sergei. At the time, neither Sergei nor Mother had plans to leave the country. There were other matters that needed attention, and by the time I would resolve one, another would crop up. Subconsciously, I was delaying our departure.

✦

In late April 1976, Yuri Orlov asked me to meet him in front of the Bolshoi. I'd first heard about Orlov back in 1956, at the Lenin Library smoking room, when one of the regulars, the fellow usually identified as "the physicist," told me about the four people at his institute who had been fired and expelled from the party after calling for further democratization of the Soviet state.

Ousted from the party and dismissed from the elite Institute of Theoretical and Experimental Physics, Orlov found a job in Armenia, earned a doctorate, and was elected a corresponding member of the Armenian Academy of Sciences.

Upon returning to Moscow in 1972, Orlov joined our circle of dissidents. He was short — shorter than I — with bushy, red hair. (The hairdo was called "Angela Davis" by friends.) Unlike many of us, he had the ability to listen. His brief, well-aimed remarks usually served one purpose: to steer any conversation in the direction that interested Orlov. Orlov was studying us. He was studying the movement that had emerged in the years of his exile.

Almost immediately after his return, Orlov's signature began to appear on dissident petitions. In 1973, when a series of newspaper articles attacked Andrei Sakharov, Orlov wrote a letter to Leonid Brezhnev. The letter invited the general secretary to answer thirteen questions about the lagging of Soviet science, stagnation of the economy, and destruction of the environment. "The most significant oversight in Marxist theory of social development is that it doesn't encompass the natural spiritual needs and qualities of a human being," Orlov wrote. "In fact, Marxism denies their very presence in human nature. Yet, this supposition isn't proven scientifically, that is, by means of experimental biology, biochemistry or biophysics."

This led Orlov to the following question: "Don't you think that our view of man and his place in society is primitive and out of balance with existing human needs and qualities?"

Orlov's final question wasn't a question at all: "Of course, you do understand that putting members of the opposition into psychiatric hospitals and maiming them with medication is a lot like sterilization of political opponents by the Nazi Reich. Here, I guess, I have nothing to ask."

Soon after mailing the letter, Orlov lost his job and was forced to make a living as a tutor. Once, at a social gathering, I heard him talk about something he called "forcing the authorities into a dialogue with society."

When he saw us raise glasses "to the success of our hopeless cause," he demonstratively refused to join in that traditional toast of

Russian democrats. "If I considered it hopeless," he said, "I would devote my time to something else."

♦

When I got to the small park in front of the Bolshoi, Orlov was waiting. We sat down on the bench closest to the Children's Theater, then, by reflex, looked around for KGB tails. Finding none, we looked at each other and simultaneously broke into laughter. We were respectable middle-aged people. I was forty-eight; he was fifty-two. We did not receive stolen goods; we didn't sell drugs. We were the kind of people you let into your house without bothering to count the silverware first.

"Lyuda, have you read the Helsinki agreement?" Orlov asked.

The Final Act of the Conference on Security and Cooperation in Europe, signed by the United States, the USSR, and thirty-three other nations eight months earlier, reaffirmed sanctity of existing borders and called for arms reduction, increased economic cooperation, freer flow of information, and greater respect for human rights. The entire document had been published in major Soviet newspapers.

I said I had glanced over the thirty-thousand-word document, found the section on human rights, then stopped reading. The section contained some nice promises, but such promises had long ago ceased to impress me.

"Lyuda, don't you see this is the first international document in which the issue of human rights is discussed as a component of international peace?

"Since human rights is presented as part of a whole, we have the opportunity to involve other countries in monitoring the Soviet performance on human rights," Orlov continued. "I can't understand why the Western governments don't protest the persecution of human-rights activists. Can't they understand that human-rights abuses in the USSR present a danger to the West? Haven't they learned any lessons after making a deal with a dictator in Munich in 1939? Can't they understand that Soviet dissidents are their natural allies? We have the same ideology, and it's not that we have borrowed it from them; we've come to it on our own."

I agreed. Our message wasn't that difficult to understand, but the West had focused its attention on the narrow issue of Jewish emigration. The Soviet democratic movement had not been able to generate such support.

If Orlov had any ideas for changing the way the West viewed our struggles, I was willing to help.

"I would like to start a group," Orlov said. The group would include active dissenters, and it would be called something like the Public Group to Assist the Implementation of the Helsinki Accord in the USSR. It was a wonderfully ironic name. The Helsinki Final Act invited the public to monitor their countries' performance, but the Soviet authorities asked for no assistance. In fact, they stood poised to punish it.

We would gather information on Soviet performance under the humanitarian articles of the Helsinki Final Act and send our reports to the nations that had signed the document, Orlov explained. Brezhnev would get a report, too.

There was logic to the idea: we would use the governments of the West to force our own government into a dialogue with us.

Before agreeing to join the group, I warned Orlov that my family was planning to emigrate, so my membership could be short-lived. "That's fine," he said. "The group will need a representative abroad." We moved on to the logistics. The new group would have no structure. There would be no voting, no application procedures. There would be no need to worry about reaching consensus on every issue. Only those who signed a document would be responsible for its content.

The *Khronika* network was producing an abundance of information on human-rights abuses. There would be no problem finding things about which to write. Offhand, though, I could foresee some difficulties: at most, a typewriter could produce ten pages at a time — a hard copy and nine carbons. To come up with a copy for each Helsinki signatory, each page of every letter would have to be typed four times. Given our tradition of long-winded writing, I could easily imagine having to produce thirty-five copies of a twenty-page, single-spaced appeal. The group had no access to copying machines, and no money to pay the typists; we would have to rely on volunteers. But who would take on such massive, dull work?

"The documents will have to be kept short — a page and a half, not a line more," I said.

After talking with Orlov, I went off to my next appointment. Two weeks later, on May 13, a friend asked me if I had heard a shortwave radio broadcast about some group formed to assist something or other.

My first reaction: "Oh my God, it's been announced. Someone could tell Mother!" I hadn't even told Kolya. Fortunately, the radio stations had not named each of the group's eleven members.

✦

On May 15, Orlov was expected to preside over a group meeting at my apartment. When he finally showed up, a couple of hours late, he said that he had been grabbed by two operatives, shoved into a car, and taken to the KGB Cheremushki regional office, where he was told that unless his group ceased its work immediately, "you will be prosecuted to the full extent of the law."

The group greeted this with silence. We'd had a sneaking suspicion that membership in the new organization would not lead to our appointment to the politburo. When you spend so much of your life under the threat of laws like Article 70 and Article 190, the penal system becomes a threat you take for granted. It's a very simple principle: if all of your friends go to Paris, you see nothing extraordinary about going to Paris; if all of your friends go to prison, you see nothing extraordinary about going to prison.

"So," said Yura, breaking the silence after delivering his account. "What will our documents be about?"

The first document protested the conviction of the Crimean Tatar activist Mustafa Dzhemiliev. The second addressed the KGB's violation of the Final Act through its interference with the mail and with telephone service in the homes of dissidents and refuseniks. The third was about the conditions of prisoners of conscience. We were issuing about two documents a month.

✦

Yuri Orlov invented nothing; he didn't bring new members into the movement. He merely focused all of our efforts. The group included Pyotr Grigorenko, Aleksandr Ginzburg, Yelena Bonner (who was married to Sakharov), and others who had been active for a decade. We weren't the first to appeal to the foreign press; Larisa Bogoraz and Pavel Litvinov were the first to appeal to public opinion worldwide. We didn't start the process of bringing *glasnost* to violations of human rights; *Khronika,* building on the philosophical groundwork of Alek Esenin-Volpin, started that with its coverage of the Galanskov-and-Ginzburg trial. We weren't the first group to demand observance of Soviet and international law; Chalidze's Committee for Human Rights in the USSR initiated that process. Nor did we invent appealing to authorities outside the USSR; that was begun by the Initiative Group. By giving our movement a new focus, Orlov made it possible for Western politicians to understand what we wanted.

Still, we needed something else: luck. And we had it. While Orlov was refining his concept of what came to be known as the Moscow Helsinki Watch Group, Millicent Fenwick, a member of the United States Congress, was refining a strikingly similar idea: setting up a commission of Congress and the administration to monitor compliance with the Final Act.

Fenwick came up with that idea after an August 1975 trip to the USSR. During that visit, she saw a number of Jewish refuseniks. "We would meet them at night at hotels in Moscow and Leningrad," Fenwick recalled in many a speech and interview.

I would ask them, "How do you dare to come see us here?"

"Don't you understand?" they would say. "That's our only hope. We've seen you. Now the KGB knows you've seen us."

I felt, my God, it's like being in the Atlantic in the middle of a terrible storm, and seeing people go by in rafts, and we are trying to pick them up, but can't. But at least we have our searchlights on them.

In Moscow, *New York Times* reporter Christopher Wren introduced Fenwick to Valentin Turchin, head of the Moscow chapter of Amnesty International. Turchin and his wife, Tatyana, later recalled that they dispatched one of their sons to get Orlov. Though Orlov was still months away from formulating the idea for the Helsinki Watch group, he and Turchin talked to Fenwick about the prospect of cooperation between the West and the Soviet human-rights movement on the basis of the humanitarian articles of the Helsinki Final Act.

On September 5, 1975, days after her return to Washington, Fenwick introduced a bill that would create a Helsinki monitoring commission. On May 5 of the following year, it sailed through the Senate. And on June 3, three weeks after Orlov announced the Moscow group, the bill was signed into law.

Thus, from the start, Fenwick's "searchlight" was upon us.

✦

Judging by attendance at our press conferences, the group was receiving constant coverage in the Western press. Our documents could be heard over shortwave radio stations just hours after being read at our press briefings.

Years later, I found out that most of the stories about us were appearing around page 19 in American newspapers. But they were appearing, and ending up in the files of Fenwick's commission — as well as in the KGB dossiers. Newspaper stories, like manuscripts, don't burn. They sit in the files and the dossiers, waiting.

The KGB could have strangled the group at birth had it decided to do so. The dossiers of every member were sufficient to put us away for many years. But the experience of the Initiative Group, whose letters to the United Nations had gone unacknowledged, had taught Andropov's KGB that appeals from Soviet citizens do not always bring response from abroad. Save for a novel commission started by an eccentric congresswoman, the West seemed unlikely to respond to the pleas of the Helsinki group.

The KGB knew precisely what was going on. Its operatives were tailing us, monitoring our phones, opening our mail. A mysterious gray van was constantly parked in front of my apartment building. A couple of times I tried to look inside, but the windows and even the windshield were draped. Something hummed from within the van — a listening device, I presume. Whenever I needed to catch a taxi from my apartment, I found myself being picked up by the same cab. On top of that, I was the only group member whose telephone didn't get disconnected. The KGB wanted to keep all communications coming from one place, to make the monitoring easier.

The KGB didn't want to overreact, especially considering that the new group included some well-known dissidents. Their arrests would cause more of an international outcry than group documents ever could. Thus, Andropov's KGB stood by, waiting for the benefits of a crackdown to outweigh its costs.

✦

Meanwhile, my family lived knowing that we no longer had any privacy. Our apartment had become a gigantic listening device. We were onstage, with the folks in the van listening, or even watching.

Foreign reporters and domestic supplicants trekked to my door by the dozen. Many of the group's press conferences took place in the larger of my two rooms. Old family rules were being wiped out: even Mother could no longer ignore my avocation. One day in the summer of 1976, she went to the Beriozka hard-currency store and, with foreign royalties from a mathematics textbook she'd coauthored, bought a Sony shortwave transistor radio.

Before the start of every press conference, she put on her apron, walked into the kitchen, puttered around for a few seconds, then walked back into her room and stayed there for a couple of hours, until news items that originated in her apartment were broadcast from Washington, London, or Munich. Still, Mother and I never discussed politics.

✦

In October, Yuri Orlov asked me to investigate the story of seven boys who had been expelled from the graduating class of a Vilnius school. All seven regularly attended Mass and visited Viktoras Petkus, a devout Catholic and a human-rights activist who had served a total of sixteen years in the camps.

At the Vilnius railroad station, I was greeted by Petkus, who'd brought along Antanas Terleckas, a Lithuanian dissident and former political prisoner, and Tomas Venclova, the poet son of the first minister of education of Communist Lithuania.

After a lifetime of hearing about "Lithuanian nationalism" and Lithuanian hatred for the Russians, I was being greeted by the honor guard of the Lithuanian national movement. As we headed for the hotel, we were followed by a dozen KGB agents. Some of them were locals, regular tails assigned to each of the three Lithuanians who met me; some were "mine." They'd accompanied me on the train from Moscow.

We spent the morning sightseeing around Vilnius, then went to lunch at Petkus's house. I, too, like to entertain, so I could appreciate the meticulous planning that had gone into every detail: the food, the table setting, the host's clothes, the guests, the way they were seated, the toasts, the subjects, and the tone of the table talk. Out of respect for the guests, everyone spoke Russian, even in conversations in which I wasn't involved.

After lunch, the conversation turned to the seven boys. Petkus suggested that I return in the evening, so I could interview the boys myself.

When I came back that evening, Petkus didn't serve wine, only tea. He and the boys drank it from the same cup, passing it around in a circle. That was their tradition.

Each of the boys told me about his encounters with the authorities. Frequently, the principal took them out of classes and passed them over to the KGB. They had been threatened, and some of them had been beaten, all for the same reason — to get them to testify against Petkus. Among other things, they were asked to "confess" that Petkus was a homosexual. In the USSR, homosexuality was punishable by six years in the camps. The KGB could not pass up insinuating that gay sex was the reason for closeness between an old convict and seventeen- and eighteen-year-old youths.

After interviewing the boys, Tomas Venclova and I went to the Lithuanian Ministry of Education. To my astonishment, Minister Rimkus himself came out to greet us in the reception room. "The son of Antanas Venclova is a welcome guest in my ministry at any time," he said.

Venclova thanked him, said that in this case he was merely an escort, and introduced me as "Ludmilla Mikhailovna Alexeyeva from Moscow."

"I am a member of the Public Group to Assist the Implementation of the Helsinki Accord in the USSR," I said.

"Which organization is this group attached to?"

"It's a public group."

"But who is in charge of it?"

"Professor Yuri Fyodorovich Orlov, Corresponding Member of the Armenian Academy of Sciences."

The title seemed to reassure the minister. Then I asked him about the seven boys.

"This has nothing to do with the Helsinki agreements. They were expelled for behavior unbecoming of Soviet schoolchildren."

"What kind of behavior was that?"

"Boguses [one of the expelled students] was rude to the principal and then brought a religious picture into his classroom, and that's forbidden by the constitution. After all, the church is separated from the state in our country."

"And this was the reason for his expulsion?"

"No, it wasn't that. I know only the general outlines of the case and cannot tell you exactly what each one of them did, but the expulsions were perfectly legal."

"Fine," I said. "We will go to the school to find out what happened."

At the school, the head of studies, a number of teachers, and the extracurricular-activities supervisor listed the transgressions committed by each of the boys expelled, but could not explain which specific actions had, in fact, provoked the expulsions. It turned out that Dobinas, the extracurricular-activities supervisor, did not have the record of the school council meeting at which the boys had been expelled. As the conversation was coming to an end, the telephone rang.

The call was from the minister. Judging by the replies to him, he had already discovered that, despite its long, official-sounding name, Professor Orlov's group did not merit the courteous treatment it was receiving.

Dobinas looked horrified. I realized that the meeting, if continued, could turn unpleasant, so I started to say good-bye. Besides, we had attained our goal. It was obvious the boys had committed no crimes, and that minutes of the meeting at which the decision to expel them was allegedly made simply didn't exist. That meant the decision had been made administratively and thus was illegal.

Walking out of the school, we were shaking with laughter. Venclova said that on an occasion like this it would be an oversight not to have a drink, so we found a bar and went inside. He ordered a glass of champagne and drank it in one gulp.

In Moscow, I compiled Document 15, "On the Expulsion of

Seven Students from the Venoulis High School." The report was issued with two signatures, mine and that of Venclova, who was now a member of the newly formed Lithuanian Helsinki group.

In late November of 1976, Petkus and Venclova came to Moscow to announce the formation of their group at one of our press conferences.

The press conference to announce the creation of the Lithuanian group was scheduled for November 27. As usual, several Moscow group members got to work preparing the documents. We rushed about madly, writing, editing, typing, correcting, retyping, and making sure there were enough copies for the reporters. We left such work for the last minute partly because we didn't want to risk losing our materials in a KGB search, and partly thanks to our genuinely Russian lack of organizational skills. That day, we worked at Orlov's apartment, where the press conference was to be held. Petkus and Venclova came prepared. Their group's documents were neatly typed and carefully collated, and there were more than enough copies to go around. Silently, they observed the sweatshop atmosphere around them.

After a few minutes, Venclova came up to me and whispered, "You know what Viktoras just said? 'Observe the way they work. That's the way the Lithuanian Helsinki group *shouldn't* work.'"

✦

Over eight months, the Moscow Helsinki group received petitions from Jewish activists, Russian nationalists, ethnic separatists, the Crimean Tatars, Meskhetians, Catholics, Baptists, Pentecostals, and Seventh-Day Adventists.

Similar Helsinki groups had sprung up in the Ukraine and Lithuania. Later, groups would be formed in Georgia and Armenia, Czechoslovakia and Poland. The US Congress had formed a commission to perform virtually the same tasks as our group. By December 1976, news stories that originated with the group began to move from page 19 to page 1 of US newspapers.

Meanwhile, the American political climate had undergone profound changes. President-elect Jimmy Carter was vowing to bring decency to US foreign policy. Our most optimistic projections now seemed within reach: it appeared likely that the new US foreign policy would include insistence that the Soviets live up to the promises made in Helsinki. The alliance of Western politicians and Soviet dissidents was starting to emerge.

✦

In December of 1976, Kolya, Misha, and I finally applied for an exit visa. Within weeks, we were told that our applications were incomplete. The visa office needed written permission from my mother and Kolya's. Misha, too, needed permission from his father.

"I won't allow it," said Valentin when Misha mentioned that we were planning to leave.

Misha was stunned.

"Why won't you? You've said to me that as a scientist in this country you are constantly restricted and that scientists in the West are more free. Don't you want me to be free?"

"The answer is still no," said Valentin. I don't know if he feared that allowing Misha to emigrate would ruin his own career. It could be that he just wanted to keep his son nearby.

I notified the visa office that all three of us were of legal age, which by any rational standards meant we were old enough to decide for ourselves. That stance delayed our emigration indefinitely.

✦

By January 1977, the KGB had concluded that the benefits of a crackdown outweighed the costs in terms of lost international prestige.

Three days after New Years', the KGB came to search my apartment. They carted off linen bags full of samizdat and Helsinki-group documents. Later that day, an official from the visa office called to ask us to furnish the previously requested permissions from our parents and from Valentin. Once again, we refused. If they wanted us out, they would expel us without the permissions, I decided.

I was right. On February 1, we were told that we could leave anyway and that we had three weeks to get out of the country. And on February 3, the KGB arrested Helsinki-group member Aleksandr Ginzburg.

That night, they came to arrest Orlov, but the founder of Moscow's Public Group to Assist the Implementation of the Helsinki Accord in the USSR was nowhere to be found. He had gone into hiding.

On February 9, at about three in the afternoon, he took a big risk and showed up at my apartment. Mother opened the door. Orlov put a finger to his lips and walked inside.

Mother picked up a Magic Pad. She had seen me use it to evade the KGB microphones.

"Would you like some tea?" she wrote in pen. The ink curdled into droplets on the gray plastic.

"No, thank you. Where is Lyuda?" Orlov wrote back.

"I don't know," Mother scrawled on the pad.

"Could you get hold of Tolya Shcharansky, please," Orlov wrote. Shcharansky was part of the group.

Mother dialed the apartment where Shcharansky was staying. "Lyuda has asked that you come over here," she said.

In a few minutes, Shcharansky was at the door. Not a word was said.

"Find Lyuda and reporters," Orlov wrote.

Shcharansky found me at Grigorenko's, where I was typing an appeal to the authorities, a plea for the conditional release of Ginzburg because of his poor health.

At the apartment, using the notepad, Orlov explained that he planned to reappear for just a short time, make a statement to the press, then go back into hiding before the KGB could locate him.

At six that evening, Shcharansky returned with Robert Toth of the *Los Angeles Times* and David Mason, the Associated Press bureau chief. At the press conference, Orlov presented a short document calling on all Helsinki Final Act signatories to declassify much of the information now labeled secret.

Meanwhile, in the hallway, Mother was on the phone talking to a friend. As soon as Orlov began speaking to the newsmen, the phone clicked, disconnecting the call. She tried to redial, but couldn't get the tone. The KGB staffer monitoring the apartment through listening devices had instantly recognized Orlov's voice.

◆

After the press conference, Orlov made a motion to leave.

"Wait a second," I said. "First, let's check the surveillance."

Shcharansky and I walked out with the reporters. We saw a man and woman kissing in the apartment building's entryway. Many Moscow couples kiss in apartment building entryways, but this couple was middle-aged and wore imported suede coats. On closer inspection, Shcharansky recognized the man as one of his KGB tails.

"Yura, you might as well stay here," I said after seeing off Tolya and the reporters. "The place is surrounded."

An hour later, at about eight o'clock, Kolya and I went to a farewell party some friends were throwing for us, but we stayed only long enough to avoid offending the hosts. When we got back home, Orlov and I went to the kitchen, where, with lights out, we talked about the future. My future was in exile, Yura's in prison. But the group had to go on.

Yura went to bed at five in the morning. At six, I woke up Misha and asked him to get dressed and check whether the building was still surrounded. He didn't even have to go outside. Three men were patrolling the staircase.

At 11:00 AM, there was a knock on the door. Minutes later, from the sixteenth-floor window, I watched eight husky men push Yuri Orlov into a prison van.

✦

The day after Yura's arrest, Tolya Shcharansky stopped by. Usually, the moment Tolya ran into my apartment, I shouted, "How much time do you have?" If he shouted back, "Five minutes!" I ran into the kitchen and threw together a sandwich he could eat on the way out. If he shouted "Twenty minutes!" I ran to heat up whatever I had in the refrigerator. Tolya was easily the most rushed man in Moscow. He ran from one refusenik to another, shepherded foreigners, translated for Sakharov, taught English, wrote Helsinki-group documents, and pushed stories to Western reporters. Frequently, he forgot to eat.

Tolya and I had been introduced a year earlier by Vitaly Rubin, a sinologist, who started out as a *podpisant,* then became a refusenik. I will never forget that introduction: "Lyuda, as you well know, it is common for a Jew to be exceptionally intelligent. Well, this young man is exceptional even among the Jews! Do you know what we tell him? We tell him that he will never be allowed to leave this country. Because, as you know, the Jews are exceptionally intelligent people, and being exceptionally intelligent they will certainly recognize that this young man is the most intelligent among them.

They would immediately elect him prime minister of Israel; he would bring everyone together, make peace in the Middle East on terms that would benefit Israel — and where would that leave the Union of Soviet Socialist Republics? They won't stand for it. Tolya, you are here for life." Considering the subject — the intelligence of his people and the intelligence of Tolya Shcharansky — I suspect Rubin was only half-joking.

I led Tolya into the kitchen, and as I was scrounging around for whatever food was still in the house, we began to talk.

"You know, with Yura under arrest, I am afraid everyone in the group will begin to fight," Tolya said.

"What makes you think so?"

"Yura has a talent for keeping people working together, and now he's gone." I understood what Tolya was saying. The Jewish movement in the USSR did not operate as peacefully as our group. The battle lines in the Jewish movement had been drawn between those who advocated emigration and those who believed in developing the Jewish culture in the USSR. There were other factions, and rival groups were known to trade accusations about collaborating with the KGB and pocketing funds sent by American Jews. Once, in 1975, one faction refused even to attend a meeting with US senator Jacob Javits if a certain other faction was present.

Shcharansky's membership in the Helsinki group was also a matter of controversy. The strategy advanced by the state of Israel called on Soviet Jews to avoid alliances with the dissidents. Dissidents, after all, supported Jewish emigration, but viewed it as an individual right no more special than the right of the Crimean Tatars to return to the Crimean peninsula. Shcharansky himself had been warned by Jewish activists to stay away from the dissidents.

"You know, these past eight months have been the happiest time in my life," Shcharansky said to me.

"I've been living like this for ten years," I said. "It's wonderful to allow yourself to think what you want and to live by what you think. There is only one drawback: it leads to prison."

Then Tolya told me how he'd found us. He'd grown up thinking that being Jewish meant being second-rate. "I would like to be tall, curly-haired, and broad-shouldered, but, instead, I am short, bald, and pudgy. So I have to make the best of what I have. Same with being Jewish. I had to make the best of it."

He coped well, until he fell in love with a Jewish woman who had come from a Zionist family. "I discovered that these people are proud of belonging to a great nation," he said. "It changed my sense of the world." The relationship went awry, but Tolya realized that Jewishness was not a handicap.

Then, through Rubin, he met Andrei Sakharov and Yuri Orlov and, eventually, was invited to join the Helsinki group. "That taught me that I can be proud not only of being a Jew, but also of being human," he said.

A bit more than a year later, in Tolya's statement to the court, I heard an echo of that conversation: "I am happy that I have lived honestly, at peace with my soul. . . . I am happy that I helped people. And I am proud that I knew and worked with such honest, brave, and courageous people as Sakharov, Orlov, and Ginzburg, who are accused of carrying on the traditions of the Russian intelligentsia."

Over the next decade, throughout Tolya's ordeal in the camps, I knew that the KGB was powerless before him. A man proud of humanity cannot be broken. He had become a hero, and that was the next step in his evolution.

✦

On February 12, our telephone was still disconnected.

"We are not going until they turn the telephone back on," I said. It was bad enough that I was leaving my seventy-one-year-old mother alone in a country with dismal medical care, but leaving her alone in an apartment without a telephone, where she would be unable to call for help, was even more terrifying.

"And what if they don't turn it on? Are you going to stay?" said Kolya. He was scared that I would stall some more and end up in prison.

"If they don't turn it on, I stay," I declared.

This was too much for my mother. "Leave!" she shouted at me. "Leave quickly!"

Mother had not raised her voice at me for half a century. Now she took that parental prerogative. After seeing Orlov arrested in her apartment, she knew very well what could happen to me. And prison was no place for her daughter.

✦

On February 22, Kolya, Misha, and I left the USSR.

Before his arrest, Orlov had asked me to represent the group in the West. At least in theory, I understood what the mission entailed. I would fight for the release of the imprisoned group members, publicize the group's documents, and do my best to galvanize governments and public opinion to pressure the USSR to live up to the promises made in Helsinki. I was ready to put my life down for the group. But I spoke no foreign languages, had no connections outside the Soviet Union, and no experience in lobbying foreign governments, let alone shaping public opinion in countries I had never seen.

There we were: three Westernizers in a westbound plane. In a few hours, we would land in Vienna. From there, we would go to Rome, then to the United States. Had we been going as tourists, it would have been a joyful occasion. But we were émigrés; we had no way back.

I could not bring myself to think of Europe or America; all I could think of was Moscow. I would never see it again, just as I would never see my mother, Seryozha, Larisa, and the crowd of friends who came to see us off at the airport. Never. Never. Never.

The instant our plane crossed the Soviet border, Kolya pulled out three shot glasses and filled them with brandy. One of our friends had slipped him a bottle at the airport. We drank up. I could sense Kolya's relief: at last he was certain that his wife would not end up in some prison camp. And prison, as everyone knows, is no place for a woman.

I did not share his sense of relief. I felt numb. It could have been the fatigue. Or it could have been that the indescribable stress of the past few months left no room for emotion. Or, it could be that numbness was my psyche's defense against all the "nevers" of life in exile.

Fourteen

Through *Khronika,* our movement covered its own demise. Issue number 58 covered the trial of *Khronika* activist Tatyana Velikanova, who was sentenced to four years in the camps and five in internal exile. The manuscript of issue number 59 was confiscated by the KGB and never came out. Issue 60 covered the conviction of *Khronika* activist Sasha Lavut, who was sentenced to three years in the camps, then rearrested at the end of his term and sentenced to three more years in exile. Issue 62 reported the arrest of Tolya Marchenko. His works would soon be classified as anti-Soviet propaganda, and Tolya would be sentenced to ten years in the camps and five in internal exile. Also in the issue was a dispatch on the death of Yuri Kukk, forty. Kukk, an Estonian who had protested the war in Afghanistan, died after a four-month hunger strike while serving three years for slandering the state.

In the Ukraine, a KGB operative snatched the purse of Raisa Rudenko, wife of Mykola Rudenko, a poet and founder of the Ukrainian Helsinki group. He was serving a twelve-year term for anti-Soviet propaganda. Raisa's purse contained her husband's poetry, which had been smuggled out of prison. The seized poetry and materials confiscated at a subsequent search were later used to convict Raisa for anti-Soviet propaganda. She was sentenced to five years in the camps and five in internal exile.

"On May 21, 1981, Andrei Sakharov turned 60," *Khronika* reported. Sakharov was in his first year of exile in the closed city of Gorky. The terse report recounted attempts by friends to reach Gorky and wish Sakharov a happy birthday.

> On May 20, former political prisoner Vitaly Pomazov arrived in Gorky. On May 21 Pomazov . . . took a taxi to Sakharov's apartment. Though the taxi stopped at some distance from Sakharov's apartment, [Pomazov was] immediately surrounded by operatives and taken to a precinct. There Pomazov was searched and, later, put on a train. (The ticket was purchased by the militia since Pomazov had no money.) He was warned against trying to get off at any station. Indeed, at every railroad station, a militia patrol prevented Pomazov from getting off the train.

Issue 64 published an open letter Sakharov wrote on January 24, the second anniversary of his exile to Gorky.

> It seems that blatantly illegal repressions against me are part of the larger plan to stifle dissent in the USSR. . . . Undoubtedly, these repressions contradict the right of free thought and exchange of information and reduce the openness of society, thereby damaging international trust, security and stability.
>
> All of this contradicts the deep interests of our country, which badly needs pluralistic reforms that could lead it out of the economic and social dead end. But today our government does not show the ability to reform itself, and, instead, directly and indirectly opposes the needed change in its sphere of influence.

That issue, dated June 1982, was *Khronika*'s last. It had survived for fourteen years, four years longer than Herzen's *Kolokol*.

✦

On September 6, 1982 — three days before her seventy-sixth birthday — Sofya Vasilyevna Kallistratova, attorney and Helsinki-group member, was charged with slandering the state under Article

190. That same day, the group announced that it would no longer be able to continue its work. (Only three members remained free to sign the group's final document.) The case against Kallistratova was then dropped. A little later, Yelena Bonner, Sakharov's wife, was accused of slandering the state by smuggling his letters to the West. She, too, was sentenced to internal exile in Gorky.

✦

By 1983, the movement was destroyed. Our old toast, "To those who cannot drink with us," had been broadened to include the émigrés and exiles. The few dissidents who remained on the streets referred to the movement in the past tense.

At the same time, people who had once helped dissidents started to look the other way. Some found a way to ease their conscience: they started to criticize dissidents for their "extremism," the impracticality of their demands, and their custom of protesting openly. The latter, critics said, was nothing less than a "provocation."

The thousand known prisoners of conscience were forgotten. They were left to themselves, and virtually all calls for the release of political prisoners came from political prisoners themselves or from a handful of their friends and relatives.

✦

Shortly after we left, the son of one of my mother's graduate-school friends asked Mother if he could stay with her for a few months until he could get his own apartment. The man's mother was a very close family friend. I had known her all my life, and called her Aunt Galya. Mother did not want anyone in the apartment, but she did not see how she could refuse. So, Aunt Galya's son Viktor and his wife moved in.

A few months passed without incident, but one afternoon Mother walked out of the apartment, discovered that she had forgotten something, and returned unexpectedly.

She walked through the corridor and pulled on the doorknob of her room, but the door didn't budge. She pulled again, then again. She knocked.

The door opened. Viktor was inside.

"Viktor, what are you doing in my room?"

"I had to change."

It was not quite clear why Viktor felt compelled to change in Mother's room. He was alone in the apartment.

After Viktor left the room, Mother looked through her desk. Everything seemed to be in place, except for Misha's yoga exercise book, which had disappeared. It was a "self-published" booklet, which is to say that someone had taken the trouble to type it up. Though it was innocent, apolitical, and legal, it fit under the semantic definition of samizdat, which made it a likely target for an eager and not terribly intelligent informant.

Mother took note, but said nothing. A couple of days later, the yoga book reappeared in her desk. Without making any explanations, Mother told Viktor to leave.

About a month later, my cousin's wife stopped by to ask if a sister of hers, together with the sister's husband, could move in for a few months. Mother did not want any more apartment mates. But this was family. The young couple, she was assured, were very nice. They had been allotted an apartment of their own, but the apartment building had not been completed. Meanwhile, they had no place to live, and since both of them were students, they were unable to rent a room at market prices. Finally, Mother agreed. And, of course, she charged no rent.

Soon after the couple moved in, Mother found that the first few pages of Misha's yoga book were missing. That night, she heard someone pecking on a typewriter. She did not know what was being typed, but it was highly unlikely that it was a term paper. As a rule, Soviet students submitted handwritten papers.

The following day, after returning from a walk, Mother discovered that the pages that had been missing the day before were back in her desk. Now, another batch of pages was missing. She heard more typing. This continued until the entire book had been reproduced.

Mother could not throw the couple out without offering an explanation. After all, they were relatives. But an explanation would have done more harm than good: the two young students would have been ostracized by the family. She decided to wait out their stay.

When the couple asked to stay another three months, Mother

declined. The following day, my cousin's wife came to ask Mother to reconsider. "No," Mother told her, "I am fed up. I am tired of their presence — but I am more tired of these kids informing on me. I am certain they are doing it."

My cousin's wife returned a few days later. "Valentina Afanasyevna, forgive us," she said. "I never thought such a thing could happen in our family."

✦

It could be that the KGB brass had convinced themselves that all dissidents worked for the CIA and that they recruited their elderly parents to do the same. Whatever their rationale, Mother's life in the USSR became unbearable.

In 1980, she applied to visit me in the United States. The first authority to consider her application was the local party organization. One thing needs to be said about our apartment building: it was originally built for the KGB. While its residents were on active duty, they belonged to the party organizations at work. After retirement, they attended party meetings close to home. Thus, the group deciding Mother's application was dominated by retired *KGBshniki*.

When they gathered to vote on Mother's application, a local librarian spoke first. "Valentina Afanasyevna has done a lot of volunteer work at the library," she said. "She is very intelligent, very thorough. She is a fine Communist, and, of course, she deserves the trust of our party organization. I suggest that we vote to allow her to visit her daughter."

A former party secretary stood up next. She was an older, sick woman, who had just resigned from her post. "Valentina Afanasyevna is always ready to help people in need," she said. "She is always ready to bring milk to people who are sick, or to watch the grandchildren for those of us who need to go to the doctor. I recommend that Valentina Afanasyevna be allowed to visit her daughter in America."

"What is your opinion of your daughter's activities?" one of the KGB retirees asked Mother.

"When she lived here, she didn't tell me anything."

"Why not?"

"She wanted to protect my nerves. You know as much about her activities as I do."

The party organization voted to allow Valentina Afanasyevna Yefimenko to visit her daughter in the United States. Mother had made friends even among the KGB. Unfortunately, the visa office denied her application. She had to choose between leaving the country forever and facing old age in solitude.

✦

In 1984, Mother chose to leave. That meant forsaking the party. Instead of going to the meeting that would consider her petition, she decided to take a nap.

The phone rang. Three women who belonged to her organization wanted to visit her.

"We came to see you because it's our duty," one of them said. "All of us have been in the party for such a long time. It is our family, no less important than our children. We beseech you to consider withdrawing your application and staying with the party family."

"I am sorry, but I have made up my mind. I have only one daughter, and I would like to stay with her."

"But we have such a fine organization! We will take care of you. If you ever need anything, we will help you with anything you want."

"I appreciate that. But I have to tell you that I have another reason for leaving. I find it disgusting that this apartment is being monitored."

There was a pause. Then one of the ladies suggested: "You could move to another apartment."

✦

Larisa stopped by just before Mother left. Mother was taking only two carry-on bags. Some of her possessions went to friends, others to family. The rest went unclaimed.

"Are you just leaving all this?" Larisa asked after seeing a well-stocked kitchen, a cabinet full of bedding, and two rooms of furniture.

"Can you use any of it?"

"I can't, but Seryozha Kovalyov is getting out of exile. So is Malva Landa. They need all of it." Landa was a Helsinki-group member.

Larisa made a few calls, rounded up a truck and helpers, and in a matter of hours the apartment stood bare. Even the ceiling lamp was gone.

"Isn't it wonderful, everything went to Seryozha and Malvochka," Mother said when I met her in Vienna.

"You know Seryozha? You know Malvochka?"

"Of course, they've come to see me."

My God, my friends were now her friends. She had become one of us.

Fifteen

Shortly after I arrived in the United States in 1977, the State Department asked me to write a two-hundred-page reference manual on all movements in Soviet dissent. Though President Carter had made the defense of human rights a US foreign-policy goal, few people in official Washington had any knowledge of dissent in the USSR. The words "dissident" and "refusenik" were being used interchangeably, and some otherwise knowledgeable people naturally assumed that most dissidents were Jewish and that the human-rights movement was an offshoot of the Jewish movement.

The State Department needed a document that brought together brief descriptions of the human-rights movement, the Russian nationalists, Russian Orthodox believers, the Ukrainians, Lithuanians, Latvians, Estonians, Georgians, Armenians, ethnic Germans, Meskhetians, Evangelical Christian Baptists, Pentecostals, and the True and Free Seventh-Day Adventists.

I was happy to take the job. It fit in with my mission as a representative of the Moscow Helsinki Watch Group. I would go through Helsinki-group documents and back issues of *Khronika*. Then I would add the bits and pieces of information I had happened to collect during a decade in the human-rights movement. I also hoped to be able to use information collected by Western

Sovietologists. I thought the whole project would take no more than a year.

I started my research with the Ukraine, but soon after I went through the obvious sources, I realized just how little I knew. *Khronika*'s coverage of the Ukraine was not systematic. It did not start from the beginning, and it was insufficiently detailed to offer a whole picture. I had to read more. I had to go through archives and look through everything I could find. It was the same with all the other movements. No one had attempted to take a bird's-eye view of disaffection in the Soviet empire.

And for all the volumes that attempted to chronicle these public movements, none offered a thorough, systematic history. At the same time, primary materials collected in archives could be measured by the crateful. Materials were being preserved at the archives of Radio Liberty in New York and Munich, at the Russian-language Khronika Press publishing house, run by my old friend Valery Chalidze, at the State Department, and at the congressional Commission on Security and Cooperation in Europe, the body founded by Millicent Fenwick.

I worked full-time, every day, for three years. By the time I completed the project, the Carter administration, whose appointee approved my project, was out of office.

The materials I found were so plentiful that, after completing the brief reference manual, I spent two more years expanding it into a book. The book was published as *Istoriya inakomysliya* ("History of Otherwise-thinking") by Khronika Press in 1984. A year later, Wesleyan University Press issued the English version, *Soviet Dissent: Contemporary Movements for National, Religious, and Human Rights.*

✦

I never thought I would get a chance to become a historian of the Soviet human-rights movement. In Moscow, I had been too busy to break down information into files and index cards. Even if I had undertaken such a project, the files would have been confiscated at the first search. Outside the USSR, I could use the treasures of our samizdat, and I had a chance to sit back and think. Similar work was being done by the KGB, but for reasons that had nothing to do with scholarly pursuit.

Fortunately, I did not have to worry about money. Kolya learned

English in a matter of months and took a job teaching mathematics. Both of us agreed that since the good Lord had saved me from prison, I had an obligation to those in the camps to tell about their sacrifices — and their reasons for them.

Hundreds of copies of my book were taken to the Soviet Union. One of them was sent directly to Larisa.

"Years go by, and with them come children, elderly parents, poor health," she wrote to me in 1986.

> Some of us are in Kazakhstan, some in Magadan, some at the Okhotsk Sea, and some doing time in Perm.
>
> I am not complaining, Lyudochka, I am just trying to explain the situation. Our Resistance had no organizational structure. That was its charm, its character. But now we face the inevitable result: a sudden end of Resistance as a social phenomenon, though inside, all of its members have remained the same, even those who threw out the white flag. We didn't have reinforcements; none were possible. The nature of the movement was such that everyone immediately ended up at the front lines. As a historian, do you think our Resistance will leave its impact on the people, the country, the Russian society? And (you can see that better where you are), on the world?
>
> I think we have yet to say our last word.

If our historical drama was indeed at an end, it ended anticlimactically, with a stalemate. Yes, we had shown the way to the square. That was all we could do. But was that enough? We had seen prison cells, camp zones, and exile, but to what end?

Larisa yearned for a more dramatic conclusion, and so did I.

✦

In November 1985, nine months after his inauguration, Mikhail Gorbachev made a series of speeches that seemed to contradict the party canons and fall outside the traditions of official Soviet oratory. The speeches did not mention the "irreconcilable differences between socialism and imperialism," the "victorious march of socialism," or the "inherent contradictions of capitalism that will inevitably lead to its demise." Instead, he talked about our small planet, where coexistence, not confrontation, is the key to survival:

• The issue is no longer the contradictions between two social systems; our choice is between survival and mutual destruction. . . . Survival has become Issue No. 1 in world politics. . . . I use the word "survival" not because I would like to dramatize the point and trigger fear, but because all of us have begun to feel deeply the realities of today's world. [*Pravda,* Nov. 22, 1985]

• The modern world has reached the point where some critical decisions must be made, for today the issue is preservation of civilization and life itself. [*Pravda,* Nov. 28, 1985]

• There can be no victory in a nuclear war. . . . It is essential to transcend national egotism, tactical considerations, arguments and rifts the importance of which is minute compared to preservation of our most important asset — a peaceful and secure future. [*Pravda,* Jan. 16, 1986]

Not long after Gorbachev made the first of his ideologically unencumbered pronouncements on world peace and arms control, the Soviet press began to refer to "new thinking." This "new thinking" was actually an adaptation of the ideas of Andrei Sakharov.

The one aspect of the Sakharov plan that was still missing from these pronouncements was democratization of the Soviet society. In fact, the author of "optimistic futurology" was going into his seventh year under house arrest in Gorky.

✦

On February 8, 1986, in an interview with the French newspaper *Humanité,* Gorbachev made the outrageous claim that Soviet courts "do not try people for their views" and that "there are no political prisoners in the USSR."

In a polite letter to Gorbachev, Sakharov begged to differ. The letter, dated February 19, pointed out that the RSFSR Criminal Code contained articles 70 and 190, which were being used to put people in jail for their views.

"In a society striving for justice there is no place for prisoners of conscience," Sakharov wrote. "Free them, solve this important problem. That would give a great push to our country's development, facilitate international contacts on all levels, and open up our society to international trust, thereby advancing the cause of peace."

The letter contained a list of political prisoners, including Sakharov's wife, Yelena Bonner, and Sakharov himself. Sakharov did not know that two days before he wrote the letter, the Soviets had released Anatoly Shcharansky, one of the best-known political prisoners, whose name also appeared on the list.

In the course of a year, thirty political prisoners, including Yuri Orlov, were released from the camps. Among those released were not only international celebrities, but a number of lesser-known prisoners.

Of course, Gorbachev knew all along that political prisoners existed.

✦

In December 1983, the guards at a Perm camp had pounded Tolya Marchenko's head against the cement floor, then left him unconscious, with his handcuffs still on. Though prison regulations allowed Tolya annual visits from relatives, Larisa had not been allowed to see him in three years. In September 1986, a letter he had written to the delegates at the Helsinki Final Act compliance-review conference in Vienna was smuggled out of Chistopol prison and reached the West.

> Gentlemen:
>
> You don't seem to be able to find a way to demand that the USSR live up to its obligations. Therefore I take it on myself to demand what was guaranteed in the agreement signed by your governments. Today, on August 4, 1986, I begin a hunger strike, and I will remain on hunger strike till the end of your conference in Vienna.

Tolya demanded amnesty for all political prisoners, an end to physical abuse of prisoners, prosecution of the guards who had savagely beaten him, and resumption of visits from his family.

By the time the letter reached the West, Tolya had been on hunger strike for over a month. I assumed he was force-fed. That would be a mixed blessing. A *zek* as stubborn as Tolya would have been tied up and held down while the food was forced through his nose.

Tolya's friends in the West did what they could. On September 24, the *New York Times* ran his appeal on its editorial page. A letter demanding Tolya's release was signed by 113 members of Congress. Secretary of State George Shultz spoke of Tolya's hunger strike at the opening of the Vienna conference. When Lane Kirkland, head of the American Federation of Labor and Congress of Industrial Organizations, asked for Tolya's release from Chistopol, Soviet authorities said Tolya would be set free if the AFL-CIO would recognize Soviet trade unions. Earlier that year, the Soviets had tied the release of Anatoly Shcharansky and Yuri Orlov to the release of spies. They were eager to keep trading.

The times were changing, but would Tolya survive till the process of change completed itself? In desperation, I decided to go to the Reagan-Gorbachev summit in Reykjavík. Only first-class tickets would be available on such short notice. All other seats were taken up by reporters on their way to cover the show. And what would I be doing there? Sightseeing in the city with a poetic name? Trying to push a news story to reporters bored by news blackouts? Anatoly Marchenko wasn't a name they would easily grasp, especially since so many of them were quite young when *My Testimony* came out.

It seemed I had paid the first-class fare only to wander the streets of Reykjavík, reliving the childhood memories of Father taking me on distant "travels" on the map that hung over my bed. Reliving childhood while Tolya lay dying in Chistopol. But what else could I do?

I was not stunned by Reykjavík. I think Father wouldn't have been stunned by it, either. I spent most of my time at the press center, watching the wide-screen television monitor. In the morning, I would see Reagan and Gorbachev enter a castle. In the evening, I would watch them leave. During the day, the screen belonged to Gorbachev's wife, Raisa. In every news shot, she was modeling a new outfit and handing out candy to the children of Iceland.

When Raisa wasn't in the limelight, Jewish activists were. They told a simple, human story: so-and-so wants to emigrate, but they won't let him. I took part in some of those press conferences, but the publicity hardly justified the trip. It was a disaster.

On the final day of the summit, Gorbachev made an hour-and-a-half long speech. He said the talks had collapsed. Still, I was moderately encouraged by what I saw. Gorbachev spoke without a prepared text, he seemed literate, and, unlike his immediate predecessors, he didn't need to be held up.

I closed my eyes and concentrated on his language. It was the language of a bureaucrat. There he stood, a peasant's son who had turned into a government official. As he spoke, the son of a railroad worker lay dying of self-starvation in a cell in Chistopol prison.

It may have been fate, but Tolya Marchenko could no more have become a bureaucrat than Misha Gorbachev could have become an intelligent. Yet both men were part of the same generation, and both were in its vanguard.

✦

On the flight back, I sat with Alik Goldfarb and Sanya Slepak, who'd come to Reykjavík to lobby for release of their parents, longtime refuseniks.

"Could this be Dubinin?" Goldfarb asked, pointing at a sculpted shock of gray hair ahead of us. I said I would not be able to recognize the Soviet ambassador to the United States.

Alik decided to investigate. He got up and walked slowly up the aisle.

"It's he," he said. "They are speaking Russian."

From then on, Goldfarb lay in wait for his opportunity. Sooner or later, Yuri Dubinin was bound to get up to go to the lavatory.

When he did, Goldfarb got up and introduced himself. I couldn't hear what was being said, but I could see that the tone was civil. It remained civil after Slepak joined the conversation. A few minutes later, I got up, squeezed in between Slepak and Goldfarb, and joined the conversation.

I felt someone tug on my sleeve. It was a reporter. "What is he saying?"

"Let me listen," I said.

"Your Western press doesn't seem to pay much attention to the Helsinki Final Act," Dubinin was saying. "It's a very important document that none of them seem to be able to grasp. You see, I was the ambassador to Spain during the Madrid conference, so I consider myself an expert."

"You know, I, too, consider myself an expert on the Helsinki process," I said. "I was one of the founding members of the Moscow Helsinki Watch Group."

A crowd of reporters formed around us. Now they were tugging on Goldfarb's and Slepak's sleeves. Three dissidents talking to the ambassador. News could be committed.

"Then, I guess both of us are experts," the ambassador said to me.

"You know why I went to Reykjavík? I went because of Anatoly Marchenko."

"I don't know who that is." Of course, he knew. Tolya's appeal that ran with the editorials in the *New York Times* had surely been placed on his desk. So had the letter from 113 members of Congress.

"Then, let me tell you. Marchenko is a writer who is now on hunger strike at the Chistopol prison. This is a matter of life and death. For us, his friends, his death would be a tragedy, and, believe me, the Soviet Union would not be better off for it. His death would damage your international prestige."

"Of course," said Dubinin. "Why don't you come to the consulate and put what you have just said in writing."

"I would be glad to," I said.

Goldfarb, Slepak, and I parted to allow the ambassador to continue on his way to the lavatory. Then we faced the press. We said that we had just had a cordial conversation with the ambassador and that he had invited us to file petitions with him at the Soviet consulate in Washington. The following day, stories about our conversation appeared in the *New York Times* and the *Washington Post*.

✦

On October 16, a day after we returned from Reykjavík, Alik's father, David Goldfarb, was released from the Soviet Union. On October 20, reporters and camera crews followed Sanya Slepak and me to the Soviet consulate. One copy of my letter went to the consulate; the rest went to the press.

My appeal requested Tolya's release, and added that if he agreed to emigrate, I would gladly invite him and his family to be my guests in the United States. By saying this, I was taking a chance. Before his imprisonment, Tolya told the KGB that he did not intend to emigrate. And since the KGB had rigged Larisa's telephone to block out all overseas calls, I couldn't ask for her guidance. I had to act on my own.

On November 13, Larisa was invited to the party's regional committee, where an official suggested that she petition for Marchenko's release "for health reasons." She did, and on November 21, the KGB suggested that Larisa, Tolya, and their son, Pavel, emigrate to Israel. "We need your decision immediately," officials said.

"I don't know if my husband wants to emigrate," said Larisa. She said that she had not seen Tolya in nearly three years and that if he was prepared to leave the country, she would join him. Then she was asked to put her demands on paper, and the paper went up through the channels.

On November 28, Tolya sent Larisa a letter requesting a food parcel. The only possible explanation for the end of the hunger strike was that Tolya had been assured of the forthcoming amnesty for Soviet political prisoners. It seemed that we were winning.

✦

On December 9, 1986, just before noon, Larisa received an urgent telegram from Chistopol: "YOUR HUSBAND MARCHENKO ANATOLY TIKHONOVICH PASSED AWAY IN HOSPITAL."

That day, Larisa, thirteen-year-old Pavel, and seven others left for Chistopol. "By 4 P.M., December 10, we stood at the gates of the Chistopol Prison," she wrote later.

> We asked to hold the burial in Moscow, near my parents' resting place. A categoric refusal: "Inmates who die in prison are to be buried by the administration in the presence of relatives."
>
> We said that we wanted to hold a Russian Orthodox funeral, with a church service. No, again. "You will view the body in the morgue, in a coffin, prepared for burial. At that point you will have the opportunity to say farewell."
>
> After several night-time telegrams and calls to Moscow and Kazan, we were allowed to delay the burial by two hours and hold a service at Chistopol's Russian Orthodox Church. Men in plainclothes, who weren't leaving us for as much as a

minute, filed into the funeral bus. The bus was followed by a *gazik* with our "escort." The bus was brought right up to the morgue door, like a prison van.

We carried the coffin into the bus. There were nine of us — three women, two boys, and four men. The bus pulled up to the church and we carried the coffin inside. Our escort, too, walked into the church and took off their hats.

The priest started the service. He conducted it with inspiration, and the choir of old ladies sang emotionally and with extraordinary beauty. The priest poured a handful of soil into the coffin and we nailed the lid shut. The old ladies, singing, followed the coffin to the bus.

The bus, followed by the *gazik,* crossed the town line, negotiating the deserted road to the cemetery. The deep grave had already been dug; on top of it lay two steel rods to lay the coffin on. Our men and boys, slipping on frozen clumps of ground, carried the coffin to the grave. Pasha, too, carried his father's coffin.

It was windy, and there was no one out, just Tolya's guards and us. Everything was ready, the shovels, the long white towel. But they realized that we would not let them near the grave, so they stayed away "until the end of the operation," as one of them put it.

Tolya's friends said a few words of farewell over the grave. We started covering the grave, first with our hands, then with shovels. An hour later we had put together a high mound. On top of it we laid live and artificial flowers, apples, bread crumbs. We put up a white, pine cross; I hope it was made by prisoners. With a ballpoint pen, I wrote on the cross: "Anatoly Marchenko. 1/23/1938–12/8/1986."

The news of Tolya's death made front pages worldwide. Warren Zimmerman, chief of the US delegation at the Helsinki Final Act review conference in Vienna, suggested that Marchenko's memory be marked by a moment of silence — a move that prompted the Soviet delegation to leave the conference floor. To maintain his image as a reformer, Gorbachev needed to do something drastic.

He had to give in to Tolya's demands. He had to admit to the existence of political prisoners. Then he had to release them.

✦

On December 15, 1986, in Gorky, the Sakharovs noticed the disappearance of the KGB detail that had guarded their apartment for seven years. The same day, workmen brought in a telephone. The following day, it rang. "We would like you to return to Moscow for patriotic work," Gorbachev said over the telephone.

That was different from releasing Shcharansky and Orlov. Shcharansky went off to Israel; Orlov, to the United States. But Sakharov was to stay in Moscow, and he was not a man who could be silenced.

An event even more astounding than the release of Sakharov followed on January 16, 1987. Yuri Kashlev, head of the Soviet delegation at the Vienna conference, announced the impending release of about two hundred people convicted on charges of engaging in "anti-Soviet propaganda." "These people, in the past, have made us uncomfortable and strained our relations with other countries," Kashlev said.

That was nothing less than the first official admission of the existence of political prisoners.

Sixteen

I will not attempt to predict Russia's future. I can say only that Westernizers, nonexistent at the time of my birth, have now become a formidable political force. The new thaw would have been unthinkable without us. Now, like the Decembrists a century before us, we have been given the reward of knowing that the country has responded to our cry for the rule of law.

"We shall win because we have no other choice," boomed Natan Eidelman, the scholar of the Decembrists, raising a glass at my house in the summer of 1989. I was happy to join him in that toast, and in that prediction.

Years ago, in our *kompanii,* no one thought that our first slogan, the demand for *glasnost,* would ever be adopted by the government. None of us thought we would see open, televised debates between People's Deputy Andrei Sakharov and General Secretary Mikhail Gorbachev. None of us could have imagined that we would see *Novy mir* and *Ogonyok* publish Anatoly Marchenko and Yuli Daniel; or that Valery Chalidze, a resident of Vermont, would become a contributor to the liberal newspaper *Moskovskiye novosti,* as well as to the "theoretical" journal of the Communist party, *Kommunist.* And, a few years ago, I would not have believed that Yuri Orlov, now a researcher at Cornell University, would ever have the opportunity to address a crowd at Moscow's Luzhniki Stadium, that *Khronika* would be studied by history scholars, that émigré Naum Korzhavin would hold readings in Moscow, that a record album with the voice of Aleksandr Galich would be pressed under the Melodiya label, that my book on Soviet dissent could be published in the USSR — or that I would see Larisa again.

The institutions that began with our grass-roots movement have evolved to their next phase. These days, public protests last long enough to have speakers. When the crowds are not so great that they require a stadium parking lot, they meet at Pushkin Square. Sometimes troops in riot gear come to disperse the demonstrators, but they keep returning, thereby paying homage to Russia's greatest poet — and to my friends who chose his monument as the site for the first independent political demonstration to be held in the USSR.

As I monitor the unfolding events in the Soviet Union, I spend little time worrying about Mikhail Gorbachev. What I think is more important is the conscience of the nation.

I see many encouraging signs. In the summer of 1989, after the miners of Kuzbass walked off their jobs, the miners of Donbass joined the strike, demanding, among other things, that the official press stop spreading lies about the events in Kuzbass and the life of Soviet miners. Eventually, nearly a million miners joined in that demand for *glasnost*. A few months earlier, when the authorities illegally arrested the eleven members of the Karabakh Committee, which had spearheaded the movement for Armenia's sovereignty, protests swept Armenia, Georgia, the Baltic republics, and Russia proper. While the committee members were still imprisoned, all of them were nominated to the Supreme Soviet. In the end, the authorities backed down and released the activists.

New independent publications continue to be referred to as "samizdat," though frequently that is a misnomer. Many of them have press runs of tens of thousands. *Express-Khronika,* edited by Aleksandr Podrabinek, formerly a member of an offshoot of the Moscow Helsinki group, is the continuation of our *Khronika.* Though the style and format are the same as those of *Khronika,* Podrabinek's journal, which comes out weekly and has a circulation of twenty thousand, is anything but a covert publication. Every Sunday at the Gogol monument, Podrabinek meets with his readers.

All over the country, samizdat collectors have organized "independent libraries" that pool unofficial publications and store them in apartments specially rented for the purpose. Somewhere in those collections there could still be an issue of *Khronika* "published" on my Mercedes typewriter.

The Lenin Library smoking room, too, has emerged from the underground. Recently, Moscow University students who called themselves the Hyde Park Group put up a sheet of plywood in the university's main lobby. The board was to be used by people of any political persuasion to display, as one of the group founders put it, "all sorts of *anti-Sovietshchina*." After many of the displayed documents had been "borrowed" by interested readers, the group raised three thousand rubles and built a locking Plexiglas stand, which at this writing still graces the lobby of my alma mater.

Now I know that I was not the only person to join the Communist party with the intention of reforming it from within. At this writing, the party leadership is finally caving in to demands from society at large as well as from the Communist rank and file, and has renounced the monopoly on power. Next on the agenda is reform of the party structure.

Our Helsinki group has given rise to an international movement. The International Helsinki Federation now includes organizations in eighteen countries. In Czechoslovakia, a Helsinki group was cofounded by the dissident playwright Václav Havel, who has since become his country's president. At this writing, Havel and Alexander Dubček, the speaker of the Czechoslovak parliament, are negotiating the withdrawal of Soviet troops from Czechoslovakia — the very issue that once brought my friends to the square.

In the summer of 1989, I was a US delegate to the Helsinki Final Act review conference in Paris. I am a consultant to the New York–based Helsinki Watch and a member in absentia of the newly established Moscow Helsinki Watch Group chaired by Larisa Bogoraz. So far, I have made five attempts to visit the USSR, but each time I have been refused. I will keep trying.

Not long ago, I received a signed copy of Natan Eidelman's final book, a comparison of the current reform with the reforms of Peter the Great and Aleksandr II. A few days after sending it to me, Natan died suddenly of a heart attack. That same month, we also lost Andrei Sakharov and Sofya Kallistratova.

Our time is coming to an end, and as we depart, one by one, we can take comfort from a homemade banner carried behind Andrei Sakharov's coffin: "Forgive us, Andrei Dmitriyevich, for not following you earlier."

It's not too late. It will never be too late.

◆

I now live a half-hour's drive from Washington, in the Virginia suburbs. The windows of my study overlook a small lake and a forest that is not too different from the woods outside Moscow. There are four of us in the house: Kolya, I, and cats Vas'ka and Murka.

The room designed to be a master bedroom is a library. So are the other two bedrooms. Archive boxes line the walls of the laundry room. Books slated for distribution in the USSR stand on shelves in the paneled family room. We don't have any beds; just foldaway couches, enough of them to accommodate our frequent house-guests. Sometimes, we have as many as seven visitors — old Moscow friends, or friends of Moscow friends, visiting the United States. Counting on more guests from the USSR, I have just put in another bathroom. Let that be the proof of my confidence in the continuation of *perestroika*.

Twice a week, shortwave radio stations beam my voice back to the Soviet Union. One program, for Radio Liberty, is devoted to the informal groups and associations that have blossomed in the USSR since the advent of *glasnost*. Another is a series of discussions of my book on Soviet dissent and its heroes, whose names have a way of showing up in the news. I am sixty-two, and at this stage I am reasonably sure that I will not have a chance to sit back and devote a year or two to studying English literature. I am too busy, and the work doesn't seem to let up.

My sons live nearby. Seryozha, who was forced out of the USSR in 1980, is a computer systems analyst. Misha is a professor of economics at George Mason University. All of us are now United States citizens.

My mother is buried here, too, at Rock Creek Cemetery, high on a wooded hill overlooking Washington. The name on her tombstone is written in Russian and English. "Valentina Afanasyevna Yefimenko, 1906–1986." A bush of lilac, Mother's favorite flower, grows beside her grave. I was told that lilac doesn't thrive in the Washington climate. But hers is doing just fine.

Another, identical, bush grows outside my house.

✦

Late in 1989, Larisa spent four weeks with me. We met at Dulles Airport. At last, we had a chance to sit back and talk about our lives, about the unexpected mission of our generation, and about growing old.

During her stay here, Larisa made a brief appearance at a convention of the AFL-CIO. Dutifully, she stood up to the applause of five thousand people. She even forced a smile.

"After such things I am sick for days," she said to me when it was over.

"Why?"

"Too many people."

That's the kind of movement we were. We came from loud Moscow *kompanii* who met in small, crowded rooms, and that's where we would like to stay. It is up to the next generation to face the roaring crowds.

Notes

We have tried, whenever possible, to quote from (and cite) published translations of Russian works. In most cases, however, we have consulted the original sources and translated the Russian into English ourselves. Unless otherwise noted below, all songs, verses, and poems were translated by Paul Goldberg. Shortened citations here refer to works listed in the Bibliography.

CHAPTER ONE

The exchange between Zoya Kosmodemyanskaya and her captors and the story of Tanya Solomakha are drawn from Kosmodemyanskaya, *The Story of Zoya and Shura*. The Esenin poem is from McVay, *Esenin*; Akhmatova's is from Akhmatova, *The Complete Poems*.

CHAPTER TWO

Lermontov's poem is from Lermontov, *'The Demon' and Other Poems;* Akhmatova's is from Akhmatova, *The Complete Poems*.

CHAPTER THREE

The exchange between Snegov and Beria is from Medvedev, *Political Diary*.

CHAPTER FOUR

The exchange between Stalin and Gelya Markizova is from Alexeyeva, "The Girl in a Sailor Suit"; Gelya's reflections on the incident are in Lebedeva, "The Girl in the Photograph." The excerpt from "GNIIPI" and the Gastev poem are from unpublished manuscripts. Akhmatova's "Requiem" is from Akhmatova, *The Complete Poems*. The exchange between Bregel, Kabo, and Khmelnitsky is from Bregel, "An Exchange after the Camp."

CHAPTER FIVE

The "Glasnost Meeting" leaflet, the "Hypocrites" article, and the Daniel-and-Sinyavsky trial transcript are from Ginzburg, *The White Book*. The Daniel excerpts are from Daniel, *This Is Moscow Speaking*.

CHAPTER SEVEN

Litvinov's exchange with the KGB is from Litvinov, *The Demonstration on Pushkin Square*. The Bogoraz-Litvinov letter and the one to the procurator general are from Litvinov, *The Trial of the Four*.

CHAPTER TEN

The report on Zolotukhin is from *The Chronicle of Current Events (Khronika)*. Marchenko's letter on the invasion of Czechoslovakia and his reaction to the Red Square demonstration are adapted from Marchenko, *To Live Like Everyone*. The Tass announcement of the invasion and the transcript of the demonstrators' trial are from Gorbanevskaya, *Red Square at Noon*. Litvinov's reaction to the Galich's "St. Petersburg Romance" is from Litvinov, "What We Did." Larisa's letters to Kaminskaya and Marchenko are in Kaminskaya, *Final Judgment*.

CHAPTER ELEVEN

The officially orchestrated responses to the invasion of Czechoslovakia are from Gorbanevskaya, *Red Square at Noon*.

CHAPTER TWELVE

The documents of the Initiative Group in Defense of Human Rights are from *The Initiative Group*. Documents of the Committee for Human Rights are from *The Chronicle of Current Events (Khronika)*.

CHAPTER THIRTEEN

Millicent Fenwick's comments and the exchange with Orlov about the formation of the Helsinki group are adapted from Goldberg, *The Final Act*. The Helsinki-group documents are from Alexeyeva, *Documents of the Public Group*.

CHAPTER FIFTEEN

Larisa's account of Marchenko's death and funeral is from Marchenko, *To Live Like Everyone*.

Bibliography

Akhmatova, Anna. *The Complete Poems of Anna Akhmatova* (bilingual ed.). Translated by Judith Hemschemeyer. Somerville, Mass.: Zephyr Press, 1990.

Alexeyeva, Ludmilla. *Soviet Dissent: Contemporary Movements for National, Religious, and Human Rights*. Translated by Carol Pearce and John Glad. Middletown, Conn.: Wesleyan University Press, 1985. Originally published as *Istoriya inakomysliya* (New York: Khronika Press, 1984).

———. " 'The Chronicle of Current Events' Turns 10" (in Russian). *Khronika Zashchity Prav Cheloveka v SSSR*, no. 28 (1978).

———. "The Girl in a Sailor Suit: Commentary on the Photograph" (in Russian). In *Pamyat*, No. 1. New York: Khronika Press, 1978.

———, ed. *Documents of the Public Group to Assist the Implementation of the Helsinki Accord in the USSR* (in Russian). 8 vols. New York: Khronika Press, 1977–1984.

Amalrik, Andrei. *Notes of a Revolutionary*. Translated by Guy Daniels. New York: Knopf, 1982.

Bogoraz, Larisa. "From Memoirs" (in Russian). In *Minuvsheye: Istorichekiy almanakh*, no. 2. Paris: Atheneum, 1986.

———. "I Wanted to Be the Master of My Name" (in Russian). Interview by Yefim Fishtein. *Forum*, no. 19 (1988).

Bregel, Yuri. "An Exchange after the Camp" (in Russian). *Vremya i my*, no. 91 (1986).

Bukovsky, Vladimir. *To Build a Castle*. Translated by Michael Scammell. New York: Viking, 1979.

Bulgakov, Mikhail. *The Master and Margarita*. Translated by Michael Glenny. London: Havril Press, 1967.

Chalidze, Valery. *To Defend These Rights*. Translated by Guy Daniels. New York: Random House, 1975.

The Chronicle of Current Events (in Russian). Nos. 1–27 (Amsterdam: Fond im. Herzena, 1979); nos. 28–64 (New York: Khronika Press, 1974–1983). English ed.: nos. 28–64 (London: Amnesty International Publications, 1975–1984.

Daniel, Yuli [Nikolai Arzhak, pseud.]. *This Is Moscow Speaking* (in Russian). New York: Waldron Press, 1966.

Dudintsev, Vladimir. *Not by Bread Alone*. Translated by Edith Bone. New York: Dutton, 1957.

Ehrenburg, Ilya. *The Thaw*. Translated by Manya Harari. Chicago: H. Regnery, 1955.

Eidelman, Natan. *Pushkin and the Decembrists* (in Russian). Moscow: Khudozhestvennaya literatura, 1979.

Galich, Aleksandr. *When I Return* (in Russian). Frankfurt: Possev-Verlag, 1981.

[Gastev, Yuri.] "On the Fate of the 'Impoverished Sybarites' " (in Russian). In *Pamyat*, no. 1. New York: Khronika Press, 1978.

Ginzburg, Aleksandr. *The White Book* (in Russian), Frankfurt: Possev-Verlag, 1967.

Goldberg, Paul. *The Final Act: The Dramatic, Revealing Story of the Moscow Helsinki Watch Group*. New York: Morrow, 1988.

Gorbanevskaya, Natalya. *Red Square at Noon*. Translated by Alexander Lieven. London: Deutsch, 1972.

Grigorenko, Petro. *Memoirs*. Translated by Thomas Whitney. New York: Norton, 1982.

The Initiative Group in Defense of Human Rights in the USSR (in Russian). New York: Khronika Press, 1976.

Kaminskaya, Dina. *Final Judgment: My Life as a Soviet Defense Attorney*. Translated by Michael Glenny. New York: Simon and Schuster, 1982.

Khmelnitsky, Sergei. "From the Belly of the Whale" (in Russian). *22,* no. 48 (1986).

Khronika Tekuschikh Sobytiy. See *The Chronicle of Current Events*.

Khrushchev, Nikita. *Khrushchev Remembers*. Translated and edited by Strobe Talbott. Boston: Little, Brown, 1970.

————. *Khrushchev Remembers: The Last Testament*. Translated and edited by Strobe Talbott. Boston: Little, Brown, 1974.

Kilinsky, Yefim. "Doctors-Murderers or the Murderers of Doctors?" (in Russian). *SSSR: Vnutrenniye protivorechiya,* no. 14–15 (1985).

Korzhavin, Naum. *The Times* (in Russian). Frankfurt: Possev-Verlag, 1976.

————. *The Weavings* (in Russian). Frankfurt: Possev-Verlag, 1981.

Kosmodemyanskaya, Lubov. *The Story of Zoya and Shura* (in Russian). Moscow: Detskaya literatura, 1961.

Krasin, Viktor. *Trial* (in Russian). New York: Chalidze Publications, 1983.

Lebedeva, G. "The Girl in the Photograph" (in Russian). *Trud,* June 7, 1988.

Lermontov, Mikhail. *'The Demon' and Other Poems*. Translated by Eugene M. Kaden. Yellow Springs, Ohio: Antioch Press, 1965.

Litvinov, Pavel. *The Demonstration on Pushkin Square*. Translated by Manya Harari. London: Harvill, 1969.

————. *The Trial of the Four*. Translated by Janis Sapiets, Hilary Sternberg, and Daniel Weissbort. New York: Viking, 1972.

————. "What We Did Was Quite Natural" (in Russian). Interview by Yefim Fishtein. *Forum,* no. 19 (1988).

Marchenko, Anatoly. *From Tarusa to Siberia*. Edited by Joshua Rubenstein. Royal Oak, Minn.: Strathcona Publishing, 1980.

————. *My Testimony*. Translated by Michael Scammell. New York: Dutton, 1969.

————. *To Live Like Everyone*. Translated by Paul Goldberg. New York: Henry Holt, 1989.

McVay, Gordon. *Esenin: A Life*. Ann Arbor, Mich.: Ardis, 1976.

Medvedev, Roy. *On Socialist Democracy*. Translated by Ellen DeKadt. New York: Knopf, 1975.

————, ed. *Political Diary* (in Russian). 2 vols. Amsterdam: Fond im. Herzena, 1972, 1975.

Mlynar, Zdenek. *Nightfrost in Prague*. Translated by Paul Wilson. New York: Karz Publishers, 1980.

Okudzhava, Bulat. *65 Songs* (bilingual ed.). Compiled and edited by Vladimir Frumkin. Translated by Eve Shapiro. Ann Arbor, Mich.: Ardis, 1980.

————. *Songs: Volume II* (bilingual ed.). Compiled and edited by Vladimir Frumkin. Translated by Tanya Wolfson, Kirsten Painter, and Laura Thompson. Ann Arbor, Mich.: Ardis, 1986.

Orlova, Raisa. "Galich as He Was" (in Russian). *Vremya i my,* no. 51 (1980).

Rozhdestvensky, S. R. "Materials from the History of Independent Political Groups in the USSR after 1945" (in Russian). In *Pamyat,* no. 5. Paris: La Presse Libre, 1982.

Sakharov, Andrei. *Alarm and Hope.* Edited by Efrem Yankelevich and Alfred Friendly, Jr. New York: Knopf, 1978.

———. *My Country and the World.* Translated by Guy Daniels. New York: Knopf, 1975.

Scammell, Michael. *Solzhenitsyn: A Biography.* New York: Norton, 1984.

Sinyavsky, Andrei [Abram Tertz, pseud.]. *Goodnight!* Translated by Richard Lourie. New York: Viking, 1989.

Svirsky, Grigory. *At the Beheading Place* (in Russian). London: Overseas Publications Interchange, 1979.

Telesin, Yulius. *1001 Jokes* (in Russian). Tenefly, N.J.: Hermitage, 1986.

Ulanovskaya, Nadezhda and Maya. *A History of One Family* (in Russian). New York: Chalidze Publications, 1982.

Yakobson, Anatoly. *The Finale of the Tragedy* (in Russian). New York: Izdatelstvo Imeni Chekhova, 1973.

Index